2004

Copyright and Multimedia

Copyright and Multimedia

by
Julián Rodríguez Pardo

KLUWER LAW INTERNATIONAL
THE HAGUE / LONDON / NEW YORK

Published by:
Kluwer Law International
P.O. Box 85889, 2508 CN The Hague, The Netherlands
sales@kluwerlaw.com
http://www.kluwerlaw.com

Sold and Distributed in North, Central and South America by:
Aspen Publishers, Inc.
7201 McKinney Circle
Frederick, MD 21704
USA

Sold and Distributed in all other countries by:
Turpin Distribution Services Limited
Blackhorse Road
Letchworth
Herts SG6 1HN
United Kingdom

Library of Congress Cataloging-in-Publication Data

Rodríguez Pardo, Julián.
    Copyright and multimedia / by Julián Rodríguez Pardo.
      p. cm.
    Includes bibliographical references.
    ISBN 90-411-8902-5 (hbk. : alk. paper)
      1. Copyright--Interactive mutlimedia. 2. Copyright--Audio-visual materials. 3.
    Copyright and electronic data processing. I. Title

K1441.R63 2003
346.04'82--dc21   2002044704

Printed on acid-free paper.

Typeset by *Steve Lambley Information Design*, The Hague.

ISBN 90-411-8902-5
© 2003 Kluwer Law International

Kluwer Law International incorporates the imprint of Martinus Nijhoff Publishers

To my grandmother, Otilia

Acknowledgment

I know this acknowledgment might seem a bit long, but, please, indulge me.

First of all, I must say thanks to Prof. Dr. Ana Azurmendi, at the University of Navarra (Spain), who taught me how to work in the Communication Law field, directed carefully this work, allowed me to have the priviledge of working close to her and gave me constantly her affection. Second, thank you to the Chancellor of the Saint Anthony Catholic University of Murcia (Spain), Prof. Dr. Antonio Montoro, who believed faithfully in my aptitudes and gave me complete freedom to teach Information Law my way; he also gave me the present of his affection through that special year at Murcia. And, most importantly, thank you to all the staff at Kluwer Law International for making this dream come true (my doctoral thesis published all around the world!!); specially Karen Knapstein, Michael Rosenberg and Karel van der Linde, for making all this so easy (and letting me express my enthusiasm!).

I would also like to thank my parents Antonio and Maria del Carmen, grandmother Otilia, and brother Juan Antonio, who give me their love, despite of our different characters and points of view in so many things; specially my parents and grandmother who always believed that the best education is the best heritage you can give to someone; I guess this is part of the results. Also, my cousins Jose Manuel and Asuncion, and my goddaughter Marta.

To my closest friends I met at so many different places: I have no doubt that the best of all this is having you in my life. I hope I will not forget any of you now: thanks to Alfonso, David, Saul, Alberto, Jorge, Pablo, Jose, Chus, Ana, Rosina, Jaime, Jesus, Carlos, Anita, Luis E., and Marta R.(La Coruña); Virginia, Rafa, Pablo, David, Asen, Maria Jose R., Alfonso V., Camino, Rosa and Miguel, Bea, Maria Jose V., Marisa, Piluca, Edurne, Alberto, Nerea, Nagore, Pia and Jose , Jose G., Nacho B., Carolina, Emilio, Alfonso and Alvaro G., Maria, Marta S., Ricart and Juan (Pamplona); Marta Roel, Marta R. Isabel, Sefi, Maloles, José A., César, Maribel, Angela and Mari Carmen (Murcia); Jordi, Pedro, Fermin, Maribel and Ismael (Barcelona); Gerardo, Pilar, Isabel M., Santi, Juanma and Abraham (Badajoz); Mark and Alberto (London).

Also, to the colleagues who have showed me their professional respect to my work and, above all, their personal friendship.

Acknowledgment

Finally I would like to show my deepest thanks to anybody reading this book, or just being casually interested on it. I feel a big responsability now that you are at the start of these pages and hope the content is stimulataing.

Any comment, whether good or bad, will be welcome at julianrodriguezpardo@ yahoo.es

Julian Rodriguez Pardo

Contents

Prologue

I start writing these lines when the Spanish audio-visual (multimedia) market has been shaken by the news of a merger agreement between the two Spanish digital platforms. This gives rise to questions about the process of media concentration, about a possible threat over the press pluralism. And despite the great political interest promoted by these kind of movements by the mass media, copyright – specially the rights in sports and cinema broadcasting – has gained a prominent position. Competition between TV stations, when negotiating prices, has been said to cause more expansive contents and financial harm when expectations on profitability have not been reached. The Spanish platforms have not been the only examples of the influence of copyright and neighbouring rights on the economic balance of communication companies; in Germany, the most recent largest mass media group, Kirch, has drowned because of an inappropriate rights management; while Italy has been the scene for another platforms merger as for the retreat of an initial government veto, after setting a series of conditions, including the breaking up of the agreements on soccer and TV cinema rights.

Other news, although not as spectacular, has been the battle between the Spanish Electronic and Communications Companies Association (ASIMELEC) and the users of Linux (free software community) against the Spanish Authors and Editors General Society (SGAE), because of the prevailing tax on recordable CDs; the promotion of thirty actions against piracy by the SGAE; or last year's important judgment of the U.S. Supreme Court, recognizing that the works of freelancers for on line information web pages require copiryght payment.

It is clear that copyright issues have economic consequences for communication companies. But there is another question, surely related to the monetary aspects of intellectual property, which has been under consideration for sometime: protection of the authors also means better or worse conditions for the payment of creativity talent, which is the authentic boost of the cultural market. In this sense, the European Union really hits when placing at this point the fundamentals of its Directive on the Harmonisation of certain aspects of Copyright and related rights in the Information Society:[1] "Any harmonisation of copyright and related rights must take as a basis a high level of protection, since such rights are crucial to intellectual creation. Their protection helps to ensure the maintenance and development of creativity in the interest of authors, performers, producers, consumers, culture, industry and the public at large. Intellectual property has therefore been recognised as an integral part or property".[2] "A rigorous, effective system for the protection of copyright and related rights is one of the main ways of ensuring that European cultural creativity and production receive the necessary resources and of safeguarding the independence and dignity of artistic creators and performers".[3]

Realities that, as the text itself recognizes, acquire new perspectives in a digital enviroment.

And it is in the dinamic context, in a non-stoping evolution, with deep economic implications, where we can place the work of Julian Rodriguez. Copyright has acquired different profiles depending on the necessities historically settled. New supports and new ways of broadcasting require creativity to fit the existing legal procedures. At the same time, the aim of the protection has remained constant: a guarantee of compensation for the author and for those who have made possible the public display of a work.

One of the indisputable merits of its analysis of the confusing views of the legal studies about New Technologies and its clarification of the central questions of copyright, distinguishing them from the secondary, but sometimes amazing characteristics illustrated today by the creations on digital support. Julian Rodriguez offers to the reader a clear and complete view of copyright in a new kind of work: the multimedia one. A product that cannot be identified with the digital signal nor the interactive possibilities of the digital technology, although it contains some of these features. The so-called multimedia work is only possible in a digital context, but cannot be simply identified with that technology, just as the work of a writer does not only consist in some narrative skills and the paper (e.g. a novel) nor in the instruments of the watercolour or the oil and the perspective, the angle, for the painting. The protectable work starts there, but above all it is an original creation fixed on a support.

---

[1] Directive 2001/29/EC of the European Parliament and of the Council of 22 may 2001 on the harmonisation of certain aspects of copyright and related rights in the information society, *Official Journal* L 167, 22/06/2001, pp. 0010-0019.

[2] *Id.*, whereas (9).

[3] *Id.*, whereas (11).

The distance between the 1994 GATT Agreement and the 1996 Bern Convention Aditional Protocol (the first specific statutes about multimedia works), and the 2001 European Directive on copyright at the Information Society, is covered here. The author shows the progressive adaptation of the legal constructions to a revolutionary reality for the social, economic and communications enviroment; which is a risky process if taking into account the development speed of these productions.

The projection of copyright in multimedia goes beyond the borders of an unique legal system, requires the inter-relation and coordination of the largest number of laws from different countries in order to contemplate an effective protection. And because of this, it is necessary to start on the international Treaties in the field, to study the evolution of the European law, and finally analyse the application of every criteria in each and every national law. From this three-step perspective, the complex overview of the copyright development is clearer. As the 2001 European Directive considers: "An harmonised legal framework on copyright and related rights, through increased legal certainty and while providing for a high level of protection of intellectual property, will foster substantial investment in creativity and innovation, including network infrastructure, and lead in turn to growth and increased competitiveness of European industry, both in the area of content provision and information technology and more generally across a wide range of industrial and cultural sectors".[4]

Actually one of the fundamental harmonised elements at the European copyright framework has been the new right of "communication to the public of the works" (also considered at the 1996 Additional Protocol to the Berne Convention). As the author of the book correctly remarks, it is about a faculty which is at a middle place between the right of communication to the public and its distribution; and it is applied specifically to "on demand interactive transmissions", which offers the fact that anybody can access to copyright works from a place and at a time individually chosen by them.

From what I have said, I must conclude that this exhaustive and rigorous work by Julian Rodriguez offers to the reader the opportunity to understand copyright in the contemporary digital convergence situation, and guess the future tendencies of these rights.

The presentation of this book would not be complete without a personal mention to the author. Every work, even a scientific one, says a lot about its author; although, as qualified witness of his research, these pages only confirm the

---

[4]   *Id.*, whereas (4)

intellectual category, the enterprising behaviour and the determination which I have seen during his doctorate years. The time I had the fortune to direct his doctoral thesis has been professionally and personally highly gratifying. Julian has given me, with the biggest flexibility, his cooperation when my Information Law lectures seemed to overflow in number of hours and students; and always has offered me his support at the tortuous avatars of an interdisciplinar knowledge field, which, from a stranger point of view, produces the mirage of being in two minds or in no men's land.

To Professor Rodriguez Pardo and his work my grateful acknowledgment.

Prof. Dr. Ana Azurmendi
Head of the Information Law knowledge field
University of Navarra
Pamplona, 21 May 2002.

Defining the Multimedia Work

In the 1960s MARSHALL MCLUHAN predicted the arrival of an essentially electronic future world, in which the traditional written linear communication – a one-way link between sender and receiver – would be replaced by new relationships of interdependence which would make mutual feedback possible.

McLuhan defined that world with the suggestive name of "the global village" and singled out as two of its main features its being unified through electric networks and the supremacy of television as compared to other mass media.[1]

At the end of that decade, virtually clashing with the arrival of man on the moon —one of the first events broadcast on television for a worldwide audience – the US Department of Defense created a new system for transmitting information based on something apparently so simple as the interconnection of computers. Thus, if a computer failed, its data could be recovered from any other part of the system – something inconceivable until then, because there were no data communications between different computer networks.

The idea, turned into the Advanced Research Projects Agency (ARPANET), gave rise to what today, thirty years later, is known as the Internet, the large information highway that links the end of the 20th century with the new millennium.

In spite of the speed at which events have developed before our very eyes, however, both in the materialization of McLuhan's theories and the creation of the Internet, it is not possible to categorically assert that man is experiencing today a real communicative revolution; carefully considered, these past thirty years have been marked by small achievements and technological advances which contributed to the idea that this age of global communication is more an evolutionary process than a leap in the dark:

The production of computers on an industrial scale, which started in 1951 with the Univac I,[2] was followed by their popularization in the 1960s and 1970s, and,

---

[1] Vid., SEMPERE, *La galaxia McLuhan*, Fernando Torres-Editor (Valencia 1975) 21-24 and MORENO, *Introducción a la comunicación social actual*, Playor (Madrid 1983) 20 and 145.

[2] Cfr. ARROYO, *200 años de informática*, Espasa-Calpe (Madrid 1991) 24.

later on, by the development of small portable machines – personal computers or PCs – that offered a user-friendly interface which made them affordable and easy-to-use tools for everyone; the vanishing of the vinyl record, whose huge success came from the early 1960s,[3] began when the Compact Disc (CD) reached the market in October 1982;[4] the great impact of terrestrial radio and television broadcasting was rivaled by cable and analog communication satellites, whose increasing deployment began in the 1970s;[5] and, finally, upon the arrival of digital technology, all these elements converged on the so-called multimedia works, which found a clear exponent in the *TV-Computer*, whose production was announced by different American companies in 1989, as a first attempt for the merging of computing and the audiovisual area.[6]

Obviously, all these advances contributed through their convergence, to the design of what is known today as the Information Society, substantially based on the use of the New Information Technologies (NITs) as working tools and also for the cultural shaping of society, in an environment where the value of information is continually increasing. Thus, the situation the European Union (EU) announced in the *White Paper on Growth, Competitiveness and Employment* (1993)

---

[3]   In 1948 CBS developed the *Long Playing* record or LP, and soon afterwards RCA launched the 45 revs per minute *Extended Play* (EP), known as *single*. However, the real starting point for the consolidation of these products took place in 1956 with the introduction of stereo and the upgrade from the medium wave radio stations that broadcast using amplitude modulation (AM) to the Frequency Modulation (FM) system, in the early sixties.
        Cfr. BAERT, THEUNISSEN and VERGULT, *Digital audio and compact disc technology*, 2nd ed., Reed International Books (Great Britain 1992) 2.

[4]   The origins of CD can be found in the Digital Audio Disc (DAD), developed in 1977. In September of that same year, MITSUBISHI, SONY, and HITACHI made their first demonstration at the *Audio Fair*.
        Id., 14-15.

[5]   The United States launched the first communication satellites into space in 1962 and 1963. Research on cable had already started in America in the forties and fifties, and then cable would have a real boom in Europe in the seventies.
        Cfr. FAUS, *La era audiovisual*, EUNSA (Pamplona 1995) 248 and 266.

[6]   "In 1989, it was announced that AT&T, INTEL, HEWLET PACKARD, ITT, DIGITAL EQUIPMENT, APPLE, IBM, MOTOROLA, TEXAS INSTRUMENTS, TECTRONIX, and ZENITH were ready to commit themselves to the development of the TV-Computer. It was a new computer with a 60-megabyte storage capacity able to receive programs via fiber-optic cable."
        Cfr. LARRÉGOLA, *De la televisión analógica a la televisión digital*, CIMS (Barcelona 1998) 176.

did materialize,[7] and was consolidated, a year later, in the communication *Europe's Way to the Information Society*.[8] That same year, U.S. vice-president Al Gore's report on the implementation of the Information Society, together with the creation of the National Information Infrastructure Task Force, served an identical purpose.

All things considered, it is just an issue of technological developments in close and interdependent historical moments, because in a way some of them cannot be conceived without the others, and all of them are links in the long chain of the communication technologies history, in development during the last fifty years.

1. The Multimedia Work

An approach to the history of multimedia works is not easy due to the very nature of these creations:[9] usually a multimedia work consists of text, graphics, sounds and images not necessarily created *ex novo*, since it can derive from elements already used in the production of other projects; that is why, under these same circumstances, it could be just an extension or derivation of previously created works and media.

Therefore, to pinpoint the exact moment of its origin is not an easy task.

Nevertheless, the first steps of multimedia came in the 1950s and 1960s, when the first computer generation appeared, since no multimedia system is conceivable without computers. The Univac models I and II, and IBM 701, 702, and 650, which had very limited capacities, were the cutting-edge technology of a market that was spreading by leaps and bounds then.[10]

A few years later, as Bill Gates recalls, there was a jump towards personal computers. By the end of 1974, Ed Roberts and his MITS company created the Altair computer, considered by Gates as the first PC or Personal Computer. However,

---

[7]   *Vid.*, EUROPEAN COMMISSION, White Paper on growth, competitiveness and employment entitled: *The Challenges and Ways Forward Into the 21st Century*, COM 700 (93), December 5, 1993, EUR-OP (Luxembourg 1993) 104.

[8]   *Vid.* EUROPEAN COMMISSION, *Europe's Way to the Information Society,* COM (94) 347 final (Brussels 1994).

[9]   Cfr. SOBRINO, *Nuevas tecnologías aplicadas a la educación universitaria. Valoración de un sistema hipermedia*, pro manuscripto, Universidad de Navarra (Pamplona 1995) 16 – 146.

[10]   Cfr. ARROYO, *op. cit.*, 24.

there are some who say that the phenomenon of the personal computer did not begin until 1977 when the first Apple II hit the market.[11]

In any case, there is consensus that those days marked the beginning of the popular use of computing devices; and that the word *multimedia* was already being used, although infrequently, to refer to any work or technological structure allowing the combination of two or more media or means of expression, regardless of the type of technical instruments and resources used in the combination.

The scope of the notion was so broad that in those days multimedia also meant the simple simultaneous projection of slides and music, synchronized using one of the audio tracks of a tape recorder, or the distribution and sale of language courses – and other educational materials – which relied both on audiovisual and textual methods.[12]

These *sui generis* uses of the term became restricted in 1978 when, in the Massachusetts Institute of Technology – where today's digital guru Nicholas Negroponte works – it was introduced the first computer and videodisc combination. The combination operated thanks to the ease with which the videodisc could be controlled from a computer screen.[13] The outcome of the system was the symbiosis of two electronic technological media and, since then, the word *multimedia* has been applied only to this type of combination.

In the 2000s the evolution of the videodisc reached the MIC 2000 board, a device worthy of that name due to its original design which combines two integrated screens – one for text and the other one for images.[14]

Finally, the next decade started with the popular acceptance of the word multimedia, a widespread term to refer to any combination of media, languages or elements, to the extent of becoming more of an advertising buzzword, as TANNENBAUM says, than a label which accurately and reliably defines the features of a given product.[15]

---

[11] Bill Gates quoted by ARMAÑANZAS, DÍAZ NOCI, and MESO, *El periodismo electrónico. Información y servicios multimedia en la era del ciberespacio*, Ariel Comunicación (Barcelona 1996) 16.

[12] Cfr. ALPISTE, BRIGOS and MONGUET, *Aplicaciones multimedia. Presente y futuro*, Ediciones Técnicas Rede (Barcelona 1993) 18.

[13] *Id.*, 11.

[14] *Id.*, 20.

[15] Cfr. TANNENBAUM, *Theoretical foundations of multimedia*, W. H. Freeman and Company (New York 1998) 3.

1.1. Formulation of its Meaning

In addition to the difficulties for establishing a definite historical period for the birth of multimedia creations, one must considered the relative youthfulness of the concept – not more than forty years – and its basic evolutionary nature as factors that hinder the formulation of a clear-cut definition of its contents.

Therefore, the multimedia notion seems vague and the experts, themselves, such as FELDMAN, emphasize its vagueness: the author lists the obstacles that prevent reaching an exact definition of the term, by pointing to the example of two technical publications which, at the beginning of the current decade, already suggested this same problem:

a) The American *Byte* magazine states in its February 1990 issue:

> "If you are not sure of what multimedia is, you will probably know it when you see it."

b) The British *Multimedia Magazine: Computing with Sound and Motion,* published since 1990, says in one of its first issues:

> "Multimedia is everything for everybody. The term can have a specific meaning or refer to anything in particular, depending on the audience. In fact, multimedia is a remarkable combination of different technologies with overlapping applications looking for a market and an identity."[16]

Nevertheless, although the definitions respond more to an intuitive criteria than to a scientific one, there is a certain affinity among them: the integration of different types of means within only one technological system is regarded as one of the main features of multimedia.

The summary of multimedia definitions made by JANKOWSKI and HANSSEN, who appropriately add that such integration must be a digital one, point in the same direction.[17]

1.1.1. Multimedia as a Combination of Textual, Audiovisual and Computer Elements

One of the most useful and necessary ways for understanding the meaning of a word is to study its etymology. In this case the word multimedia comes from Latin

---

[16] For both quotations, cfr. FELDMAN, *Multimedia*, Blueprint (United Kingdom 1994) 1-2.

[17] Cfr. JANKOWSKI and HANSSEN eds., *op. cit.*, 4.

and consists of two distinctive parts: *multi* – from *multus, multa, multum* – and *media* – from *medium, medii* – whose combined meanings imply "many means" or "several means".[18]

Therefore, the roots seem clear and confirm the meaning assigned to the term until now. However, in spite of having a Latin signifier so easily translatable and understandable, the word multimedia is not univocal. On the contrary, in time it has been loaded with a polysemic value following a process that has taken place mainly in the communications area:

a) The terms *multimedia* or *media conglomerate* are used to describe the commercial enterprises that diversified their investments among different types of media, moving away from their focus on only one segment of the market[19] and expanding their activities to different areas of this business.

As a result of this business stance, this group of companies has been identified as multimedia communication conglomerates, known for being established as such, either with regard to the number of means owned, or to their different activities – press, radio, television or digital communications —, or both.

Their distinctive feature, business diversification, is closely related to the issues related to the market predominance of one enterprise, or just a few, which could easily turn into the establishment of *de facto* monopolies or oligopolies.

b) The word *multimedia* is used to refer to the applications and creations resulting from the integration of elements typical of conventional media – fixed or animated images, graphics, text and sound – using interactive digital technology, by means of software programs used as a basic tools for such integration.

As FELDMAN indicates:

"Multimedia is the simultaneous integration of data, text, any kind of images and sounds within a single digital information environment."[20]

---

[18] In Latin, the word *medium, medii* means "central," as in "central position," and not as a means for communication. It was the development of communications that gave this new meaning to the term. Cfr VOX ed., *Diccionario ilustrado. Latino-español, español-latino*, Bibliograf (Barcelona 1997) 296 and 311.

[19] *Vid.*, GINER, "La prensa del futuro y el futuro de la prensa," *Nuestro Tiempo*, no. 403/4 (Pamplona 1988) 28-128.

[20] Cfr. FELDMAN, *op. cit.*, 4.

And, as VAUGHAN, TREJO, and VIVANCO say:

> "*Multimedia* is any text, graphic art, sound, animation and video combination that reaches you through your computer or through other electronic means".[21]

Obviously, there is a clear coincidence when it comes to point out the basic elements of these works. There is a tendency to incorporate interactive features,[22] given that digital technology enables the user to communicate with the multimedia work which performs the commands it receives – though, for VAUGHAN, TREJO, and VIVANCO, the presence of digital technology is not essential for a work to be described as "multimedia".

According to these authors, one of the distinctive features of multimedia is the possibility of a linear or non-linear development of the display sequence; that is, if it is a non-interactive creation, it will run continuously from beginning to end and the user will not have an option other than to stop it. If, on the contrary, it has such ability, there will not be a compulsory sequential order and the work will be played following the user's requests.[23]

Therefore, can only the works combining each and every of the aforementioned elements be considered multimedia?

c) The word multimedia – in reference to its original meaning "many means or more than one means" – can be easily applied to any product or work that combines, through digital technology or otherwise, at least two of the aforementioned elements, provided that such integration is obtained by means of a computer program.

This third meaning, which is a practical and conciliatory solution, is based upon two points: from a strictly linguistic point of view, there is no clear and absolute need that all the listed elements should be present for the existence of a multimedia work, as the Latin meaning of the word might suggest. On the other hand, and from a historical perspective, the facts mentioned in the beginning of

---

[21]   Cfr. VAUGHAN, TREJO and VIVANCO, *Todo el poder de multimedia*, 2ª ed., McGraw-Hill (México 1995) 4.

[22]   The importance of interactivity is underlined also in *The cyberespace lexicon* in this definition: "Multimedia: term applied to works of art which include the use of combined materials (means), but generally it is used as short for *interactive multimedia.*"
    Cfr. COTTON and OLIVER, *The cyberspace lexicon. An illustrated dictionary of terms from multimedia to virtual reality*, 2ª ed., Phaidon Press (Spain 1995) 136.

[23]   VAUGHAN, TREJO and VIVANCO, *op. cit.*, 6.

Section 1 proved the word *multimedia* had been originally related to a simpler type of combinations.

Thus, this "compromise solution," has been spread almost without objections, as it can be verified in other definitions offered for the term:

i) The French legislation, always seeking some conceptualization as a first step toward finding legal solutions, has established the following parameters:

December 1993 decree: "Multimedia is, according to Article 4, Paragraph 8, Act of June 20, 1992, any document combining in one medium two or more of the previously mentioned media."

The media included in the Decree are mentioned in the definition of the same word proposed by the Information Technology Task Force from the *Association Française de Normalisation (AFNOR)*:

"Multimedia (adj.): related to the combined use of several media. Note: a multimedia representation can combine sounds, images and graphics created by computer."[24]

ii) From a legal point of view, DELGADO says:

"[...] The multimedia production we are dealing with here includes: a) elements belonging to several of the mentioned genres, which may be the expression either of preexisting works (adapted or not) or of specific contributions to the production involved; b) a computer program; and, c) a structure or plan that enables, through the operation of that program, accessing or retrieving the aforementioned elements as well as the 'non-sequential' navigation or browsing within the same."[25]

iii) TANNENBAUM clearly settles this issue from the theoretical point of view:

"Multimedia is defined as an interactive computer presentation, which includes at least two of the following elements: text, sound, fixed images, images in motion or animation."[26]

---

[24] For both definitions, cfr. DEMNARD-TELLIER ed., *Le multimedia et le droit. The Internet, off line, on line,* Hermes (París 1996) 1- 2.

[25] Cfr. DELGADO PORRAS, "La propiedad intelectual ante la tecnología digital: las obras multimedia", chapter of AA VV, *Los derechos de propiedad intelectual en la nueva sociedad de la información. Perspectivas de derecho civil, procesal, penal e internacional comparado,* Comares (Granada 1998) 39.

[26] Cfr. TANNENBAUM, *op. cit.,* 4.

1.1.2. Concepts Distinction: Hypertext, Multimedia, and Hypermedia

Thanks to the definition of multimedia, it is now possible to compare how it differs from other terms linked to the New Information Technologies (NIT) which, although may be part of a multimedia system, should not be considered as having equivalent meanings.

Therefore, we must distinguish hypertext from multimedia and hypermedia:

a) Hypertext: works that enable accessing the information contained in them through a system of links or *hyperlinks* – also known as nodes – which display that information gradually, as the user requests it by clicking on the hyperlinks.

Hypertext forms a network whose distinctive feature is the displaying of contents from a general perspective first, from which the user navigates at will towards more concrete and specific levels.

The birth of hypertext, according to ORIHUELA and SANTOS, is found in VANNEVAR BUSH's 1945 article "As we may think," in which he deals with the main problems faced by the scientists of his time when they had to access certain scientific works while carrying out their researches.[27]

Against the traditional alphabetical or numerical cataloguing, Bush suggested the use of an associative formula in which the information is connected by links, so there is no need to exit the system and start again every time the researcher needs to search for new information.

The influence of "As we may think" was great and, in subsequent years, different researchers dared to put forward alternative formulas for indexing data, whose evolution is reflected in the current hypertext features and among which the non-linearity or non-sequentiality of the information stands out. [28]

Due to this feature the hypertextual structure is also known as tree or branch structure, though it is true that the latter is, according to the ORIHUELA and SANTOS' scheme, just one of seven basic structures it can present: linear, branched, parallel, concentric, hierarchic, reticular or mixed.[29]

---

[27] Cfr., ORIHUELA and SANTOS, *Diseño of comunicación digital. Concepción y desarrollo de proyectos interactivos*, Digitalia (Mutilva Baja 1999) 14.

[28] Ted Nelson coined in 1965 the word "hypertext" to refer to a way of linking documents using links. *Id.*, 13-22.

[29] *Id.*, 30-37.

b) Multimedia is the creation resulting from the combination of text, fixed or animated images, sound and graphics, by means of digital technology and over a digital medium, and with a larger or lesser degree of interactivity.

c) Hypermedia is the combination of the two prior systems or applications; that is, the structuring of a multimedia work through a hypertextual or branched system to retrieve information whose elements are linked to each other. [30]

VAUGHAN, TREJO, and VIVANCO say, on the other hand, that only in case that the system allows the user to choose to some extent the sequence of the presentation of elements, that is, if it is an interactive system, it can be called hypermedia:

> "Multimedia is, as already described, the combined use of text, graphic art, sound, animation and video. When you enable the end user – the viewer of a multimedia project – to control certain elements and when they should be displayed, this is called interactive multimedia. When you provide a structure of linked elements through which the user can navigate, the interactive multimedia is called Hypermedia".[31]

1.2. Formulation of a Typology of its Own

In the light of what has previously been said it seems obvious that the description of multimedia works is more complex than can be expected *a priori;* in fact, the above analysis shows doubts regarding what specific creations should be analyzed as "multimedia" for the purpose of this work.

The polysemic nature of the term and the difficulty to find a particular creation that clearly matches all the parameters that hypothetically should constitute these works, make this problem even more acute.

---

[30] ORIHUELA and SANTOS reject the use of the term hypermedia and push for the exclusive use of the term hypertext: "On the one hand, the distinction between hypertext and hypermedia is a legacy from the Analogical Media Age and from the early days of the Digital Age [...]. In analogic media there was a connection between information formats and media [...]. On the other hand, the modern understanding of text includes any information format, exceeding the idea of written text, it is possible to speak of audiovisual text or radio text, for example [...]. Therefore, the term hypermedia is, partly anachronistic and partly redundant [...]". *Id.*, 39.

[31] VAUGHAN, TREJO and VIVANCO, *op. cit.,* 6.

Regarding this, two are the possibilities and both, apparently, could be considered correct: to understand that a multimedia work should have all the elements mentioned in its definition; or, to accept those more flexible opinions, which only require the presence of two of them.

Both options are however questionable: Is there any multimedia product showing all the features mentioned? Assuming that the presence of all these elements is not essential, should a creation combining just text and video be analyzed as well although, for example, it may be only a subtitled movie?

The first and probably most fundamental distinction, according to GÓMEZ SEGADE,[32] should be made between products or works edited in a physical medium and products or works available on an electronic network: the former are also known as *off-line creations*, because they are displayed individually and on tangible media; the latter, on the other hand, are known as *on-line creations*, precisely because they are works that only exist in a network and do not occupy a definite physical space.

Computer programs, CD-ROMs and CD-Is, and databases contained on tangible media are considered off-line works; on the other hand, networked databases and web pages are considered on-line creations.

a) Computer Programs

Though their technical features and content prevent them from being defined as real multimedia works, the fact that they constitute the basis of these creations, the technical medium over which their different elements are integrated, constitutes sufficient ground for including them within this typology, since the existence of a multimedia work is not possible without a computer program supporting and articulating it.

First and foremost one must make a distinction between the two basic components of any computer equipment: hardware and software.

Hardware is, as stated by FERNÁNDEZ MASÍA, a "set of physical elements which form the computer itself,"[33] that is, the machine or appliance strictly speaking; software, on the other hand, is constituted by the computer programs which

---

[32] Words of GÓMEZ SEGADA, quoted in ESTEVE, *La obra multimedia en la legislación española*, Aranzadi (Pamplona 1997) 26.

[33] Cfr. FERNÁNDEZ MASÍA, "Informática y propiedad intelectual: *software*, bases de datos y creaciones asistidas por ordenador," Chapter of AA VV, *Los derechos de propiedad intelectual en la nueva Sociedad de la Información*, 4.

instruct the machine to perform different operations and that simultaneously enable their execution.

Nevertheless, though in informal speech software and computer program are usually considered equivalent, FERNÁNDEZ MASÍA points out that "the latter is included in the former", since software actually consists of three elements: "the computer program, the description of the program and the supporting material."[34]

However, including the description of the program and the supporting material as integral to the software is, to say the least, disputable, since both elements are included in the software "packages" as instructions for the use of the computer program more than as part of the same.

In short, and maybe as a possible explanation to the current confusion, it should be pointed out that in the beginning, in the 1960s, hardware and software were marketed together, and it was only in the next decade that they began to be sold separately, just as today.[35]

b) CD-ROM (Compact Disc Read Only Memory) and CD-I (Compact Disc Interactive)

McCRAKEN and GILBART say that "it is frequently assumed that the term *CD* is a generic name for all digital and interactive formats,"[36] when in fact it is only a medium on which certain creations may be contained.

Even so, it is true that the popular use of the word has given it a meaning that does not agree with its own nature. The CD-ROM is often considered a multi-media work itself, but its analysis shows that it is only the physical substrate on which some of these productions are contained and distributed.

However, a similar widespread use has not changed the contents of the concept of a computer diskette. A diskette, although sharing similar features with the CD-ROM as a container for the storage of different types of creations, has always been considered a simple medium.

In any case, and since this typology deals with the analysis of what most people understand today as multimedia, CD-ROMs and CD-Is are considered, in their material aspect, as physical means used to store video games, databases or computer programs, among other options.

---

[34]   *Id.,* 4.

[35]   *Id.,* 2.

[36]   Cfr. McCRAKEN and GILBART, *Buying and Clearing Rights. Print, Broadcast and Multimedia*, Blueprint (London 1995) 31.

In this sense, their use has been aimed toward three basic purposes up to now: as databases; as complementary educational methods; or as products designed for leisure time and personal entertainment – e.g. video games.

As for its success, since the beginning the widespread use of the CD-ROM resulted from its low cost, which has turned it into an affordable medium for the presentation of multimedia projects. In 1997 there were over twenty million players worldwide.[37]

And compared to the ancient CD linearity, the CD-I adds user-machine interactivity as a distinctive feature.

c) On-Line and Off-Line Databases

From a historical perspective, LUQUE and GÓMEZ NIETO set the origin of this term in the mid-1960s. In those days, the information was contained in computer files – a great step forward compared to paper file classification systems. However these files were still too rigid for choosing and displaying collected data because they did not allow free combinations or the comparison of different points of view on a same data.[38]

With the evolution of computer systems, relational databases started to play a new significant role thanks to the new designs and dynamic structures that allow the continuous updating and display of information.

The elimination of the rigid formats in which the information was presented, together with the particular criterion that each creator uses for setting up a database, will turn these works into a universal classification methodology and information storage system rather than the final result of the particular method employed for their deployment.[39]

Today, as LUQUE and GÓMEZ NIETO point out, the versatility and speed of databases for accessing information are two of their main features, but they are not the only ones. When evaluating the quality of databases, one should also consider the speed of access, the stored data redundancy or lack thereof, the ease and simplicity of operation, the integrity and accuracy of the indexed information, and the quality of the protection safeguards.[40]

---

[37]   Cfr. VAUGHAN, TREJO, and VIVANCO, *op. cit.*, 7.

[38]   Cfr. LUQUE and GÓMEZ-NIETO, *Diseño y uso de bases de datos relacionales*, Ra-Ma (Madrid 1997) 1.

[39]   *Vid.* GILLENSON, *Introducción a las bases de datos*, McGraw-Hill (Mexico 1988) 1-27.

[40]   *Vid.* LUQUE and GÓMEZ-NIETO, *op. cit.*, 2-6.

d) Web Pages

It seems obvious that any current attempt to explain the origin of the so-called Web pages, inevitably, refers to the birth and development of the Internet, the electronic network used as a medium for their dissemination.

The creation of the Internet in the 1960s, as already noted, took place in the Cold War international political climate, in which there was a constant diplomatic tension between the United States and the then Union of Soviet Socialist Republics (USSR).

In the next decade, away from the political and military connections of the Internet, a new consolidation step was taken when the American academic community started to use it, as they found in the Net an excellent medium for the exchange of scientific knowledge.

This is how the first *newsgroups*, forums for regular intellectual dialogue, were established. In 1985 this lead to the creation of the National Science Foundation (NSF) network, devoted to the spreading of its discoveries and to the improvement of education in the United States.

But what actually triggered the current success of the Internet was the 1989 creation of the *World Wide Web (WWW)*, a technological application through which a huge variety of contents can be presented using different languages, by means of hypertextual structures and with a high degree of interactivity.[41]

In 1993, the *graphic interface* – or browser – Mosaic, followed by Netscape Navigator and Microsoft Explorer, simplified the use of the Web, and so helped it to achieve its indisputable success.

As TREJO says, in a concise and metaphorical description of the whys and the wherefores of the Internet "the net developed until 1983 when it was called, still with military functions, MILNET," but "[…] soon, as a report of that development says, the Net was dominated by a Woodstock spirit, including the respect for common good and individual freedom of speech."[42]

---

[41]   *Vid.*, ORIHUELA and SANTOS, *op. cit.*, 22-24.

[42]   Cfr. TREJO, *La nueva alfombra mágica. Usos y mitos de Internet, la red de redes*, Fundesco (Madrid 1996) 53-54.

Description of Copyright and its Basic Features Throughout its History

A multimedia work is, as already seen, a product of its time, fruit of a technological evolution which, as any technical advance, involves new forms of expression and communication, and at the same time gives rise to situations that require the setting of an appropriate legal framework.

One of these situations, as has been seen, does tally with the new forms of commercial transactions of said works and the infringements which, consequently, could be committed against copyright – a right which should also evolve to adapt itself to the new technological circumstances surrounding –creative activities.

If in the case of the multimedia work it was necessary to formulate a typology of its own to define part of the purpose of this survey, in the case of copyright the situation regards a legal concept deeply rooted and consolidated in most national law bodies. Therefore, there is no need to formulate a new concept of copyright. On the contrary, it will be just necessary to improve on an already existing setting.

Apparently copyright share some common features in the laws currently in force in Western countries, which contrast with the fact that not all countries have the same legal tradition – consider, for instance, Continental Law and Common Law. For that reason, one might wonder: what has happened then? Has copyright derived from the same common origin? Or does the resemblance of certain features come from a subsequent process of mutual influence and legal convergence?

As there are just a few works detailing the origins of copyright, compared to those devoted to explain its current contents, its genesis remains partly in the dark. From what is known, however, and as it will be seen in the following pages, it is possible to draw a first conclusion: copyright is not a revolutionary concept, such as multimedia works, but a concept that has been constantly evolving from the fifth century BC to our times.

Just as it happened in the case of multimedia works where it was possible to draw an evolution timeline in order to understand the current meaning of the term, in copyright there is another line, similar although much longer, which also helps to understand the current principles sustaining this fundamental right.

Thus, and although the most solid traces of this right can be found the 18th and 19th century laws, it cannot be asserted that the genesis of copyright took place then – at least, as far as its concept is concerned.

Although it is true that the Statute of Queen Anne (1709) is considered the first copyright law, the search of its real origin requires a through study of ancient Greece and Rome, where, even though their legislation did not include this right, there was a social and moral recognition, as well as a certain defense, of the authors' work.

More than two thousand years had to elapse between the fifth century BC and the enactment of the English law. Authors and their work then received a crucial stimulus with the invention of the printing press (1450), which not only helped to create a literary industry and fostered widespread literacy, but was also a starting point for devising a suitable legal framework for the printing business.

Nevertheless, it would not be the authors the beneficiaries of this environment, but rather the printers, who were favored with the use of printing privileges that granted them a true monopoly right to print books regardless of the authors' wishes and alleged rights.

However, copyright's two thousand five hundred years path does not show an uninterrupted series of periods of legal interest. In fact, it is only in the 18th century when it is really possible to witness the birth of copyright; but there is, definitely, a long incubation period that a thorough research cannot discard, since it was then when a series of circumstances took place without which, probably, this right would have never seen the light.

From then on, each country, in accordance with their legal tradition, would advance in copyright's consolidation through the passing of specific legislation that, although regulating the same right, maintained the specific features of the national law.

At the end of the 19th century, in order to settle the disputes which started with the international circulation of literary, artistic and scientific creations, the need to join forces through consensual principles in the Public International Law became apparent.

1. Antecedents

1.1. The Social Significance of Authors in Greece and Rome (Fifth Century BC)

Copyright started its history in ancient Greece and Rome, since it was only then that the value of the individuality of the artist, creator or author – anonymous until then – was revealed for the first time, thanks to the qualitative change from the oral transmission of tradition to the creation of handwritten works.

During the fifth century BC both countries witnessed the takeoff of the arts, and the appeareance of the first playwrights, poets, philosophers and jurists that came to be known up to this day, who could at that time "use their own words and thoughts as opposed to the oral bard, always submitted to the control of the attentive audience of his performance."[1]

Thus, it was there and then when it became evident the close relationship bonding the author with his work – which today forms the figure and the purpose of the author's right – as a link that exists since humankind is capable of intellectual creation.

That is why the sensitivity of that period was permeated by the fulfilling idea which asserted that intellectual property is one of the properties most intimately bonded to man,[2] as PUTNAM states in the following passage:

> "The literary property concept was known in the Ancient World. Some kind of reward for the author was seen as a natural law, and anyone infringing this concept was considered almost a thief." [3]

This however did not mean the existence of a formal legal recognition of copyright, nor of a registry to safeguard the authorship of the works – a fact partly denied by DETIENNE when he states that tragedy poet-playwrights kept their manuscripts in the city registry after their being performed.[4]

---

[1] Cfr. DETIENNE dir., *Les savoirs de l'écriture. En Grèce Ancienne*, Presses Universitaires de Lille (France 1988) 340.

[2] Cfr. STEWART, *International Copyright and Neighbouring Rights*, Butterworths (London 1989) 4.

[3] Cfr. PUTNAM ed., *The Question of Copyright*, The Knickerbocker Press (New York-London 1891) 38-39.

[4] Cfr. DETIENNE dir., *op. cit.*, 331.

There is, on the other hand, evidence that society had a clear idea of the correspondence of author's rights to their works, as compared to the rights of those who attempted to copy their creations.

Plagiarism, whose Latin term *plagiarium* comes from the Lex Fabia on kidnapping, was always construed as detrimental to the author and, therefore, it was set within the bounds of the so-called unlawful conducts. Its origin, GIURATI says, quoting Vettore Randi, the royal procurator, stems from the fact that "Roman plagiarism was a form of violence," therefore "literary plagiarism must have been called that way because the plagiarist, deleting the name of the real author and replacing it with his own name, would appropriate another person's work, just as the masters did with their slaves' labor."[5]

But it was in Greece where the authors' protection was most clearly introduced through social condemnation, focused on a series of items comparable to the creators' moral rights of this day. BAYLOS notes that:

"[…] In the Ancient World it was believed that, from a personal and spiritual point of view, the work belonged to the author and the misappropriation of authorship, publication without the author's consent and plagiarism were unlawful."[6]

Therefore, the following acts were condemned:

a) To counterfeit the authorship of a work.

b) The unlawful copy of a work's content without the express consent of the author.

c) The publication of a work under those same circumstances.

In parallel to the commission of these acts, usually in the performance of a play the actors were not faithful to the original text, whether due to forgetfulness or on purpose, and largely ignored the script during the stage show.

This practice offended the Athenian playwrights who finally managed to compel actors to be faithful to the original text when performing a play.

With this aim an Athenian law appeared in 330 BC which, without having been created to specifically ensure the recognition and regulation of the right of authors,

---

[5]   However, Giurati himself objects the use of this term. Cfr. Giurati, *El plagio*, Imprenta de Gabriel L. Horno (Madrid 1922) 40.

[6]   BAYLOS, quoted in ROGEL, *Autores, coautores y propiedad intelectual*, Tecnos (Madrid 1984) 16.

would legally protect what today is considered one of the moral powers of this right: to prevent the distortion or mutilation of the work.

For this purpose, and also in order to be able to carry out the appropriate verifications in case of infringement, the concept of deposit as a compulsory provision finally came up to protect the creations of the great authors of Greek literature.[7]

Comparatively, there is more information available regarding the protection of authors in ancient Rome, where, regardless of their particular artistic inclination, genre or performance, authors would be recognized as *artifices*, just as CALABI notes:

> "The authors of marble or bronze statues and portraits, of paintings and murals, of mosaics, of any work of art and of all the objects suitable for improving the appearance of houses, tombs, theaters and any other building of the Romans' social and public life; the craftsmen of luxurious utensils made of silver and gold, ivory, precious stones, coral, glass; [...] they were all called craftsmen in Latin, whether they created original works, they were inspired by other works, or whether they used forms and casts for mass production."[8]

Their efforts and the fruits of their efforts were recognized at different levels, according to which the work of art had three different purposes: to earn money for its author (*pecunia*), to offer him fame (*gloria*) and to give his work a sense of transcendence (*religio*) – because it was considered that the artist pretended to be a god when taking part through his work in worship, if the artist produced religious works.

However, the artistic work was included in the common category of *operae* and its legal profile did not show differences with other types of work. In fact, its contractual features depended on the type of work that the creator was hired to perform.

In Rome, the social status of each person defined its work, and served to differentiate between works. Thus, the artist called *libero* enjoyed a special consideration allowing him to work anywhere, without limits to his creative activity, as compared to those whose work had always to be performed at a particular place.

---

[7]   Cfr. LIPSZYC, *Derecho de autor y derechos conexos*, UNESCO and CERLALC (Buenos Aires 1993) 28.

[8]   Cfr. CALABI, *Studi sulla società romana. Il lavoro artistico*, Instituto Editoriale Cisalpino (Milan-Varese 1958) 9.

But, despite all these indications on the status of the literary, artistic or scientific creator, the search in Roman Law for any *actio* dealing with the legal protection of intellectual rights remains fruitless. It is only possible to mention, although with great reservation, the *actio iniurarium* as the closest to a provision protecting the author's rights, since to "counterfeit" the authorship of a work was seen as prejudicial to the original creator's honor. The contents of this *actio* have certain similar nuances to what now is known as injury.

Nevertheless, GARCÍA GARRIDO excludes this possibility when he explains the meaning of this action, pointing out that it has a very general content – and is therefore applicable to many fields – to restrain damages or offenses to dignity, since it is an action regarding injury and its application within the scope of copyright would be an example of a concrete application, but never a right created with this aim.[9]

Therefore, although there were no particular laws protecting copyright or providing for transactions involving intellectual rights; this does not mean that Roman jurists showed no interest in intellectual property. They were interested from a theoretical point of view, basically focused on the consideration of the formal expression of ideas as well as of their property.

Thus, Roman jurists asked themselves what granted the property right of intangible assets, such as those created by the intellect:[10]

a) Proculus' disciples held that it was the use of a material substrate, turning it into something new, what granted a property right to whom had crafted it.

b) The School of Sabinus, instead, defended the idea that the owner of the base material should obtain title on what had been made with it.

c) Justinian, choosing an intermediate solution previously indicated by Gaius, offered as an idea for solving the problem, to determine the possibility of returning the material to its original form, and consider what was more essential: the base material or what had been made with it.

   Both views apparently referred to a particular case – the property of a table with a painting on its surface – in which the decision was taken in favor of the artist, since it was interpreted that the property of ideas relied on the form of its expression.

---

[9] Cfr. GARCÍA GARRIDO, *Derecho Privado Romano*. Edición Abreviada, Dykinson (Madrid 1993) 298.

[10] Cfr. PUTNAM ed., *op. cit.*, 40-42.

On the other hand, there is evidence of the Roman social consideration of the rights of the authors, not only as regards their moral dignity, but also regarding the practice of certain proprietary powers.[11]

KLOSTERMANN indicates that the agreements reached between authors and sellers for the reproduction and sale of the artists' works demonstrate that there existed a true recognition of the artist's property, in addition to consider unlawful any infringement of the seller's right on a work which eventually had been transferred to him.[12]

a) Terence's *The Eunuch* was sold for performance and it was so successful that it was resold to third parties by the first buyer, with the provision that it would be performed just one time before an adult audience; the author also negotiated his work *Hecyra*, which he sold to Roscius.

b) Atticus traded the works of the jurist Cicero, at his request, and acted like what today is known as a publisher.

According to STEWART, the profits Atticus brought to Cicero were so significant that, after the sale of his *Speech for Ligarius*, Cicero offered Atticus the trading of his future works.[13]

c) The poet Martial had four different publishers in charge of selling his works, one of whom was a slave set free by the *Lucensis* family, who made a special pocket edition of the *Epigrames*.

d) Horace referred to the Sosius brothers as his publishers, to whom the sale of his works brought large profits.

e) Statius would have starved had he not sold his tragedy *Agave* to Paris, who was an actor.[14]

From these five examples the first signs of the principle of assignment can be inferred, as well as the birth of the concept of the publisher. However, from what has been said it cannot be concluded that ancient Rome would have known how to

---

[11]   It should not be overlooked that the Roman legal system, like the Greek one, established a clear difference between "to own a thing and to be its owner."

Cfr. HARRISON, *The Law of Athens. The Family and the Property*, Clarendon Press (Oxford 1968) 204.

[12]   KLOSTERMANN, quoted in PUTNAM ed., *op. cit.*, 39.

[13]   Cfr. STEWART, *op. cit.*, 13.

[14]   Cfr. PUTNAM ed., *op. cit.*, 40.

protect the right of the authors. In fact, there is not a single trace of the explicit creation of laws in that regard, and those sales were based on natural justice, according to COPPINGER, since "no man can have a right to benefit from the sale of the work of another without the author's consent."[15]

All in all, the social respect given to authors in those days – whose signature was the most common advertising medium – can be inferred from the actual existence of these commercial transactions.[16] However, the signature of the work was not customary for Roman creators; so much so that it is possible to say that the lack of a signature did not mean that the work was lacking in significance, originality or beauty.[17]

In the case of sculptures, the works with signatures represented only a small fraction of a sculptor's entire collection, part of which included unfinished or mutilated works. Nevertheless, from the signed sculptures that have survived to this day it is possible to assume that the signature consisted of the name of the artist, in nominative or genitive case; with the name followed by *fecit* or *sculpsit* (made or sculpted); and, occasionally, with the name in genitive followed by *manu* (by hand).[18]

Concerning the trading and promotion of a writers' works, a good example is the case of Martial, who personally prepared epigrams advertising his works for his sellers, indicating the price of each book as well as the place where to buy them.[19]

1.2. Invention of the Printing Press (1450) and the Birth of Privileges

In the times of ancient Greece or Rome, copyright – in the modern sense of the term – had not been consolidated as such; likewise the Middle Ages did not show any progress regarding the author's rights, as this period was some sort of temporary halt before the printing press would give a boost to creative activity.[20]

---

[15] *Id.*, 40.

[16] Cfr. CALABI, *op. cit.*, 88.

[17] *Id.*, 90.

[18] *Id.*, 90.

[19] Cfr. PUTNAM ed., *op. cit.*, 39.

[20] As PUTNAM points out, "it is after the invention of the press where one look for the genesis of *copyright.*" *Id.*, 13.

After the Fall of the Roman Empire, scripting – particularly copying – was no longer done by the *librarii* and slaves and was transferred to the monasteries.[21] There the monks, away from earthly concerns, spent their time studying and copying by hand – *amanuensis* – the great treatises and compendia of knowledge that they possessed in their libraries, to the point of virtually becoming the sole guarantors of the survival of the written culture and science of those days. Later on, they would gloss and read aloud those works to facilitate their dissemination.

To be precise, the word *scriptoria* designated the group of monks in charge of manufacturing books, and this term was also used to name each one of them, regardless of the step of the process they were involved in.[22]

Copyists considered their work a real form of asceticism, because it required a lot of effort to decipher a text – which was often poorly written – and reproducing it correctly. So much so that sometimes, when a book was completed its offering to God would become some sort of liturgy. A 9th century volume of Flavius Josephus of Stavelot, reads as follow: "*Suscipe, Sancta Trinitas, Oblationem huius codicis* [...]."[23] Naturally, this intense activity resulted in the revival of the Christian message.

In any case, aside from considering the spiritual point of view of the work of the *scriptoria*, it seems obvious that, thanks to this work – particularly in the 9th and 10th centuries – and to the work of the universities and their laymen copying workshops, nowadays the libraries both of Europe and the Americas are well furnished with handwritten copies.[24]

It is precisely in the Middle Ages when the universities, together with the monasteries, were the most significant cultural centres.[25] The cultural revival

---

[21] Cfr. FUIANO, *Libri, scritorii e bibioteche nell'alto medioevo*, Libreria Scientifica Editrice (Naples 1973) 56.

[22] Cfr. LECLERCQ, *The Love of Learning and the Desire of God. A Study of Monastic Culture*, 1ª ed. in New American Library (New York 1962) 127.

[23] The effort the copyists had to make is described, in this same work, by the Abbot of Fleury: "To copy a book was like praying and fasting, a means to correct those overcame with passion." Cfr. LECLERCQ, *op. cit*, 127.

[24] Cfr. FUIANO, *op. cit.*, 49-50.

[25] RASHDALL advocates the significance of the cultural role of the universities, leaving the activities of the monasteries aside: "It is possible to say that the universities and their most immediate products were the most important achievement in the intellectual field in the Middle Ages." Cfr. RASHDALL, *The Universities of Europe in the Middle Ages*, vol. I, 2ª ed., Oxford University Press (London 1936) 3.

of the 11th century, enhanced by the political stability of European states, was mostly due to a recovery of the educational values, marked by the rediscovery of the ancient thought of authors like Aristotle or Plato and also by the birth of scholasticism.

Although the prestige then acquired by universities like Bologna, Salerno, Oxford or Cambridge was undeniable, the University of Paris was certainly pre-eminent in the book trade field. The *stationarii* and the *librarii*, publishers and booksellers, saw their business flourish under the wing of these institutions: the former employed writers to increase the production of books; the latter, sold copies to students and to all those interested in the acquisition of new knowledge. Sometimes, a sale was replaced by the lending of the copy in exchange of a sum as a deposit for the possible damages that might be caused to the work. In any case, before the circulation of a new work, the authorities of the university had to be informed about its publication and content.

1.2.1. The Privilege: A Right in Favor of Printers

But between 1438 and 1450 a real revolution in the arts and communications world took place: Johann Gensfleisch von Güttemberg invented his printing press, which was gradually improved during that twelve year period. The invention began to revitalize various literary genres that had almost sunk into oblivion, and which were unknown to most citizens.

In 1451 Güttenberg printed his first book with movable types in Mainz. In 1464 Caxton installed the first press in England; in 1465 two Germans started to develop the printing industry in a monastery near Rome – city to which they would move two years later. In 1469 John of Spyre started this same activity in Venice; and that same year Louis XI sent Nicholas Jenson to Mainz so that he would bring the invention to France on his return.[26]

Thanks to the printing press a significant number of copies of the same work were easily reproduced at relatively low cost. For that reason, the literary, artistic and scientific creations began to benefit from an incipient geographic mobility unknown until then – due in part to the scarcity of copies of each work.

In parallel, the increase of literacy originated new potential markets for the authors, whose works eventually left the monastic cloisters to move into the

---

[26]   Cfr. PUTNAM ed., *op. cit.*, 13.

booksellers' stores and printing workshops, being now subject to mechanical reproduction.[27]

The work of the printers was focused, at first, on Bibles, prayer books and such; but in 1465 Fust and Schoeffer published Cicero's *Officios* – "the first tribute paid by the new art to social literature," according to HALLAM.[28] This provided the necessary incentive to revitalize the genres that seemed lost – like the novel or the classical tragedy – to which the monks had barely devoted themselves, due to the excessive cost that represented copying and publishing manuscripts.

"Back then," LECLERCQ says, "a manuscript represented a capital investment, a huge block of paper was necessary to supply the required material to copy a book of Seneca or Cicero."[29]

This explains why so many authors remained anonymous until well into the Renaissance, not because they did not wish to exploit their works commercially, but rather because they could not reach an agreement with printers and publishers. For that reason, the concept of patron of the arts, as a promoter of literary and artistic creations, acquired an important status.[30]

All things considered, and according to STEINGBERG, "the printing press had a very important influence on political, constitutional, religious and financial events, and on all social, philosophical and literary movements, to such a degree that it is not possible to understand any of those without taking this influence into account."[31]

Paradoxically, authors were not the most favored from the invention of the printing press, but rather the printers, who thanks to their skill in the use of this invention played a leading role in the cultural revival of the time, often being at the same time publishers and booksellers.

However, the feudal rulers, lords and monarchs, overwhelmed by the power given to the printers by the printing press, decided to establish an administrative-

---

[27]   *Vid.* GRAFF, *Storia dell' alfabetizzazione occidentale*, Il Mulino (Italy 1987).
        However, the appearance of the press did not mean, at all, the end of the work of the monks as copyists.
        Cfr. EISENSTEIN, *Le rivoluzioni del libro. L'invenzione della stampa e la nascita dell'età moderna*, 1st. ed. in Il Mulino (Bologna 1995) 24.

[28]   HALLAM, quoted in PUTNAM ed., *op. cit.*, 14.

[29]   Cfr. LECLERCQ, *op. cit.*, 128-129.

[30]   Cfr. SEIGNETTE, *Challenges to the Creator Doctrine*, Kluwer Law and Taxation Publishers (Deventer-Boston 1994) 10.

[31]   STEINBERG, quoted in EISENTEIN, *op. cit.*, 18-19.

legal concept which would allow them to exert an absolute control over Güttem-berg's invention use: it was called "the privilege".

This new concept consisted in the obligatory authorization, granted by the ruling classes, given to a printer as his sole right to print and sell books within the law. Thus, a certain control was exerted over the disseminated content, as well as over the printer – although there is evidence that some privileges were granted by feudal lords in compensation for the contribution made by authors to increase the standard of general education in a given territory.

Therefore, anyone interested in printing a work should have a *privilege* and also a *placet* for the reproduction and subsequent distribution of the work. This also prevented the sale of the same book at different prices depending on the printer.

This provision, besides being a means of prior censorship, also turned the printers' craft into a monopoly – which is still nowadays blamed on copyright – since only those who had been authorized could devote to the printing business.

The privileges granted had a simple typology: a) general privileges, which not only authorized the printing of a given work, but also its adaptation or translation, for instance; and b) simple privileges, which only allowed the publication of a given work.

Despite everything, the concept of *privilege* did not prevent the development of a cultural industry. At the end of the 15th century the three main European printing centers – Venice, Paris and Lyon – reported a volume of forty thousand, twenty-five thousand and sixteen-thousand works, respectively.[32]

Curiously enough, to a certain extent the *privilege* shares some features with what today is known as copyright, due to the exclusive nature of both concepts. Nevertheless, there is a noticeable difference: while the creator of the work holds a copyright, the privilege consisted in a right granted to printers, not by the authors, but by the feudal monarchs and lords – who never conceived it as an intellectual right, although in practice it would turn into a concept regulating the publishing business.

Four were the elements that defined the features of the privilege, which are now present, *mutatis mutandis*, in copyright:

   a) The exclusive right enjoyed by printers.

   b) A time limit on the validity of this right.

---

[32] Cfr. MARTIN, *op. cit.*, 29.

c) The adoption of coercive measures to prevent unauthorized printers from printing protected works.

d) And the printer right to claim a compensation, in case of any infringement of his vested right.

Unlike what happened in classical cultures, when the moral rights of authors were specially vindicated, the invention of the printing press diverted the attention from authors to printers and booksellers, aside from emphasizing the now so-called economic rights of copyright: the exclusive assignment of the right to copy, the limited duration of the right and the adoption of coercive measures and compensation remedies to protect an industry which was starting to flourish.

Nevertheless, and according to ROSE, it should be taken into account that in this period there were also minor and occasional privileges awarded to authors only. One of these privileges was granted in 1486 to the Venetian historian Marco Antonio Sabellico for his work *Decades rerum Venetarum*, allowing him to choose the printer to whose care he would entrust the publication of his work, as well as formally condemning any printer to pay a five hundred ducat fine if found guilty of printing unauthorized copies of that work.[33]

1.2.2. International Spreading of Privileges and the Shaping of their National Features

The consolidation of privileges, through its application in different countries would eventually give birth to the first laws dealing with copyright, whose features, however, would differ from country to country.

In this regard, the first traces of the broadening of privileges and their subsequent development into copyright go back to 1469 Venice.[34] In those days, the city Senate granted a monopolistic authorization in favor of one printer, John of Spyre, to enjoy an exclusive five-year right to print Cicero's and Plinio's epistles.[35]

---

[33] Cfr. ROSE, *Authors and Owners. The Invention of Copyright*, Harvard University Press (United States 1993) 10.

[34] Cfr. PUTNAM ed., *op. cit.*, 15.

[35] Contrary to this fact, WIPO states that the first privilege granted in said city dates from 1474 and is called *Parte Veneziana*. However, WIPO indicates that this privilege was planned to protect inventions, not literary works. Cfr. WORLD INTELLECTUAL PROPERTY ORGANIZATION ed., *Introduction to Intellectual Property. Theory and Practice*, Kluwer Law International (London 1997) 17.

This privilege was passed into law in 1603 with no changes to its basic content, and therefore, it can be considered as the first formal regulation on copyright – thus replacing the Statute of Queen Anne (1709), according to MARANDOLA.[36]

This law granted authors the right to sell their works to third parties for commercial purposes for a term of twenty years, after which they would enjoy a right to reversion.

Previously, in 1481, the Duke of Milan granted Andrea of Bosiis the right to publish Jean Semonet's *Sforziade*, for a five-year period.[37] And in 1491 the publicist Peter of Ravenna was granted, together with the publisher that he would choose, the exclusive right to copy and sale his work *Phoenix* – a concession that, according to PUTNAM, constituted the first direct privilege granted to an author.[38]

Other Italian states also granted privileges to various printers for terms of about fourteen years, aiming to promote the new industry of printing, which would eventually contribute to the revival of literature, regarded as an asset to the community.

In addition to the Italian case, in order to understand the singularity and importance of this concept it is also necessary to watch its evolution in another three countries – Germany, France and Great Britain -, besides the obvious reference to the Spanish case:

a) In Germany each privilege was confined to a *land*, therefore its effect had a very limited geographical scope. So, to provide an effective protection of the rights of printers and booksellers, the *länder* had to reach mutual agreements in order to ensure a better defense of the works circulating throughout the whole country.

The privileges – of which the first one was granted in Nüremberg in 1501[39] – used to be valid for ten years and, although they were particularly protective of printers, these usually acted within the knowledge and consent of authors.

In any case, FEATHER extends this privilege to all works to be printed within the Venetian territory during those five years. Cfr. FEATHER, *Publishing, Piracy and Politics. An Historical Study of Copyright in Britain*, Mansell Publishing Limited (London 1994) 11.

ARMSTRONG, instead, quoted by SAUNDERS, sets the first privilege in Wurzburg (1479). Cfr. SAUNDERS, *Authorship and Copyright*, Routledge (London-New York 1992) 80.

[36]   Cfr. MARANDOLA, *Diritto d'autore*, Associazione Italiana Biblioteche (Rome 1996) 7.

[37]   *Id.*, 11.

[38]   Cfr. PUTNAM ed., *op. cit.*, 15-16.

As far as PUTTER is concerned, quoted by PUTNAM, also states that this was the first privilege granted in the Middle Ages, and dates it January 3, 1491. *Id.*, 43.

[39]   Cfr. PUTNAM ed., *op. cit.*, 16.

The poet Conrad Celtes was granted the privilege of Nüremberg over the work of the poetess Hroswista, who had been dead for six hundred years, to encourage the printing of her writings.[40]

Between 1510 and 1514 Emperor Maximilian granted privileges for the sermons of Geiles Kaiserberg and the writings of Schottius and Stabius, among others.

In 1525 Luther published a pamphlet entitled *Notice to Printers* in which he warned about the serious economic consequences arising from illegal printing. In this pamphlet he also quoted a decision from the Court of Nüremberg banning the imitation of painter Dürer's signature on the illegal copies made of his work – but although the painter resorted to the appropriate legal channels, he was unable to prevent the unlawful copying.

Nine years later, Luther himself obtained from the Elector of Saxony, in Wittenberg, a privilege to print his translation of the Bible.

In the 16th and 17th centuries the cities of Frankfurt and Leipzig were the main German literary trade centers,[41] in which, occasionally, the privileges only became effective once the works had been published.

More than a century later, from 1660, the passage of some general laws helped to protect the privilege and its holders, at the same time setting forth penalties for making illegal copies and their sale: in Frankfurt, in 1657, 1660, and 1775; in Nüremberg, in 1623; in Saxony, in 1661; and by the Imperial government, in 1646.[42]

Some of these laws pursued the protection of printers, to compensate the heavy financial investment required for the reproduction of a book, and at the same time printers were compelled to obtain the authors' written consent, which could be understood either as a simple moral justification of their work or as rights duly assigned.

b) In France the privilege concept had a significant impact between the reign of Louis XII and the turn of the 16th century, being its distinctive feature the death penalty imposed on those who violated a privilege.

Also, any book intended for publication had to be previously authorized by the Royal Chancery, a body which prior to releasing the works for printing controlled

---

[40]   *Id.*, 47.

[41]   Cfr. SEIGNETTE, *op. cit.*, 11.

[42]   *Id.*, 48.

their contents – save for theological texts, which were reviewed by the Paris School of Theology.

There was an indisputable close relationship between the development of copyright and censorship.[43] No publisher or author would be granted any privilege if the royal censors did not approve the contents of the book to be published, as the Edict of Moulins (1566) shows. This Edict banned "any person from printing or encouraging to print any book or treatise without permit or consent of the king, and the requisite letters patent."[44]

On April 30, 1504 André de la Vigne, chancellor of King Charles VIII, filed a claim against Michel Lenoir before the Parliament of Paris, requesting not to grant Lenoir an authorization to publish *Vergier d'honneur* – an anthology of poems which collected some compositions of the Royal Chancellor.[45]

On May 11, 1504 the Parliament granted De la Vigne a two-week period to find witnesses. Meanwhile Lenoir obtained an authorization to finish printing the copies that were already at the printer's, although he was not authorized to sell those copies.

On June 3 the Parliament delivered its final decision banning Lenoir, and any other person with exception of De la Vigne, to print or sell the works *Vergier d' honneur* and *Regnars traversant*, until April 1, 1505:

> "It is hereby stated that said Court has rejected and rejects to approve the petition of Le Noir and he and other printers and booksellers of the city of Paris, except the defendant De la Vigne, are forbidden to print or sell the books entitled *Vergier d'honneur* and *Regnars traversant*, until next April 1, under penalty of an indeterminate fine and confiscation of said books; furthermore, the Court condemns the applicant to pay court costs, whose determination is reserved to this Court."[46]

Almost seventy years later, in 1571, Charles IX would recognize the existence of intellectual property; and in 1576 Henry III would support this idea by establishing letters patent.

---

[43] ARMSTRONG, quoted by SAUNDERS, dissident of this opinion. Cfr. SAUNDERS, *op. cit.*, 80.

[44] Cfr. SEIGNETTE, *op. cit.*, 18.

[45] Cfr. BROWN, *Poets, Patrons and Printers. Crisis of Authority in Late Medieval France*, Cornell University Press (United States 1995) 1.

[46] Archives Nationales, Conseil 1509: from November 12, 1503 to December 7, 1504. *Id.*, 1.

In 1618 the French government forced Parisian booksellers and printers to form a guild which, in return for a printing monopoly, would censor the works to be published. The concept of the censor, created back then by the Guild of Printers and Booksellers of Paris, survived until the beginning of the French Revolution, when the system of privileges had already virtually disappeared everywhere in Europe.[47]

The French system of privileges was completed by implicit permits – *permissions tacites* – which during the 18th century granted non-exclusive printing rights. As SAUNDERS explains, these rights should not be disregarded as thanks to them important works like Montesquieu's *L'esprit de lois*, and Diderot's *Encyclopédie* came to be published.

That is why, almost every work printed before the French Revolution carried the following legend:

"Royal Patents (address and name of beneficiary):

To our friends and loyal advisors, to the people representing us in Parliament… and to any other in charge of administering justice, to all those who protect our bookstores and printers, and to other people of any quality and status whatsoever, against the introduction of foreign works in any part of our domains."[48]

c) In England the system of privileges was initiated by Henry VII in 1485, when he granted the first privilege – First Royale Printer – to Peter Actors, in the following terms:

"Privilege for life to Peter Actors, born in Savoy, granted by the office of the King's *Stationer*; also, license to import, so often as he likes, from parts beyond the sea, books printed and not printed into the port city of London, and other ports and places of the Kingdom of England, and to dispose of the same for sale or otherwise without paying customs dues, and without rendering any type of account."[49]

---

[47] Cfr. SEIGNETTE, *op. cit.*, 13.

[48] *Id.*, 45.

[49] Cfr. PATTERSON, *Copyright in Historical Perspective*, Vanderbilt University Press (Nashville 1968) 81.

Nevertheless, the system was not consolidated until 1529,[50] almost a century after the invention of the printing press in its more rudimentary form, when foreigners were banned from setting up any type of printing shop. The reason for this delay was due to the liberalism of Charles III, English monarch of that period, who in 1483 enacted a statute establishing the free printing and import of books.

The ideas contained in this text caused the massive arrival of foreign authors to England in order to have their works printed without restrictions, under the protection of a legal system which, although not intended to regulate the rights of authors, gave literary creators the opportunity to publish their works under more favorable conditions than in their own countries.

However, when Henry VIII came to power this policy against monopolies ended. The new monarch considered that the arrival of foreign authors on the island could jeopardize the survival of English national culture and, due to this, he decided to restrict the right to print with the passage of two laws in 1523 and 1528. He also ordered the compulsory inspection of the contents of all books by the Privy Council. A year later, in 1529, the system of exclusive privileges was definitely established under the name of Printing Patent System.

Though it was intended basically to control the contents of books and publications, in practice it made of the publishing business an exclusive system, because only a few favored printers would enjoy said privileges, which fell into two categories:

  i) General printing patent on a generic group of works – usually legal texts, basic education, prayers or almanacs.

  ii) Particular printing patent on a specific book for a term of seven to ten years, first applied to *The Latin Sermon Preached by Richard Pae at St. Paul's Cathedral on the Peace Between England and France.*[51]

On May 4, 1557, King Philip II and his wife Mary granted the Stationers' Company[52] a different type of privilege, allowing a new way of exerting a printing monopoly not based on the censorship of contents applied by the Privy Council, but with a similar purpose.

---

[50] PATTERSON fixes the consolidation date of the privilege system in 1538. *Id.*, 81.

[51] *Id.*, 87.

[52] The origin of the *Stationers' Company* goes back to 1403, date in which the Mayor of London granted to the participants in the book business the right to set up a professional association.

The royal charter in favor of the Stationers' Company required all printers to be registered in the company's register, which since then, started to exert a close control over the publication of writings against the Catholic faith – a system which, once again, would give rise to printing monopolies not in any way related with censorship.

> "No person within this our Kingdom of England, or of its domains, shall practice or exercise by itself, its ministers, its servants or through any other person, the art or mystery of printing any book or any thing for sale or trade within this our Kingdom of England, or of its domains, unless that same person at the time of such impression is or will be a member of the guild of said mystery or art of the Stationery in said City, or has our authorization or that of the successors of our Queen by means of letters patent."[53]

Thus, a period of coexistence between two systems started in which, in both cases, the right of a work's author was turned into a right of the printer, which does not mean that creators were kept completely out of the reproduction and trade of their works. However, the recognition given to authors was more an expression of the wish of the Stationers' to publish works without any competition, than an actual and fair recognition towards authors, who sometimes would receive a certain amount of money upon giving their authorization to the Stationers' Company for the publication of their writings.

Thus, the Anglo-Saxon copyright received at birth, through the system of privileges, a very special characterization: "Common law copyright is the right of first publication."[54]

Nevertheless, and to avoid oversimplifying this analysis, it should be pointed out that at least these agreements used to recognize the sole right of authors to modify their works, as it can be inferred from the *Stationers'* notes, when Doctor Bright's work *A treatise of melancholie* was registered in 1586. Nonetheless, and as it will be seen, the basic setting and intention were commercial, foreign to the moral conflicts of the author's rights:

> "Memorandum stating that Doctor Bright has given his word not to interfere by increasing or altering said book until John Windet's edition is sold."[55]

---

[53] *Id.*, 32.

[54] *Id.*, 70.

[55] ARBER, quoted by PATTERSON. *Id.*, 71.

But the coexistence of both systems was no easy task. Between 1571 and 1576 many young apprentices who started to serve at the Stationers' realized how the Printing Patent System was preventing them from taking their first steps in the business, since there was not enough work for any person wishing to reproduce and sell books.

In 1578, several members of this group of young apprentices wrote the document *The petition of the poor*, which they sent to the House of Lords with the purpose of putting an end to this discriminatory situation. The aim was partially achieved, since the Chamber only recognized their right to print the works nobody else wanted.[56]

Naturally, this concession did not mean the end of the controversy, since it was considered insufficient. As of 1580, in addition to these complaints, members of the Stationers' started to print illegal copies – violating granted privileges – led by John Wolfe, who was defending the right of any man to print any book out of his own free will.

Eventually, peace would be reestablished on May 23, 1586, although by means of a restriction, with *The new decrees of the Star Chamber for orders in printing*, requiring printers to register with the Stationers' and confining printers to London and its surroundings, except for one press each at the university cities of Oxford and Cambridge.[57]

In 1637 the Star Chamber Decree banned the printing of any work which had not been previously registered with the Stationers', not only exerting control over printers, but also over the works they published.

In spite of the national differences seen in the study of the privileges, printers of all the small states of Europe, during the Holy Roman Empire, had as a common concern the need to apply for privileges in foreign states as the only way to protect their interests in a commercial activity which was seeing an increasing international expansion. Thus, when in 1553 the *Pandecta* were published in Florence, the publisher ensured his privileges not only in that city, but also in Spain, the Two Sicilies and France.

---

[56] About its precedents, *id.*, 92-93.

[57] *Id.*, 29.

> Three years before, in 1583, a report written by a special committee, established by royal order, recommended the abolition of *general patents*, the restriction on the number of printers and apprentices, and price control, as a way to rearrange the book trade. *Id.*, 134.

However, it was difficult for a non-resident to secure these privileges in the country where he was seeking that protection and, in fact, the safeguards actually offered were minimal.

The difficulty encountered for the publication of works in the 16th and 17th centuries, consolidated the patronage system as a customary way to publish personal creations. Therefore, when the copies were ready at the printer's, the authors requested their share of copies and sent one of them to their patrons together with laudatory letters. Furthermore, this difficulty hindered some humanities scholars from meeting their expectations of becoming authors, and so had to settle for a job as print shop "proof-readers".[58]

This notwithstanding, in view of the vast business opening up in the literary field, the authors were soon able to assign their writings for a consideration. La Fontaine and Molière put this into practice with their comedies and tragedies; Ribou, a bookseller, after acquiring Molière's *Précieuses ridicules*, once published it without the author's consent and then he was granted a privilege which, eventually, would be revoked.[59]

Erasmus, for his part, when criticized by his rivals for obtaining money from his booksellers in exchange for the printing and sale of his works, argued that he only received money from his friends when he gave them signed copies. This was not true, since being well renowned, the author had a network of agents all over Europe.[60]

In England, on April 27, 1667, Milton sold the original of his *Paradise Lost* for five pounds, and his publisher, Samuel Simons, would add other five pounds once the first edition of one thousand three hundred copies would be sold out – a procedure to be repeated in subsequent editions.[61]

In France, the mid-18th century bookseller Praul paid Voltaire one thousand pounds for his *Enfant prodigue*. For his part, another well-known figure, Rousseau,

---

[58] The University of Paris, a book trade center in amanuensis copies times, was a wonderful exponent of these new relationships.

[59] *Vid.* EISENSTEIN, *The Printing Press as an Agent of Change. Communications and Cultural Transformations in Early-Modern Europe*, vol. II, Cambridge University Press (United States 1979) 520-543. Cfr. FEVRE and MARTIN, La aparición del libro, UTEHA (Mexico 1962) 175.

[60] *Id.*, 173.

[61] *Id.*, 173.

received twenty-five louis for his *Discours sur l'inégalité*; thirty louis for *Lettre à d'Alembert*; and six thousand pounds for *Emille*.

Nevertheless, by the end of the 16th century many authors began to print their own works after realizing that, if the work were successful, they would obtain greater earnings and benefits.

Germany is a singular example of these initiatives, since authors like Lessing resorted to this method and, even, publishing cooperatives were created, among them the famous Klopstock's Republic of Scholars (*Gelehrtenrepublik*), in 1774.[62]

2. The Statute of Queen Anne (1709): First Positive Materialization of a Right in Favor of Authors

2.1. Contents: Recognition of a Time Limited Exclusive Right

Although MARANDOLA points to the Venetian law of 1603 as the first copyright rule, jurists consider, in general, that this title should be assigned to the Statute of Queen Anne (1709), passed in England. As opposed to the Venetian case, this text did not arise from a privilege, but rather from an independent attempt to solve different conflicts causing unrest in the 17th century English arts scene and, in particular, in the copyright field:

a) The influence, in the 16th and 17th centuries, of John Locke's ideas, who held that certain rights were inherent to the individual, and did not need the state authorization to be enjoyed; including the right to the fruits of one's labor.

Thus, he considered copyright as the recognition owed to the authors for the time and effort invested in the creation of their works.

Specifically, Locke demanded that the protection of the author's rights should be extended to between fifty and seventy years, in a much closer stance to the interests of authors than of printers.

b) The strict control of the system of privileges, established by Henry VIII, and in effect until 1642. By this date the House of Commons prohibited the members of the Stationers' Company to print any book without its author's consent.

---

[62] *Id.*, 176.

However, twenty years later, Charles I reinstated the system of privileges favoring once again printers and booksellers, rather than authors, through the Licensing Act of 1662, which reorganized a chaotic scene after a civil war and Cromwell's dictatorship.

An Act for Preventing Abuses in Printing Seditious, Treasonable and Unlicensed Books and Pamphlets, and for Regulating of Printing and Printing Presses – the full name of the law – survived due to its successive renewals until 1698. On this year *An Act for the Better Regulation of Printers and Printing-Presses* was passed, to censor contents and compel the inclusion of the name of the publisher and owner of the press, and the place of publication, on every book.[63]

c) The growing importance of the Stationers' Company, an organization that gathered most of the English printers and booksellers – mainly from London — and was highly regarded by printers, and which tried to become the only regulatory agency of the printing industry of the country.

The convergence of these three factors led to the writing and passage of the Statue of Queen Anne, in 1709, whose official name was *Act for the Encouragament of Learning by Vesting the Copies of Printed Books in the Authors or Purchasers of Such Copies During the Times Therein Mentioned*,[64] and whose most immediate cause had been the constant demand from the members of the company to secure a printing monopoly.

Thus, the Statute of Queen Anne, in effect as of April 10, 1710, gave rise to the following rights:

a) In the case of works created after the enactment of the law, their authors were granted an exclusive right for twenty-eight years from the date of first publication, after which the work could be freely used; or the author could waive this right and transfer his work for its exploitation for two periods of fourteen years.

> "[...] The Author of any Book or Books... and his assignee or assigns, shall have the sole right and Liberty of printing and reprinting such Book or Books for the term of fourteen years..."[65]

---

[63] Cfr. PATTERSON, *op. cit.*, 134.

[64] *Vid.* ROSE, *op. cit.*, 31-48.

[65] Cfr. PATTERSON, *op. cit.*, 145.

"Provided always, That after the Expiration of said term of fourteen years, the sole Right of printing or disposing of Copies shall return to the Authors thereof, if they are then living, for another term of fourteen years."[66]

b) A right for twenty-one years, in favor of those who had a copyright from the Stationers' Company, to the works published before the enactment of the law, whose holder could be:

"[…] the Author of any Book or Books already printed, who hath not transferred to any other the Copy or Copies of such Book or Books… or the Bookseller or Booksellers, Printer or Printers, or other Person or Persons, who hath purchased or acquired the Copy or Copies of any Book or Books."[67]

c) Duration of the rights granted by the Printing Patent System.

Other two interesting ideas, included in the Statute, established that the illegal copy of a protected creation would be fined, and that any author would have to register his works with the Stationers' Company to evidence his authorship. If the Company refused to register a work, "being thereunto required by the Author or Proprietor of such Copy,"[68] then it would only be necessary to publish a notice in the Gazette.

However, as it can be deduced from one of the excerpts transcribed above, the authors and printers were not the only ones who benefited from the Statute of Queen Anne, since during the 18th century the rights of booksellers were also increased, causing a confrontation between them.[69]

In short, two different ways to understand copyright were constantly contrasted: one based on the recognition through positive laws, benefiting printers and booksellers; and the other based on the author's natural rights, therefore, favoring his rights.

---

[66] *Id.*, 146.

[67] *Id.*, 145.

[68] *Id.*, 146.

[69] As KENT and LANCOUR say, *copyright* before 1709 was a *stationer's right* or *publisher's right*, which explains the confrontation between one and the other upon approval of the Statute of Queen Anne.

Cfr. KENT and LANCOUR, *Copyright. Current View Point on History, Laws And Legislation*, R. R. Bowker Company (New York-London 1972) 2.

According to JOHNSON,

"Apparently authors have a property right stronger than the one which is obtained through occupation; a metaphysical right, a creation right, let's say, which due to its nature should be in perpetuity; but nations are reluctant to accept it, and even the reason and interests of learning are against it."[70]

2.2. Application: *Donaldson vs. Beckett*

In 1767 the bookseller Andrew Millar sued Robert Taylor for printing James Thomson's *The Seasons*, which the plaintiff had acquired directly from the author in 1729 and registered at the Stationers' Company.

The term of protection in favor of Andrew Millar, in accordance with the Statute of Queen Anne, had ended, since thirty nine years had elapsed from its beginning, therefore the Court stated that neither Taylor, nor Millar had any right to exploit Thomson's work, since the author had recovered the right to his creation.

"If the copy of the book belonged to the author, there is no doubt he could transfer it to the plaintiff. And though the plaintiff, by assignment, had become the owner of the copy, there still exists a small doubt on whether the defendant has caused him damage and violated his right: therefore, this claim is the appropriate remedy.

But the term of guaranteed protection […] has expired."[71]

The decision, which curiously never mentioned that the work had already entered the public domain – just as laid out in the Statute of Queen Anne — was supported by the booksellers who consider it as a guarantee that copyright was still favoring their monopolies against possible third party interference.

Referring to its contents, Lord Mansfield said:

"[…] It is just, that an author should reap the pecuniary profit of his own ingenuity and labour. It is just, that another should not use his name without his consent. It is fit that he should judge when to publish, or whether he will ever publish. It is fit he should not only choose the time, but the manner of publication; how many; what volume; what print. It is fit, he should choose to

---

[70] Cfr. PATTERSON, *op. cit.*, 157.

[71] *Id.*, 169.

whose care he will trust the accuracy and correctness of the impression; in whose honesty he will confide [...]."[72]

But, in 1768, Andrew Millar died and his copies and rights were sold a year later, giving Thomas Beckett, and fourteen of his colleagues, the opportunity to purchase the rights to several of Johnson's poems.

Nevertheless, the Statute of Queen Anne established that, after twenty-eight years from the first publication and register of a work – and, consequently, from the beginning of its protection – it should enter the public domain; therefore Alexander Donaldson, who had been excluded from the sale, claimed his right to publish those works without paying for them.

In addition, the London booksellers had, prior to the passing of the Statute, control over virtually all the books published in the country, thanks to the strong presence and power of the Stationers' Company, and behaved as if they had perpetual rights on all the works.

Due to this fact, and protected by the new legislation in force, booksellers outside London expressed their opposition to the continuation of such attitudes, arguing that they had hardly enjoyed some printing and sale privileges on the most successful works. This had been always detrimental to them as compared to the London booksellers.

Based on the Statute of Queen Anne and its disposition regarding the entering of works into the public domain after twenty-one or twenty-eight years of protection – depending on the first date of publication – they decided to print and sell those titles that could yield some profit.

The London booksellers reacted swiftly and the confrontation turned into a lawsuit which would be settled in Court.

Once the action was brought, the First Instance Court decided in favor of the London printers, acknowledging them a perpetual right to printed literary works, according to the current standards of Common Law.

However, when the booksellers from outside London, and Donaldson, entered an appeal against this first decision, the case was heard again by a Court who, in 1774, rendered an adverse final judgment.

The content of the court decision stated that, due to the coming into force of the Statute of Queen Anne, all disputes regarding works already published should be

---

[72] *Id.*, 170.

governed by this rule and that, therefore, out-of-London printers and booksellers were allowed to reproduce and sell works already in the public domain.

In addition, the court decision had two other remarkable consequences:

a) Any future dispute, regarding author's rights, should be settled by resorting to the legislation in force, that is, the Statute of Queen Anne. Thus, since the prevailing idea of copyright under Common Law vanished, the author's right was no longer considered a perpetual right but a time limited right.

b) It made a clear legal distinction between published works and unpublished manuscripts. The latter did not enjoy the specific author's right granted by the Statue after publication, since they had not been registered at the Stationers' Company.

3. Creation and Consolidation in the National Laws (18th – 19th Centuries)

3.1. England and the Search of a Balance between Author's Right and Copyright

With the enactment of the Statute of Queen Anne, in 1709, England decided to find a balanced legal system securing both the printers and booksellers rights, obviously without neglecting the rights of the creator – putting an end to the tradition of the Common Law which had considered the author's right as exclusively a right to copy.

Hence, the term *copyright*, which is still in use today, was coined in England to refer to the author's right within the Anglo-Saxon legal system.

In 1701 the Stationers' Company composed a document in which this term was mentioned for the first time, although not as a single word, but two: *copy* and *right*. Since then, the linguistic interaction that allowed the natural separation of these two words gave rise to two types of rights:

a) The *right in copy*, or the right in the original copy, which would put it on a level with the author's right.

b) The *right to copy*, or copy right, which would put it on a level with the printer's right.

In both cases it can be deduced that the right of the author – which includes the power to copy – begins when the creative idea of the author is materialized, and not before.

No matter how, in the last quarter of the 18th century and during all the 19th century, the English studies on copyright focused on the comprehension and theoretical construction of literary property as a private property, together with the development of the laws that, successively, broadened the contents of this right.

The Copyright Act (1814), introduced a term of protection of twenty-eight years after the first publication, or the lifetime of the author. In 1842, the Copyright Amendment Act fixed that term in forty-two years after the first publication or seven years after the death of the author, and spread the use of contracts between authors and publishers as a way to reflect their respective interests – a provision which, initially, was understood as an affront to honor and dignity in a society governed by the "word of honor".[73]

In the 1850s and 1860s, the appearance of magazines including literary fiction published in episodes gave a new boost to the editorial business, where Charles Dickens excelled as one of the most solid and important writers, thanks to works like *All the Year Round*.[74]

Nevertheless, as the English legal evolution tried to keep in line with the general legal tradition of the country, it did not consider the author' right as an extension of the author's character and personality, although it established the protection of continental moral rights by punishing offenses against honor and reputation.

3.2. The English Influence in American Copyright

During the 18th century the European migration – composed mainly of Anglo-Saxons – to North America gave rise to the thirteen original American colonies which, subsequently, would be the basis of what today is the United States.

The settlers' European origin helped the spread of European thought, particularly the philosophical, cultural and political Anglo-Saxon and French ideas.

Accordingly, the idea of the copyright imported from England had a great influence on the Colonies, aiming not only to protect the rights of the author, but

---

[73] Cfr. SAUNDERS, *Authorship and Copyright*, Routledge (London-New York 1992) 136.
    An example of the content of the agreements makes reference to the agreement, in 1855, between William Gaskell and the publisher Chapman & Hall – considered by SUTHERLAND as the first evidence of an agreement establishing the payment of *royalties*:
    Cfr. SUTHERLAND, *Victorian Novelists and Publishers*, Athlone Press and the University of London (London 1976), quoted by SAUNDERS, *op. cit.*, 138.

[74] *Id.*, 142.

also to promote the education, the regulation of book trade and the prevention of monopolies.

Thus, the Statute of Queen Anne imbued the spirit of the first laws on copyright enacted in 1780 and 1787 (date in which the American Constitution was adopted).[75]

On May 2, 1783 the Continental Congress passed a resolution which "recommended the several states, to secure to the authors and publishers of any new books … the copyright,"[76] for not less than fourteen years renewable for another similar term, and including the right of printing, publishing and vending.

During the 1780-1787 period, twelve of the thirteen colonies passed laws on copyright, modeled on the English Statute. Maryland, Connecticut, and Massachusetts were first in doing so.

However, since the colonies were not yet an independent and unified political entity, it was agreed that the principle of reciprocity would be applied, by which the authorities of a colony would secure the copyright of the works protected in other colonies, based on a protection principle similar to the one established in the German *länders*.

No state law, with the exception of the rules in effect in South Carolina and Virginia, gave the publisher or the purchaser of the copy any right; on the contrary, the authors were the main beneficiaries.

In 1790 the Federal Copyright Act provided a widespread protection – once the colonies became a political unity – although restricted only to works created and published within the American territory, but it did not accord any protection to foreign authors.

The wide range of state laws demanded the passing of a federal law enforceable in all the territory; therefore the Congress was empowered to legislate in that regard. Thus the first reference to copyright can be found in the Congress Minutes of August 18, 1787, compiled by James Madison and Charles Pinckey, who had submitted to the House a list of powers that it should exert, to wit, "To establish a university. To promote, by means of rewards and other measures, the progress of science and useful arts," apart from the power "to grant patents to useful inventions" and "… by securing for limited times to authors and inventors the exclusive right…"[77]

---

[75]   Cfr. STEWART, *op. cit.*, 24-25.

[76]   Cfr. PATTERSON, *op. cit.*, 183.

[77]   Cfr. ELLIOT, *The Debates in the Several State Conventions on The Adoption of the Federal Constitution. As Recommended by the General Convention at Philadelphia in 1787. To*

Finally, the approved clause stated:

"To promote the Progress of Science and useful Arts, by securing for limited Times to Authors and Inventors the exclusive right to their respective Writings and Discoveries."[78]

The text gave rise to the first Federal Act (1790), whose full name was *An Act for the Encouragement of Learning, by Securing the Copies of Maps, Charts and Books, to the Authors and Proprietors of Such Copies, During the Times Therein Mentioned.*[79]

Thus, the act protected books, maps and charts, making a distinction between published and unpublished works:

i) The copyright holders of the works already published would be the author or authors, citizens of or residents in the United States, who had not transferred to any other their rights; or their executors, administrators or assignees, or who had purchased or acquired that right in order to print, reprint, publish or sell a given work, for a term of fourteen years.

ii) The copyright holders of unpublished works would be the same above mentioned individuals, with the only difference that the term would be extended for fourteen additional years.

This rule would be in effect for more than a century, until 1891, when a new law on copyright granted foreign works equal treatment – provided that the works were printed in the American territory, and that the author's country of citizenship accorded reciprocal protection. Until then foreign works only arrived to the American market as a consequence of intellectual piracy, since there was not sufficient legal protection for the authors.

---

gether with the Journals of the Federal Convention, 5 vols., 2ª ed., Lippincott (Philadelphia 1836), quoted in PATTERSON, op. cit., 192.

About the *iter legis* of the Copyright Federal Act (1790), cfr. LIBRARY OF CONGRESS, *Copyright in Congress 1789-1904*. A bibliography and chronological record of all proceedings in Congress in relation to copyright from April 15th, 1789, to April 28th, 1904, 1st session, to Fifty-eighth congress, 2nd session, Government Printing Office (Washington 1905) 112-113.

[78]   Cfr. PATTERSON, *op. cit.*, 192.

[79]   *Id.*, 197.

This provision, still discriminating against most foreign authors, would be in force until 1976, when the current US Copyright Act was enacted, settling this issue.[80]

On the other hand, throughout the 19th century the law in effect since 1790 was broadened, while the courts developed and defined legal principles.

In 1828, Richard Peters, a Supreme Court reporter, decided to publish the Court's decisions in a six-volume collection including also the work of his predecessors. Its title was *Condensed Reports Cases in the Supreme Court of the United States*.

Two of his predecessors, Wheaton and Donaldson, claimed their right in their work by suing Peters and his publisher, saying that Peters had published the transcriptions that Wheaton had previously collected and compiled, by himself, without any alteration, modification or addition. Therefore, both works were identical and Wheaton's copyright was infringed.

While the Circuit Court merely confirmed that copyright was a privilege granted by the Government, and not a right, the Supreme Court, categorically and unanimously pronounced in its ruling:

> "It may be proper to remark that the Court are unanimously of opinion, that no reporter has or can have any copyright in the written opinions delivered by this Court," although it is possible to have a copyright on "the marginal notes, tables of cases and decided issues, abstracts of briefs and its evidence, and the indexes of different volumes."[81]

In 1833 copyright protection was extended to public performances and representations; in 1862 to works of art in general, and twenty years later, this protection reached musical creations.

It was then when the term of protection was extended to twenty-eight years with the possibility of a renewal after the first term expired.

Thus, and for more than two centuries, lawmakers found in copyright a suitable way to protect the works of American authors, whose influence was considered essential in a young country, then virtually without historical roots, with no cultural tradition of its own and subject to the influence of ideas coming from Europe.

---

[80] Cfr. STEWART, *op. cit.*, 25.

[81] Cfr. PATTERSON, *op. cit.*, 207.

3.3. The French Formulation of the *Droit d'auteur* as a Property Right

The confrontation that took place in England between London booksellers and out-of-city booksellers was echoed in France by the printers that had not been privileged by the Monarch. They were at a disadvantage with those who enjoyed the royal favor, because they were unable to conduct their business fairly and reasonably.

Thus, in 1776 the *Mémoire à consulter. Pour les librairies & imprimeurs de Lyon, Rouen, Toulouse & Nimes. Concernant les privilèges & continuations d'iceux* was published, requesting that once a book was published for the first time it should enter into the public domain, abolishing the system of privileges.[82]

As a consequence of the uprisings that took place in France, Louis XVI enacted six Royal Decrees in August, 1777, subsequently completed with other provisions adopted in 1778.

However, and contrary to the printers' expectations, the King chose a system which gave a right to the printers, but also recognized to authors the right to sell, print and publish freely their work everywhere they wished, as well as a perpetual right on it.[83] According to SAUNDERS, this fact should not lead us to believe that the French legislation had adopted from its beginning the author's moral right approach.[84]

Since the provision did not please the printers, Louis XVI decided to grant them some right to safeguard their investment when publishing a work. Then the printers were entitled to exercise these two rights – to print and sell – provided that they had the author's authorization and that this exercise was limited in time.

But the precarious stability of this system collapsed with the outbreak of the French Revolution, in 1789, which established a regime in which the royal prerogatives became meaningless – since the Revolution aimed at the equal protection of all citizens under the law. Therefore on August 4, 1789 a decree abolished all existing privileges in France.

---

[82]   Cfr. SAUNDERS, *op. cit.*, 86.

[83]   Cfr. STEWART, *op. cit.*, 18-19 and LIPSZYC, *op. cit.*, 32-33.

[84]   However, and against printers expectations, the King chose a system in which both printers and authors were recognized a right to sell, print and publish their work wherever they wanted, enjoying in addition a right to such works in perpetuity – which, according to SAUNDERS, should not induce to believe that the French legislation adopted from the beginning the literary moral right approach.

In 1791 the newly elected Assembly decided to consider the right of authors a Property Right, as a singular element of a set of related rights, a move that had two important and immediate consequences:

i) It put the author's brainwork on a level with other types of property.

ii) It based the author's right on the Economic Right, but still recognizing that it was a moral right of the author.

The Assembly established, also, the lifetime of the author plus five years after his death as a new term of protection – after which, the work would enter into the public domain. This provision suggested a certain transcendence of the author's right beyond the natural life of the author, which was rather surprising in a country apparently only concerned about the economic side of the right.

> "The French Constitutional Convention adopted, in January, 1791, a document prepared by Chopelin which stated: 'the most sacred, the most incontestable, and, if I may say, the most personal of all properties, is the work resulting from a writer's brainwork'."[85]

In addition, it was established that the authors should give their written consent to the performance of their works.

In 1792, the National Assembly protected the interests of playwrights, by compelling authors to announce that their rights of performance were reserved, as well as to deposit the work in a notary's office. A similar warning should be included in the text headline.[86]

A year later the term of protection was extended to ten years after the death of the author, and included musical and artistic works which previously lacked legal protection in France. Also, the exclusive nature of the right to copy was consolidated as belonging to the creator only.

The decree, approved on July 10, contained the following preamble from Lakanal:

> "[...] Of all properties, the least questionable one is that related to the work of one's own ingenuity: and it is amazing to think that a property needs to be recognized, that a positive law is required to secure its free exercise; that a

---

[85]   Cfr. PATTERSON, *op. cit.*, 36. For an interpretation of these words, cfr. SAUNDERS, *op. cit.*, 91.

[86]   *Id.*, 92.

great revolution like ours was necessary to reintroduce this matter, as so many others, simple elements of the most common justice.[87]

Since then the legislative history of the author's right in France has been based on the rethinking and evolution of the laws that, while keeping their basic features, began to include rights like copyright and public performance rights.

In 1838 the term *droit d'auteur* was first used in the law, and then again in 1866 when regulating the rights of heirs and successors.

In 1844, 1854, and 1866 substantive laws on this right were enacted which, however, and according to SAUNDERS, did not shape the moral right of authors, which actually developed from the construction that courts made of said rules.[88]

Thus, on July 17, 1845, in the *Lacordaire* case, the Correctional Court of Lyon affirmed that "[…] in terms of his moral personality and interests, the author should always be entitled to examine and review his work, to ensure that it has been adequately reproduced, and to decide the time and manner of publication." Seven years later, the Civil Division of the Court of the Seine decided that "[…] no publisher shall be entitled to make essential changes in the signed work of an author. […] Should this be tolerated, then the reputation and status of authors would fall into the printers' hands."[89]

Nevertheless, it was not until 1898, with the *Lecocq* case, when the dual vision of copyright would be consolidated as a combination of economic and moral elements. In the court decision (1902) on the division of assets of the musician Lecocq after divorcing from his wife, the Cassation Court of Paris noted that, though the literary and artistic property of any of the spouses might be divided, this fact cannot limit "[…] the artist's ability, inherent to his most intimate personality, to make changes in his creation, or even to take it away, since this cannot be construed as an unfair treatment toward his spouse or agents."[90]

STEWART notes, as a conclusion of the study of the French case, a questionable idea: the development of the rights of authors was based on terms and features which were closer to economic rights than to the moral rights of authors.

---

[87] *Id.*, 92.

[88] *Id.*, 103.

[89] *Id.*, 103.

[90] *Id.*, 104.

"There is a distinction between copyright, first developed in England with the Statute of Queen Anne (1709), and which spread to all the English-speaking countries, and the *droit d'auteur*, a French creation, which spread to the countries of the Latin legal system and also to most of the European continental countries. That is a fallacious argument. The development of this right took place simultaneously throughout Europe from the 15th to the 18th centuries. The two approaches split up in times of the French Revolution with the decrees of 1791 and 1793. And became closer again with the Berne Convention."[91]

3.4. Germany and Copyright as a Moral Right

The disintegrating role played by privileges, hindering the wide circulation of the works, had been overcome in Germany thanks to the agreements of reciprocal protection signed between the various *länders*.

In 1794 the Prussian Parliament passed the laws on author's rights – accepted by other states, except Wurtemberg and Mecklenburg – under which all German and foreign authors, whose works were presented by their publishers in the book fairs of Franckfurt and Leipzig, would be protected against any unauthorized reproduction in all the German states.

As a consequence, throughout the 19th century a stronger national unity for the protection of the authors' interest was gradually achieved – which however did not prevent the development of rampant book piracy industry in Germany.

In 1815 thirty-eight states adhered to the Law of the German Confederation, whose article 18 pointed out the need to legislate on author's rights:

"The Diet shall consider, in its first meeting, some plan to uniform the legislation related to the freedom of the press, and also the steps that should be taken to guarantee authors and publishers that their author's rights will not be violated."[92]

In 1832 the Alliance of German States ensured an interstate protection of privileges and put an end to the legal differences between the States; in 1837 the protection granted would last for ten years; and in 1845 the term was extended to thirty years after the death of the author.

---

[91] Cfr. STEWART, *op. cit.*, 16.

[92] Cfr. SAUNDERS, *op. cit.*, 107.

Finally, in 1871 the first national unified act on this right was passed, laying down as a basic principle that the right to reproduce a work by mechanical means belonged exclusively to the author.

Probably due to this *länder* unity image, and the scarce disputes over this issue, in Germany the legal studies on author's rights were based on philosophical-legal grounds.

In England Locke's ideas had created a certain social awareness that the recognition of authors and creators was important, while in Germany mainly Kant and Gierke devoted their efforts to find a solid axiological root where to plant and develop these rights.

At the end of 18th century Emmanuel Kant in *Of The Injustice of Counterfeiting Books*[93] stated his conviction that the author's right should be considered as a moral right, since it referred to an object imbued with the spirit of the human being who had conceived it, regardless of its materialization in a medium.

The legal thought of Kant – collected in *The Metaphysics of Morals*, consisting of *Metaphysical First Principles of the Doctrine of Rights* and *Metaphysical First Principles of the Doctrine of Virtue* – argued that there is a natural law and a positive law, the first one "derived from nature," and the second one, "deriving from the lawmaker's will".[94]

Within the right of personality sphere, and specifically in the author's right, there are two components:

i) A real right which survives in the material copy of the work.

ii) An authorial right of personality (*Persönlicheitsrech*) which survives in the work, regardless of its materialization in a medium, and which is unalienable for three reasons:

– Because any work comes from the author's individual intellectual powers.

– Because the intellectual activity of building one's own thoughts can only belong to the author itself.

– Because it is a right innate to the author, existing by nature, regardless of its materialization in positive laws.[95]

---

[93] Original German version (1785), entitled *Von der Unrechtmässigkeit des Büchernachdruckes*. *Id.*, 109.

[94] Cfr. COLOMER, *El pensamiento alemán de Kant a Heidegger*. Volume I: La filosofía trascendental: Kant, Herder (Barcelona 1986) 280-281.

[95] Cfr. SAUNDERS, *op. cit.*, 113.

Kant also considers that there is a clear and close relationship between author, work and publisher: the publisher is a middleman who offers the work of the author to the public, but he is not its owner and although certain rights are transferred to him, an unalienable part of them remains with the author.[96]

Nevertheless, author and work are separated by a line which divides what is transcendental from what is empirical, being the author the basis required for the development of the positive rights regulating the publication and book trade process.

> "The book, on the one hand, is a material product (*opus mecanicum*) which can be imitated (by he who legitimately posses a copy of it) and, consequently, there is a right *in rem;* on the other hand, the book is a discourse from publisher to public, and this no one can reproduce publicly, without first having from the author the authority to do so, such that it is a matter of a personal right. The error consists in confusing these two rights."[97]

As far as he is concerned, Otto von Gierke continued this line of thought, endorsing the idea that the work of the author had to be considered as an extension of his personality, emanating from within the author himself.

Gierke's line of argument rests on two levels: the existence of a set of specific attributes of the personality, among which one can find the intellectual creations right; and the existence of a subordinate and derivative right, constituted by property.[98]

This philosopher thinks that, since the author's right is a moral right, its holder has an exclusive right to control the publication and reproduction of his creation, in such a way he ensures the pecuniary profit of the publication of his works.[99]

The theoretical contribution of both philosophers can be understood as the recognition of the creative ability of man as one of his most intimate and transcendental powers, permeating to every work created, in such a way that the author's right is considered to be an inherent right to every man. Therefore, this very fact casts a doubt about the appropriateness of granting a time limited term of protection to works which, according to this idea, are beyond being just a material asset.

---

[96] *Vid.* STOCKHOLM, *Le droit moral de l'auteur en droit Allemand, Français et Scandinave,* P. A. Norstedt & Söners Förlag (Stockholm 1967).

[97] KANT, quoted by SAUNDERS. Cfr. SAUNDERS, *op. cit.,* 111.

[98] *Id.,* 116.

[99] Cfr. SEIGNETTE, *op. cit.,* 27.

But later, and in line with this same doctrinal ideas, a third track was born in Germany offering an intermediate solution: to consider the author's right as an economic right – since the work is defined by the physical materialization of an idea in a medium which can be traded – as well as a moral right – insofar the resulting physical object came from a creation made by the human intellect.

Josef Kohler supported this dualist theory of rights – *Doppelrecht* – which differs from the prior approach in which it does not subordinate a right to the other, but puts them at the same level of importance, as a consequence of a continuous dialectics between the spiritual and the material. Both exist, thus, autonomously and independently, but form a synthetic whole.

> "The authors of an intellectual production and a material product are so different as Homer's poems and Jacquard's loom. But both have the same right: the right to request a complete protection for their creative personality."[100]

This third track – where some moral rights match up with economic rights (*Inmaterialguterrec*) – will eventually draw together a greater number of followers, both from the doctrinal and legal point of view, as it is evidenced by the division of copyright according to its economic and moral powers, where some do not derive from the others, but rather coexist peacefully.

The German approach combined at the end of 19th century with the French legal doctrine approach, since as STROMHOLM says, the German doctrine constituted "an empty structure in search of contents," and the French jurisprudence was just "contents in search of a structure".[101]

In any case, the complementary nature of the material and immaterial elements does not represent a new idea, since 2500 years before, in the 5th century BC, it had already been perceived by Greco-Latin thought.

---

[100] SAUNDERS, *op. cit.*, 116.

[101] *Id.*, 120.

International Treaties for the Protection of Copyright and their Application to Multimedia Works

The consolidation of the first copyright laws brought about the take off of this right, whose development during the 19th century was characterized by national legal traditions, being Continental Law and Common Law the most relevant ones.

The various positive laws enjoyed then a certain autonomy and independence, while in previous years the legislation of some countries had influenced the legislation of others, as was the case, for example, of English copyright on the laws of the American colonies.

Thus, and after the efforts made to consolidate the concept of copyright, this right started a stage of development in which its would extend its protection to literary works, drama and musical works, to include the most common types of creative expression of each period.

The strong development of international trade had meant an incentive for the wide spread of culture, science and art, which gave authors a new significance for their work or, rather, a renewed significance for it: the economic one. But the very international circulation of the works left them unprotected: as soon as the creations were sold abroad it was almost impossible to earn royalties and protect the authors' rights.

How could then the rights of authors and printers be regulated? What changes could national laws undergo to solve this issue? And, how to reach a supranational legal consensus in this regard?

The idea of concluding bilateral agreements for the protection of intellectual property proved to be insufficient and expensive, due to the investment in time required to achieve country by country agreements, individually, until reaching an admissible degree of protection. Therefore, following several meetings held in the last quarter of the 19th century, authors and publishers suggested the development of some general legal principles of international validity through treaties and agreements, which could be signed by many nations.

Finally, this idea was materialized at the signing of the Berne Convention of 1886, establishing at this first stage a system in which the author of a work takes precedence over those who could not be considered its actual creators. From the very beginning, the Berne system relied on three basic principles that are still in effect today and inspire different international initiatives that are being carried out in this field, to wit:

a) The principle of national treatment, is that works originating in one state must be given the same protection in each of the other contracting states as the latter grants to the works of its own nationals.

b) The principle of independence of protection, is that the works published in a given nation are protected regardless of whether or not they are legally protected in their country of origin.

c) The principle of automatic protection, is that protection must not be conditional upon compliance with any formality.

But law-makers from every country and organization promoting the international treaty system always wish copyright to respond effectively to the new ways of expression provided by continuing technological development. For that reason, the rapid strides and development of different media, as driving forces for the creation of new works, will cause the convergence of the system of Berne, national laws and technological developments.

Thus, the close relationship between copyright and the world of communications was reestablished, a relationship which had started four hundreds years before with the invention of the printing press.

Therefore, since the end of the 19th century and during all of the 20th century, radio, television, satellite or cable TV, for example, compelled the constant reexamination of the Berne Convention,[1] as well as the conclusion of new treaties to extend copyright protection to new ways of creation and transmission, by formulating new legal principles to broaden the subject matter and contents of copyright.

Furthermore, in the last two decades of the 20th century, due to the birth of the Information Society the international copyright protection system regained its leading role when it became evident that national laws were unsuitable to face up to this technological challenge.

Nevertheless, is international copyright protection for multimedia works or covering the global dissemination of any literary, artistic or scientific creation possible? In fact, could it be asserted, today, the existence of sufficient legal protection or, on the contrary, are we to conclude that we are facing an undecided issue?

---

[1]   The revisions of the Berne Convention are quoted in STEWART, *op. cit.*, 101 and (Switzerland 2002).

Contrary to expectations, the guarantee of protection is now unquestionable: On the one hand, the GATT Agreement of 1994 and the Protocol to the Berne Convention of 1996, specifically regulate the copyright protection of computer programs, databases and interactive digital communication; on the other hand, and as it will be discussed in the next pages, the mere application of the contents of the treaties signed until then would be reason enough to speak of a protection, theoretical at least, of said right.

1. Introduction: The Berne Convention of 1886, and its Promotion as a Result of Technological Development. From the Protection of Printed Works to the Protection of Distribution by Wire

As has been pointed out, the Berne Convention of 1886, is considered the real starting point for international copyright protection, aside from minor initiatives such as the Spanish Intellectual Property Act of 1879, which only afforded protection to foreign authors if their own country legislation recognized the rights of Spanish authors.

The Berne Convention origins can be traced to a joint initiative of authors and publishers from three leading associations during the last decades of the 19th century: the *Association Litteraire Internationale* – established in France in 1878 and which became, in 1884, the *Association Litteraire et Artistique Internationales* (ALAI) – the *Société des gens des lettres* and the *Boersen-verein der deutschen Buchändler*.

In 1882 representatives of these three associations met in Rome to discuss copyright protection in the international arena. The results were included in a draft showing the participants' desire to create a permanent international association, which could be able to solve any type of dispute related to copyright.

For this, the participants in the Rome meeting of 1882, met again in Geneva in three additional occasions. There, they outlined the particulars that would eventually become the text of the Berne Convention for the Protection of Literary and Artistic works.[2]

Its original version had twenty-one articles organized in four subject areas: the basic principles of the treaty, the minimal protection terms for works and their

---

[2]   Cfr. STEWART, *op. cit.*, 100. LIPSZYC, *op. cit.*, 617-621. ELSEMORE, http://www.ccls.edu/ iplaw/qmw_web_page.html (United Kingdom 1996) and WIPO ed., *Introduction to Intellectual Property. Theory and practice*, 385.

authors, the formulation of special provisions for the developing countries and the creation of the Union of Countries as a permanent body for the administration of the Convention.[3]

1.1. Developing a Right for Printed Works

The international copyright protection system, established in the Berne Convention, defined the first works to be protected by this right. The protection, as it was expected according to the contents of national laws, went to printed works, whose trade had been eased by the printing press since the 15th century.

Broadly speaking, the Berne Convention grants international protection to the creators of written works, whether literary or artistic; in particular, books, pamphlets and other writings, dramatic, musical compositions with or without words, works of drawing, painting, sculpture, engraving, lithography, illustrations, maps, plans, sketches, three-dimensional works relative to geography, topography, architecture or science.

In short, and as it is stated in effective and ample terms in the last paragraph of Article 4, "all in all, every production in the literary, scientific and artistic domain, whatever may be the mode or form of its expression".[4]

But, although this paragraph actually extended the protection to new works regardless of their actual existence, their widely different features made it advisable to adapt the original text to the new creations through their specification in the draft of the Convention.

This happened in 1896, when the Berne text underwent its first revision with the Paris Act, made – among other circumstances – to include photographic works in the catalogue of works protected by copyright:[5]

On August 10, 1839 Françoise Arago presented in the Academy of Science and Arts of Paris a revolutionary invention, the daguerreotype, created by Niépce and

---

[3]   Cfr. STEWART, *op. cit.*, 101.

[4]   Cfr. LIPSZYC, *op. cit.*, 624-625.

[5]   Contrary to STEWART's opinion, who states that photographic works were included in the Paris Act of 1896, LIPSZYC states they were included in the Berlin revision of 1908.
       Cfr. STEWART, *op. cit.*, 104-106 and LIPSZYC, *op. cit.*, 630-633.
       NORDEMANN, VINCK, HERTIN and MEYER have no comment to make in this regard.
       Vid. NORDEMANN, VINCK, HERTIN and MEYER, *International copyright. Commentary*, VCH (Germany 1990) 39-58.

Daguerre, allowing to take pictures and its subsequent reproduction, which several years later would turn into the photo camera.[6]

Photography, the result on paper of an optical and chemical process, became a new and twofold copyright object, since its protection was considered from two different aspects:

a) Conventional artistic photography was protected.

b) And also, photos, which were not original creative works *per se*, but that contained the picture of some artistic object that could be protected due to its characteristics.

In other words, the Paris Act included two possible beneficiaries of the copyright on a same work: the author of the photography and the author of the photographed object.

Taking as a starting point the photographic reproduction, copyright protection was extended to cinema films, since they were creations produced by a process similar to photography, though with the basic and important difference of capturing moving images.

Such eventuality was also anticipated in Paris, giving rise to the first protection for a product from an invention that, as STEWART points out, would result in a new activity which would soon be a revelation to creators and public alike: the motion-picture industry.[7]

1.2. Protection of Cinematographic, Sound and Audiovisual Works

Although the Paris Act of 1896, opened the door to the protection of cinematographic works thanks to their analogy with photography, it was soon realized that the most suitable way for their protection was to include it in the text of the Convention, which took place in its Berlin revision of 1908.[8]

In 1895, just before the completion of the Paris Act, the Lumière brothers had filmed and exhibited by means of their cinematographic system some workers

---

[6] Cfr. AZURMENDI, *El derecho a la propia imagen. Su identidad y aproximación al derecho a la información*, Fundación Manuel Buendía y Universidad Iberoamericana (Mexico 1998) 18.

[7] Cfr. STEWART, *op. cit.*, 104.

[8] In addition to the works included in the Berlin revision, which are specifically discussed in this epigraph, the official text laid down the protection for choreographic works, entertainments in dumb shows and works of applied art.

leaving their Parisian factory, creating thus the first cinema film, though was non-fiction, but basically a documentary work.[9]

The Berlin text laid down the right of mechanical reproduction in addition to the right to reproduce printed works, allowing the copyright protection for the result of the Lumière brothers' invention. Nevertheless, as it was understood that documentary movies did not involve creative talent on the part of their author, just as was the case in the photography of objects, it was established that in order to be protected, films should have a personal and original nature in "the setting or combination of represented events"[10] as a *sine qua non* condition for enjoying the legal benefits of this right.

The author's contribution, in the case of documentary movies, was limited to start a recording device and, so, it seemed logical to wonder where were the creativity and the personal style entitling an author to the protection of his work.

Finally, since the Rome revision of 1928, the protection of cinematographic works would be granted regardless of their being expressive of the author's personality or of the existence of signs of originality in his work. In fact, the Brussels revision of 1948 recognized all cinematographic works as being original in themselves, putting an end to this issue.

Nevertheless, according to its own definition, the right to mechanical reproduction could not be limited to cinematographic works. Although in 1877, Edison's mechanical phonograph revolutionized the world of communications allowing the recording and reproduction of sounds, there was no provision for this in the Berne texts of 1886 and 1896.

In 1908, the author's right in sound recordings – which, in those days, had been improving from the first prototype designed by Edison – was afforded protection with the mechanical sound reproduction right.[11]

In parallel to this right, and since the device allowed the reproduction of recorded sounds, the right of the author to authorize the public performance would come up as his right to authorize or prohibit the public performance of his recordings.

---

[9]   Cfr. PALAU, *Historia del cine*, Seix Barral (Barcelona 1946) 9.

[10]   Cfr. STEWART, *op. cit.*, 633.

[11]   *Vid.* MORENO MORENO, *La música en la radio: transformación de un contenido en un concepto de programación*, tesis doctoral, *pro manuscripto*, Facultad de Comunicación, Universidad de Navarra (Pamplona 1998) 99-124.

However, the apparent logic of this legal provision did not mean its acceptance by all the sound recording industry. The most conspicuous case was that of the record companies, who were strongly against a right that seemed to grant too much power to authors and limited the strong decision power on recordings that companies enjoyed at the time.

Soon after, however, in the decade following the end of the First World War a new technological advance appeared, with a similar impact, perhaps, to that of the printing press: in 1920, in Pittsburgh, a radio station broadcast for the first time, thus consolidating the United States' leadership in the technological world and giving rise, as a consequence, to the public birth of radio.[12]

That was the time to advance a step further in the development of copyright, so that works broadcast through the radio waves, which serve as a medium or channel, could obtain their legal recognition.

The broadcasting right, introduced in the Rome revision of 1928, entitled an author to authorize or prohibit the communication of his works to an undetermined public via the propagation of waves through space.

Nevertheless, the introduction of this new right raised a number of issues that would soon be settled through new international agreements: What role did radio stations play in broadcasting? Which rights were they entitled to, if any? If a station purchased a given creation captured on a recording, was the author still entitled to authorize or prohibit its broadcasting?

The Rome revision provided, in addition to sound broadcasting, protection for certain oral works whose creative and economic value was more than questionable: conferences, addresses, sermons and the like. Not protecting them at all was, obviously, out of proportion, while giving them the same protection of recitative texts – such as drama and poetry – gave rise to serious doubts on the fairness of this comparison. However, settling this issue would also take some time.

Also in 1928, and with these questions still unsolved, appeared a new communication medium whose impact has been virtually unequaled in the history of social communication: television. The interest of the public moved then toward a

---

[12] Cfr. BORDERÍA, LAGUNA and MARTÍNEZ, *Historia de la comunicación social. Voces, registros y conciencias*, Síntesis (Madrid 1996) 380.

About this same subject, *vid.* KEITH and KRAUSE, *The Radio Station*, 3ª ed., Butterworths-Heinemann (United States 1993) 1-6.

Attending to the British Encyclopedia the first radio broadcast was made in Argentina, by the Argentina Radio Society, on August 27, 1920.

communication system that has far exceeded radio, due to the huge additional value of the moving images.

The first experiences with television took place in the United States in 1928, though it was in Germany, a year later, where the first television programs were broadcast using the method invented by the British electrical engineer John L. Baird.[13]

The Rome revision would have become, therefore, obsolete just one year after its ratification, unless TV broadcasting would be covered by the broadcasting right, regardless of what was broadcast (sounds and/or images). This was an era of incredible changes, as Marcel Plaisant, official reporter of the Berne Act of 1948 would say twenty years later:

> "During the last twenty years we have witnessed such an incredible development of inventions and means of dissemination of thoughts that we are astonished at the progress of science and the yet unforeseen methods it can impose to the trade of the works of the spirit. At the same time, the world, and particularly Europe, has undergone, due to this long war and its consequences, political and social changes so drastic that we are powerless to conceive its foreseeable image in a developing society. Our mission has been, then, to ensure copyright protection in times when books have been largely surpassed by electronic and mechanical means and by other new means yet to be invented. This Conference was devoted above all to broadcasting, records, cinema, artificial or natural screens. Having brought copyright, a spiritual essence, into line with those material realities, at the same time so strong and changing: that is your great contribution".[14]

Finally, this Berne Act assimilated TV broadcasting into the broadcasting right, which not only protected the broadcasting of sounds, but also that of still images and moving pictures. At the same time, the right of communication to the public was established, distinguishing it from broadcasting, as a new right covering transmissions by wire or cable, while radio broadcasting was limited to the transmission by wireless means – which in those days was done exclusively through radio waves.

---

[13]   Cfr. BODERÍA, LAGUNA and MARTÍNEZ, *op. cit.*, 396.

[14]   Cfr. LIPSZYC, *op. cit.*, 646-647.

"Art. 11 bis, § 1. Authors of literary and artistic works shall enjoy the exclusive right of authorizing:

(i) the radio broadcasting of their works or the communication thereof to the public by any other means of wireless broadcasting of signs, sounds or images.

(ii) any communication to the public by wire or by rebroadcasting of the broadcast of the work, when this communication is made by an organization other than the original".[15]

From a terminological point of view, the wording was confusing because it might be deduced that there was an act of communication to the public whether by radio broadcast or by wire or cable transmission. Therefore, do we have to understand that the communication to the public is not a right in itself? Is it, rather, a general right covering the radio broadcasting right? Is the communication to the public only limited to communication by wire? And, regarding the subject matter of this paper, would not this "communication to the public by wire" be capable of protecting the current communication of works by means of digital technology?

Even so, this apparent arbitrariness of terms would not be the major problem of the Berne Act. The text also brings up an interesting issue regarding TV broadcasting, since the works covered by its articles would only be protected provided their being recorded before their transmission; that is, the legal protection of copyright for television shows was limited to prerecorded programs, excluding the protection of live television broadcasts.

This incomprehensible omission would not be solved until 1967 when, during the Stockholm revision, the need to "capture" the broadcast images by means of a process analogous to photography and cinematography, was replaced with the possibility to "express" them by means of an analogous process, not requiring then their prior fixation or capture to be protected.

1.3. A Point of Contact with the New Technologies: Protection of Satellite and Cable Broadcasting

After the Berne revision of 1948, the international development of copyright came to a brief standstill, since it would not be until the sixties when technological advances in communications would once again create new challenges for this right.

---

[15] Cfr. STEWART, *op. cit.*, 914.

In that decade the first telecommunication satellites were launched, allowing the transmission of television shows over wider geographical areas than the areas reached until then by terrestrial TV broadcasts, giving rise to the internationalization of broadcasting.[16]

Again the United States led the field by launching, in 1962 and 1963, the Telstar and Syncom satellites.

The Rome Convention of 1961, which for the first time dealt with related or neighboring rights, made no reference to this new medium,[17] consequently the possible regulations options seemed to be only two: to either opt for the TV broadcasting right, according to the Brussels Act of 1948; or the ratification of a new treaty defining a new satellite broadcasting right.

However, before taking a final decision, the possibility of revising the International Telecommunications Convention of 1971, together with its Regulation was also considered, as well as the inclusion of this new communication medium in the Rome Convention of 1961 for the protection of Related or Neighboring Rights. Eventually, the extremely technical nature of the regulations governing communications, together with the scarce international ratification of the Rome Convention, would tip the balance in favor of a new agreement.

The preliminary negotiations of the new agreement contents were conducted by UNESCO and the *Bureaux Internationaux Réunis pour la Protection de la Propriété Intellectuelle* (BIRPI).[18] "The problems arising for the copyright protection of the interests of performers, producers of phonograms and broadcasting organizations by satellite broadcasting" became evident in these negotiations.[19] The sign of the agreement would take place in Brussels, in 1974, recognizing the following rights:

a) The right of the satellite broadcasting organizations to authorize or prohibit the re-broadcasting of their transmissions.

b) Their right to authorize or prohibit the transmission of these broadcasts by cable.

---

[16] Cfr. BODERÍA, LAGUNA and MARTÍNEZ, *op. cit.*, 398. About this same subject, *vid.* FAUS, *op. cit.*, 248.

[17] Cfr. LYPSZYC, *op. cit.*, 872.

[18] *Vid.* OMPI ed., Información General, http://www.wipo.org/spa/infbroch/infbro98.htm (Geneva 1999).

[19] Cfr. STEWART, *op. cit.*, 872.

c) Their right to authorize or prohibit the communication to the public of the same broadcasts by any other means.

d) Recording rights over their programs and over the broadcast of those same recordings.

Soon after the birth of telecommunication satellites cable broadcasting appeared,[20] which was not considered an autonomous broadcasting medium, but rather a way for distributing signals from other broadcasting organizations transmitting via satellite or microwave. Its conception would mean a new technological improvement, giving rise to the concept of *distribution*:

"Art. 1, § 1. Distribution is the operation by which a distributor broadcasts derived signals to the general public or to a given segment of it".[21]

However, the text did not provide a specific protection for the works televised by direct broadcasting satellites (DBS), which did not have any intermediate organizations between the transmitter and receiver; therefore, these transmissions were protected by the wireless broadcasting right, as another way of TV broadcasting in accordance with the Berne Act of 1948.

2. The GATT Agreement of 1994, and the Berne Protocol of 1996: Protection of Multimedia Works through New Copyright Categories

The copyright protection granted to satellite broadcast and wire distribution did not represent the end of the development of this right. At the same time that in 1974 this right was being recognized, the computing industry was starting its expansion by selling lower cost computers as very useful working tools and, later on, for entertainment and communication purposes.

Thus, the appropriate basis was laid for the popularization, years later, of multimedia works and other digital creations. In parallel, the 1970s and 1980s would become a fruitful period of changes in communication technologies, mainly focused on transmission channels gradually empowered by the strength of an element whose value is still on the rise today: information.

---

[20]   Cfr. FAUS, *op. cit.*, 266.

[21]   Cfr. NORDEMANN, VINCK, HERTIN and MEYER, *op. cit.*, 622.

2.1. First Multimedia Copyrights Covered by International Treaties: Software and Databases in the GATT Agreement of 1994

The importance of the economic aspect of multimedia creations was emphasized in 1994 upon the signing of a new agreement by GATT members – an organization responsible for the regulation of international trade which, every soon often, set new rules to attain its aim.[22]

In a strongly commercialized world, where technology and information play an increasingly crucial role, this new agreement reached through the negotiations of the Uruguay Round, emphasized the huge economic interest aroused by intellectual property today; and so devoted a full paragraph of the final text – entitled Trade-Related Aspects of Intellectual Property Rights (TRIPS) – to the regulation of these rights.

The text, resulting from the round initiated in 1993 with the Punta del Este Statement, and concluded in Marrakech a year later, attempted to set some flexible legal principles on copyright in order to obtain a greater international support than the adhesion achieved by the Berne Convention.[23]

However, GATT did not just consider only its own approaches for its proposal, but it also used the ideas and projects submitted in the 1980s and 1990s by the World Intellectual Property Organization (WIPO) workgroups created for the research of copyright and, specifically, for the study of its application to multimedia works.[24]

The result of their work – included in Section 1, part II of the final text – besides having a bearing on certain general aspects of copyright,[25] focused on the regulation of two specific types of multimedia creations: computer programs and

---

[22]   About this same subject, cfr. MONTAÑÁ, *La OMC y el reforzamiento del sistema GATT*, McGraw-Hill (Madrid 1997) XVII-XVIII and 1-3, and WIPO ed., *Introduction to Intellectual Property. Theory and practice*, 475.

[23]   Cfr. GEUZE, "Droit d'auteur, droit moral, droits voisins. Le projet ADPIC", AA VV, *L'audiovisuel et le GATT*, Presses Universitaires de France (Paris 1995) 46.

[24]   The close relationship existing between GATT and WIPO became evident through the signing of a collaboration agreement between the latter and the World Trade Organization (WTO) on December, 1995.

       Cfr. WIPO ed., Agreement between the World Intellectual Property Organization and the World Trade Organization, http://www.wipo.org/spa/iplex/wipo-wto.htm (Geneva 1999).

[25]   About these aspects, cfr. WIPO ed., *Introduction to Intellectual Property. Theory and practice*, 475.

databases. As regards them, it laid down some rather simple legal principles of protection which would be included in the legal texts drawn-up by WIPO with the same aim, two years later.

2.1.1. Computer Programs Protected as Literary Works: Objections to this Assimilation

Once established the need to give computer programs an adequate protection, the GATT opted for laying down its protection through copyright and its assimilation to literary works, according to the basic text of the Berne Convention.

Thus computer programs were offered a similar protection to that of literary works, both for their source code – that is, for the technical language used to write the original program – and for their object code – that is, for the translation of the original man-made coding by an automated machine-language compiler, so that the resulting program can be executed by a computer.

> "Art. 10, § 1. Computer programs, whether source or object, shall be protected as literary works in accordance with the Berne Convention (1971)".[26]

There is no doubt that this option is an effective measure, but this does not prevent from asking the following questions:

Is copyright the most appropriate protection for software? Are its basic features the ones required for its protection through this right? Is it possible to say, in fact, that a computer program is a literary work? Is it not closer to being a scientific work, considering its particular language? There is no doubt that anyone can sense *a priori* that between a literary work and a computer program there are differences in their appearance, which also extend to their nature, purpose and structure, as it is verified upon the thorough analysis of both concepts.

Just as it was pointed out when studying its structure in Chapter I, all computer programs have two codes: source code and object code.

a) The source code is the set of technical instructions of a program in its first version, that is, in the version directly written by its creator and which later will be compiled or translated into an object code that is machine readable.

---

[26]   Cfr. CORREA, *Acuerdo TRIPs. Régimen internacional de la propiedad intelectual*, Ediciones Ciudad Argentina (Buenos Aires 1996) 58.

"Source program: program written in assembly language or in a high-level language".[27]

"Source language: programming language for the writing of source programs readable by a given compiler (automated translator into machine code)".[28]

"Source code: program to be compiled or translated to convert it to the equivalent object code".[29]

"Source program: program written in code language or symbolic code which is later translated into an object program".[30]

On the other hand, and as it can be deduced from the foregoing, the object code is the compiler-made translation of the source code into a machine-readable language, also known as "machine language".

"Object code: output generated by a compiler, which translates the 'source code' of a program into an 'object code'. The object code may be pure machine code, which may be loaded directly to the memory, or it may be 'relocatable' binary code."[31]

"Object program: program written in an object language, which may be executed".[32]

"Object program: Like the object code, it is the output generated by a compiler. The object program is the translation of the source program into an object language."[33]

---

[27] Cfr. LARA dir., *Gran enciclopedia informática. Diccionario informático*, vol. XVIII, Nueva Lente (Madrid 1986) 91.

[28] Cfr. ISO/AFNOR, Diccionario de la informática. Inglés-español/español-inglés, AENOR (Madrid 1992) 262.

[29] Cfr. DÍAZ DE SANTOS ed., Diccionario Oxford de Informática. Inglés-español/español-inglés, AENOR (Madrid 1985) 452.

[30] Cfr. ZUBIRI ed., *Terminología de la informática*, Zubiri (Bilbao 1970) 44.

[31] Cfr. LARA, *op. cit.*, 33.

[32] Cfr. ISPO/AFNOR, *op. cit.*, 197.

[33] Cfr. DÍAZ DE SANTOS ed., *op. cit.*, 330.

"Object program: or absolute program, a program whose instructions were written in machine language."[34]

b) As for the literary work, its content, structure and features are defined by the WIPO glossary of terms – very useful for the study of copyright – which recognizes that the essential features of these works are aesthetics and emotions, although when regarding copyright these essential characteristics are left aside.

> "Strictly speaking [...] [a literary work] is a highly valuable writing for its beauty and for the emotional effect of its form and content. From the copyright point of view, however, a general reference to literary works is understood as any type of original written works, whether they have stylistic beauty, or just a scientific, technical or merely practical nature, regardless of their value or purpose."[35]

Therefore, it seems evident that an assimilation, according to the criteria of WIPO , is possible, since in order to consider a creation a literary work it only needs to be a written work.

Nevertheless, and with a lot of common sense, philological researchers consider as literary works those that match the usual stylistic parameters. For instance, WELLECK distinguishes between literary, common and scientific use:

> "In contrast to the last two, Welleck says that literary usage is 'connotative', that is, ambiguous and with a wide capacity of association; 'opaque' (as compared to the transparency of the scientific use, according to Ullman's term) and 'plurifunctional', that is, not only referential, but also and at the same time, expressive and connotative."[36]

TRABANT and MARTÍNEZ BONATI take a further step in distinguishing literary works from computer programs, by pointing out two notes of the former which, although not essential, anyone can recognize in this type of creations:

---

[34]   Cfr. ZUBIRI ed., *op. cit.*, 40.

[35]   Cfr. WIPO ed., WIPO Glossary of Terms of the Law of Copyright and Neighboring Rights, WIPO (Geneva 1980) 146.

[36]   WELLECK, quoted by TALENS, COMPANY and HERNÁNDEZ in "Lenguaje literario y producción de sentido", chapter in DÍEZ BORQUE coord., *Métodos de estudio de la obra literaria*, Taurus (Madrid 1985) 527.

"Literary texts are considered art, only when they are an act of special oral expression: 'aesthetic reading'."[37]

"The fictitious speaker is an element required in all literary expressions (poetry). Sometimes, there is a similarity or correspondence between the fictitious speaker and the author, as there is between the latter and some character."[38]

From now on it is possible to assume that both the source code and object code have a different nature, content and structure from literary works, with the peculiarity that the object code has a double and simultaneous content: the machine readable instructions and their on-screen display, as seen by the user.

Nevertheless, in neither case it is possible to say that these are literary works: the object code is not only a symbolic or algorithmic representation, since it can be displayed on screen as a set of textual, graphic and audiovisual elements, in such a way that, occasionally, it could be considered more an artistic work than a literary work – as, for instance, in video games.

How is it possible to state, then, that MS Word or Excel are similar to Don Quixote? Is it possible to include both kind of works in the same category?

A possible explanation of this assimilation would be the need to use a general category to include works that, although enjoying a similar formal layout – in writing lines – do not share common features as regards their content and purpose.

But if this simplification is, as a rule, inadequate, in the case of computer programs the difference between both types of works is even greater: Do computer programs share more features with scientific works than that with literary works? And if this is true, is there any point to include scientific works in the literary work category and, at the same time, to include the former in a different category?

LIPSZYC points out that "scientific works are those in which the topics are developed following the requirements of the scientific method" and, though this author does not explain the meaning of "scientific method," she enumerates what works are included in such category:

"They include both the works relative to the exact, natural, and medical sciences, etc., and literary works of scientific nature, as well as educational works, technical writings, scientific publications, practical guides, etc., maps, graph-

---

[37] Cfr. TRABANT, Semiología de la obra literaria. Glosemática y teoría de la literatura, Gredos (Madrid 1975) 15.

[38] Cfr. MARTÍNEZ BONATI, *La estructura de la obra literaria*, Seix Barral (Barcelona 1972) 152.

ics, designs and three-dimensional works relative to geography, topography and, as a rule, to science."[39]

On the other hand, the WIPO glossary defines scientific works as:

"A work dealing with issues following the requirements of scientific methodology. The coverage of this category is not exclusively circumscribed to the natural sciences or to literary works of scientific nature. A computer program could, under certain circumstances, also be a scientific work. Under copyright legislation, a scientific work often includes any type of work different from artistic works or works of fiction, such as technical writings, reference books, popular scientific writings or practical guides. However, scientific works protected under copyright do not include scientific inventions, discoveries, research projects or scientific actions."[40]

According to these two definitions, it seems that the "scientific method" notion is a key element to determine the possible assimilation of computer programs to scientific works.

Philosophers have defined this concept, considering that it belongs to the Philosophy of Sciences and making it clear that each science has its own method, therefore the methodology of Physics, for example, cannot be judged using the criteria of Mathematics.

SIMARD states that "[...] it is a matter of following a scientist in the laboratory and watching how he defines his concepts, establishes his laws, formulates and changes his theories."[41]

In other words,

"We understand the term *science* in the expression *scientific methodology* in its modern sense. Its aim is to put forward the proceedings used by the experimental sciences and to determine the value and scope of its principles and conclusions."[42]

---

[39] For both quotes, cfr. STEWART, *op. cit.*, 87.

[40] WIPO ed., WIPO Glossary of terms of the law of copyright and neighboring rights, 236.

[41] Cfr. SIMARD, *Naturaleza y alcance del método científico*, Gráficas Condor (Madrid 1961) 16.

[42] *Id.*, 20. A similar opinion is held by GARCÍA GARCÉS and LÓPEZ-BARAJAS.
     Cfr. GARCÍA GARCÉS, *Compendio de metodología científica general*, Coculsa (Madrid 1945) 15 and LÓPEZ-BARAJAS, *Fundamentos de metodología científica*, UNED (Madrid 1988) 56.

The requirement, therefore, that a scientific work has to be based on scientific methods refers to the fact that creations in the experimental science field are made according to basic scientific principles, something with which, *a priori*, computer programs comply, since in the resolution of a given problem – the purpose for which the software is frequently created – it turns to the Computing method itself.

Besides, when taking into account some features of a computer program the suitability of this protection becomes evident, upon revealing its closeness to technical writings:

    i) Both computer programs and technical writings are composed by a set of identical instructions.

    ii) The language used in both their sequences has this same nature.

    iii) And they are created following their own methodology that is used, successively, in the resolution of the problems caused by the development of the software itself.

2.1.2. Patent Rights as an Alternative to Copyright Protection of Software?

But the features of computer programs themselves, which make them eligible for a most suitable protection as scientific works, are the basis for questioning whether copyright is the more effective legal option for the protection of their creators or, on the other hand, a more relevant legal protection should be sought.

In addition to the technical language used in the creation of software, it must be taken into account that software development is often undertaken to solve a practical problem, in the industry or services field: computer programs are widely used both in office, sales and manufacturing applications.

Would not it be simpler then, at least whenever computer programs are used in industrial and corporate applications, to protect them under patent rights? And, at the same time, would not this solution prevent the problem of their difficult assimilation to literary works protected under copyright?

Patent rights protect industrial property and covers "inventions," which OTERO defines as "immaterial goods solving technical problems in industry and allowing to obtain a positive result." [43]

---

[43]   Cfr. OTERO GARCÍA-CASTRILLÓN, Las patentes en el comercio internacional. La empresa española y la disciplina de la Unión Europea y de la Organización Mundial del Comercio, Dykinson (Madrid 1997) 34.

The relationship between an invention and an inventor is safeguarded by the protection of patent rights, which is a government grant, although meeting this requirement is not difficult.

WIPO has stated in one of its works the conditions that a creation has to fulfill to claim protection under this right:

"[…] An invention shall be taken to be new, it shall involve an inventive step (or, at least, something not obvious to a person skilled in the art), and shall be capable of industrial application." [44]

Also, the American, French, British and German national law bodies, for example, all agree that an invention must have these three features to entitle its creator to enjoy patent rights:

i) It should be a new invention.

ii) It should involve an inventive step, that is, not being obvious and evident, and that, therefore, it must require a certain intellectual effort for its conception.

iii) It should be capable of industrial application.[45]

American legislation on patent rights, which is based on the Lanham Act of 1976, and in the American Inventors Protection Act of 1999, states:

"US Code Title 35.

Section 101. Whoever invents or discovers any new and useful process, machine, manufacture or composition of matter, or any new and useful improvement thereof, may obtain a patent […]".

British legislation, based on the Patent Act of 1977, states:

"Section 1 (1) (a). 1. An invention shall be taken to be new if it is does not form part of the state of the art. 2. The state of the art in the case of an invention shall be taken to comprise all matter (whether a product, a process, information about either, or anything else) which has at any time before the priority date of that invention been made available to the public (whether in the United

---

[44] *Id.*

[45] About these legal texts and their amendments to date, cfr. CONGRESS OF THE UNITED STATES, US Code. Title 35, http://thomas.loc.gov/cgi-bin/query/z?c104:S652.enr (United States 1999),

Kingdom or elsewhere), by written or oral description, by use or in any other way."

The German Patent Act of 1980, and its current amendments, states.

"Art 1. Patents are granted to new inventions, involving an inventive step and capable of industrial application.

"Art. 3. An invention is new if it is not part of the state of the art. All the knowledge that, prior to the priority date of a patent application, has been made available to the public by oral or written description, by use or in other way is considered state of the art."

Finally, the French legislation, quite comprehensive when it comes to consider these three features, includes in its Intellectual Property Act, Book VI, a title relating to the so-called *Brevets d'invention*, which is in keeping with the Industrial Property Act 90-1052 of November 26, 1990.

"Art. L. 611-10. 1. New inventions involving an inventive step capable of industrial application are patentable."

"Art. L. 611-11. An invention is new if it is not part of the state of the art. The state of the art shall be taken to comprise all matter which has at any time before the priority date of the patent application of that invention been made available to the public, by means of a written or oral description, use or any other way."

"Art. L. 611-14. An invention shall be taken to involve an inventive step if it is not obvious to a person skilled in the art."

"Art. L. 611-15. An invention shall be taken to be capable of industrial application if it can be made or used in any kind of industry, including agriculture."

In the supranational field, the actual subject of this chapter, international treaties also provide for patent protection: The Paris Convention for the Protection of Industrial Property (1883); the Patent Cooperation Treaty (Washington, 1970), and its Regulations (1992); the GATT Agreement (1994); and, the WIPO Patent Law Treaty and its Regulations (2000).[46]

---

[46] Cfr. WIPO, Treaties on Industrial Property, http://www.wipo.org/treaties/ip/plt/index.html (Geneva 2002).

However, only the GATT text refers to the owner, subject matter and content of patent rights, as well as to the conditions that an invention has to fulfill to enjoy this protection:

"Art. 27.

1) [...] patents shall be available for any inventions, whether products or processes, in all fields of technology, provided that they are new, involve an inventive step and are capable of industrial application [...]".

"Art. 28.

1) A patent shall confer on its owner the following exclusive rights:

    a) where the subject matter of a patent is a product, to prevent third parties not having his consent from the acts of: making, using, offering for sale, selling, or importing the product for these purposes;

    b) where the subject matter of a patent is a process, to prevent third parties not having his consent from the act of: using the process, and from the acts of: using, offering for sale, selling, or importing for these purposes at least the product obtained directly by that process.

2. Patent owners shall also have the right to assign, or transfer by succession, the patent and to conclude licensing contracts."[47]

The rest of the aforementioned supranational texts only establish the procedures required for the international filing of patents, and provide a general classification. However, two issues should be considered in this regard:

    a) The principle of national treatment, established by the Paris Convention, according to which signatory countries committed themselves to protect foreign inventions with the same protection that their respective laws grant to nationals.

    b) The priority to file a patent in a foreign country, to which a person is entitled if he has previously filed it in his country of origin, provided that said country is a signatory of the Agreement.

---

[47] Cfr. GATT ed., Los resultados de la Ronda Uruguay de negociaciones comerciales multilaterales, Centre William Rappard (Geneva 1994) 395-396.

In principle nothing prevents, therefore, computer programs from receiving legal protection under patent rights, which can give a more appropriate protection than copyright, since there is no need to assimilate them to other works of similar characteristics. In fact, this idea is reinforced when realizing that the term of protection granted to an invention seems more appropriate to the actual life span of a computer program than the fifty years of copyright granted under the GATT Agreement:

> "Art. 33.
>
> The term of protection available shall not end before the expiration of a period of twenty years counted from the filing."[48]

After all, is there any sense to grant a term of protection of no less-than fifty years for a product that, approximately, every five two or three years is marketed in a higher version with new features and capabilities?

However, the patent option, allowed by the latitude of the international treaties on this matter,[49] is questioned when interpreting said principle of national treatment: What would happen if the legislation of a signatory country of the Paris Convention would provide for the protection of software under patent rights and the legislation of another signatory country would not? According to the text of the Convention, it would not be possible to file for a patent in a country whose national legislation does not provide for the application of this system for the protection of software. And although this could seem a simple theoretical formulation, this does happen, for example, in the French, English and German cases, as opposed to the American case:

French *Code de la Propriété Intellectuelle* :

> "Art. L. 611-10.
>
> 1. New inventions are patentable when they involve an inventive step capable of industrial application.

---

[48]   Cfr. PUTNAM ed., *op. cit.*, 399.

[49]   The GATT Agreement text of 1994, when listing the works that could not be covered by patent rights, did not include computer programs, therefore their protection seems possible in accordance with this solution.

Cfr. SCHIUM, "TRIPS and exclusion of *software* 'as such' from patentability", *IIC: International Review of Industrial Property and Copyright Law*, vol. 31, no. 1, VCH (Weinheim 2000) 37.

2. The following are not considered inventions in the sense of the above line:

   a) a discovery, scientific theory or mathematical method;

   b) an aesthetic creation;

   c) a scheme, rule or method for performing a mental act, playing a game, or doing business, or a program for a computer;

   d) the presentation of information.

3. The provisions of the above paragraph only exclude the patentability of the elements mentioned if the patent application deals with said elements in isolation".[50]

British Patents Act of 1977.

   "1. Patentable inventions.

   [...]

   (2) It is hereby declared that the following are not inventions for the purposes of this Act:

   a) a discovery, scientific theory or mathematical method;

   b) a literary, dramatic, musical or artistic work, or any other aesthetic creation whatsoever;

   c) a scheme, rule or method for performing a mental act, playing a game or doing business, or a program for a computer;

   d) the presentation of information;

   but this prohibition to consider said elements as inventions, for the purposes of this Act, is only valid if the patent refers to these elements taken individually as such."[51]

---

[50]   Cfr. CABINET BEAU DELOMENIE, *op. cit.*

[51]   Cfr. BUTTERWORTHS ed., *op. cit.* In the American case, quoted as an example in the main text, the law does not contain any specification about patentable creations, therefore it is assumed that the protection of software may be covered by this solution.
   Cfr. U.S. PATENT AND TRADEMARK OFFICE ed., Qualifying for a patent, http://www.nolo.com/encyclopedia/articles/pct/pct3.html (United States 2000).

German *Patentgesetz* of 1980:

"Art. 1.

[...]

2. The following elements shall not be considered inventions according to the meaning given to this term:

a. discovery, scientific theory and mathematical method.

b. an aesthetic creation.

c. a schemes, rule or method for performing mental acts.

d. the presentation of information.

3. The provisions adopted in subsection 2 would only exclude patentability if the protection is claimed for these elements as such."[52]

Therefore, the international protection of computer programs under patent rights would depend, in practice, on the content of the national laws.

2.1.3. Protection for Databases as Compilations According to the Selection or Arrangement of Contents

For the first time, the GATT Agreement of 1994 also provides for international protection for the rights of the authors of databases – also known as data banks – whose data was previously collected on paper and, thanks to computing technology, are now available on various supporting media, in a wide range of designs and sorted in new ways, making these works different from simple lists or catalogs of words, codes, sounds or images.

This protection is granted by the conceptual assimilation of these works to compilations, but this would only be possible regarding to the originality of the selection or arrangement of the contents:

---

[52] Cfr. DEUTSCHE PATENTAMT ed., *Germany Patent Law*, copy supplied by the German Patent Office (Munich 1993).

"Art. 10.

[...]

2) Databases or data compilations, whether in machine readable or other form, which by reason of the selection or arrangement of their contents constitute intellectual creations shall be protected as such. Such protection, which shall not extend to the data or material itself, shall be without prejudice to any copyright subsisting in the data or material itself."[53]

As opposed to the software, the key for the protection does not lie now in an assimilation, but in the conditions which any database must meet to reach the status of an original creation.

Therefore, it is not a question of discussing whether an encyclopedia can be identified with a database according to the meaning given to this word when speaking, for example, about personal data files. It is rather a question of understanding that a database, regardless of the type of content and medium in which it is contained, will only be protected according to its structure, to the "architecture" given to it by its author and which makes it an interactive or non-interactive work, visually attractive or poor as regards its design, user-friendly or not, etc., being these the features which mark its originality and novelty.

Therefore, the deciding factor, as it is correctly stated in the GATT Agreement text, is the selection or arrangement of the contents: the selection turns a database into something new and original due to the fact that its elements were until then scattered; the arrangement determines its aesthetic and operative parameters; and both establish the difference with other works which, although containing some similar data, arrange them differently.

Aside from the criteria required, it is possible to raise two other issues regarding the protection of these works:

a) Going back to their assimilation to compilations, and in the name of scientific rigor, it must be established that some databases currently available in the market are different from compilations, mainly because the latter collects data or information previously published, while databases may include contents never disseminated before.

---

[53] Cfr. CORREA, *op. cit.*, 58.

Therefore to put databases on a level with compilations is somehow inappropriate, since the preexistence of the contents is the feature which more clearly differentiates one work from the other.

While a compilation will always fit in the database category provided it collects scattered materials and arranges them to facilitate their access, not all databases constitute a compilation, since a database containing new elements is not a compilation.

As shown in some definitions of both concepts:

"Compilation: (From Latin *Compilatio, -onis*) f. The act or process of compiling. 2. To gather in a work information, rules or doctrines from other sources."[54]

"Database: a set of related data stored in one collection, without unnecessary redundancies and complying with three fundamental conditions:

– The data can be stored on several information media, so as to be program-independent.

– Its use is not limited to a single application, since it may be accessed by several applications, even simultaneously.

– In order to manage the information contained in the database, different specially designed procedures are used to optimize the system operation."[55]

"Database.

Structured collection of data: information arranged for search and retrieval by a computer. Many hypermedia programs (like encyclopedias and illustrated dictionaries) apply sophisticated database techniques to store the data contents. Interactive multimedia techniques can be used to provide a user-friendly access to the database."[56]

Both definitions of a database seem to share an essential element: the use of a computer is a *sine qua non* for a work to receive this name, although in fact this is not absolutely true. Thus, while *The Cyberspace Lexicon* states this issue

---

[54] Cfr. REAL ACADEMIA ESPAÑOLA DE LA LENGUA, *op. cit.*, 369.

[55] Cfr. LARA, *op. cit.*, 18.

[56] Cfr. COTTON and OLIVER, *op. cit.*, 58.

explicitly, LARA's definition mentions it implicitly, since the data interrelationship which it demands, together with the existence of the other features he attributes to these works, are only possible if the constituting elements are integrated by a computer.

And although nothing prevents a compilation to be carried out using a computer, it is the lack of novelty of its content that prevents it from being called a database.

b) On the other hand, the utilitarian purpose with which these works are usually used could make them eligible, as in the case of computer programs, for their protection under patent rights.

However, and unlike what happens with software, it seems that the industrial application of a database is not significant enough and, therefore, it would not comply with the criteria required for claiming protection under this right.

Furthermore, a database – as a kind – is more like a system of classification, management and access to a given information, than an invention. There is no provision for the protection of the methods of classification or the presentation of information in current national legislations, with the exception of the U.S.A.

Computer programs, on the other hand, not only manage information and data, but also control the operation of industrial machines, spelling checkers, design tools and video games, among a wide range of possibilities that certainly include their industrial application.

2.2. New Copyright Protection for Multimedia: The WIPO Treaties or the Protocol to the Berne Convention of 1996

Two years after the signing of the GATT Agreement, the Copyright Treaty and the Performances and Phonograms Treaty, known as the Protocol to the Berne Convention of 1996, were signed in Geneva, sponsored by WIPO.

As stated in the preparatory agendas of 1991 and 1992, "the Protocol would be mainly devoted to specify the rules in force or to establish new rules whenever the current text of the Berne Convention is not clear as regards the field of application of such Convention. Thus some voices of dissent were raised, and some might be raised in the near future, regarding certain subject matters to be protected (for example, computer programs, phonograms, works made by means of computers); regarding certain rights (for example, right of rental, right of public lending, right of circulation of copies of any type of work, right to display on a computer screen), regarding the applicability of a minimal protection (absence of formalities, protection duration, etc.) and regarding the obligation of granting national treatment (without reciprocity) to foreigners."[57]

Since 1982 a "Group of Government Experts in Copyright Issues Raised by the Use of Computers to Access or Create Works" works in the draft of a report for WIPO and UNESCO, carrying on with the work the former started in 1978 with the publication of a series of provisions for the protection of software, alerting to the effect on copyright of the extended use of computing technology.

The conclusions of the report of both organizations focused on this same problem and pointed out some ideas which, later on, would cause some controversy when they were included in different legislations:

a) That the use of protected works in a computer system implies the commission of an act of reproduction (replay) in a medium allowing the reading of such works, as well as their fixing in the computer memory as provided for in the Berne Convention and the Universal Copyright Convention of 1952.

b) That the extraction of protected works from a computer system must be under the protection of copyright regardless of the medium selected to fix (record) it; this may be a diskette, any machine readable format, the transmission from that system to another one – with or without an intermediary – or the images and sounds reproduced on a screen in a such a way that the work may reach the public.

c) That the protection of the author's moral rights in computer media must be taken into account, as well as the lawful use of protected works without requiring authorization.

d) That licenses should only be compulsory when it is impossible to obtain a voluntary license from the author.[58]

Since 1989, and in the meetings held between GATT and WIPO members, prevailed the idea of drafting a new treaty to update the Berne Convention and to adapt it to the most recent technical developments.

It was understood that the text had to be presented as an addition to the Agreement and not as a substantial revision of it, though in fact that would be its practical consequence upon broadening copyright protection to new right holders, subjects and contents.

---

[57]   Cfr. LIPSZYC, *op. cit.*, 720-721.

[58]   Cfr. WIPO ed., *Introduction to Intellectual Property. Theory and practice*, 584.

With this aim, a Committee of Experts met in Geneva in 1991 and raised the question of digital and multimedia issues as one of the high-priority fields that should be approached regarding copyright.

But the agreement reached in this Committee was minimal and in the end its contribution was just to assert that copyright was the most adequate way for the protection of computer programs and databases – provided the latter comply with the originality criterion for its protection as compilations – instead of other possible ways of protection, such as patent rights.

Obviously, a second Committee of Experts was necessary, which met in 1992, and who pointed out a series of specific proposals to work on in the future:

a) The redefinition of the word "reproduction," to include the storage of works in computer systems in order to seek protection for them in the conventional right of reproduction.[59]

b) The unlawful nature of personal reproduction or private copy – lawful until then – of digital works, since it is easy to copy them, and their high technical quality make it difficult to distinguish between an original work and its copy.

c) The proposal to create a new right – the right of public performance or communication to the public – including the protection for the displaying of a work on a computer screen.

d) The invention of electronic copy management systems as a practical and effective method for controlling the unauthorized reproduction.

2.2.1. The Attempt to Afford Protection to Databases Makers was a Failure

Taking these issues into consideration, new sessions began in 1993 to discuss the final document that would be submitted for the approval of WIPO members. The sessions went on until September 1995, when the last meetings took place before the call of the Geneva conference in which the final text would be approved.[60]

---

[59] About the right of reproduction applied to a display on a computer screen, cfr. LUCAS, "La propiedad intelectual y la infraestructura global de la información", *Boletín de derecho de autor*, no. 1, UNESCO (Paris 1998) 4.

[60] Cfr. FICSOR, "Towards a global solution: the digital agenda of the Berne Protocol and the new instrument. The Rorschach test of digital transmission", HUGENHOLTZ, *The future of copyright in a digital environment*, Kluwer International Law (Holland 1996) 116.

Among the documents under consideration in those two years, there was a draft treaty on the protection of databases[61] including some significant and appropriate provisions that finally were not approved in the plenary sessions of December 1996.[62]

> "The production and distribution of databases has become a significant economic activity which is expanding rapidly worldwide. The production and distribution of databases may be viewed as the 'content industry' within the information industry, and it may be expected that this industry will be a major source of employment […].
>
> The production and distribution of databases requires considerable investment. At the same time, exact copies of whole databases or their essential parts can be made at practically no cost. The increasing use of digital recording technology exposes database makers to the risk that the contents of their databases may be copied and rearranged electronically, without their authorization, to produce similar competing databases or databases with identical contents […]".[63]

The draft relied, as one of its main driving forces, on the support of the Delegation of the European Union which, during 1994, informed WIPO Committees of Experts of their progress in the study of copyright protection for databases, as well as their plans to enact an EU Directive in this regard – eventually passed in 1996 – and therefore they favored a similar protection in the international field for these creations.

The proposal was also favorably received by the Delegation of the United States, who was working then on similar regulatory principles which, finally, would be included in their legislation.

Since both the Delegation of the European Union and the Delegation of the United States supported the regulations proposed, the content of the draft was written as follows:

---

[61] Cfr. WIPO ed., Basic proposal for the substantive provisions of the treaty on intellectual property in respect of databases to be considered by the diplomatic conference, photocopy supplied by WIPO (Geneva 1996).

[62] *Id.*, 8-10.

[63] *Id.*

a) The obligation that the creation of a database represented a substantial investment devoted to the collection, assembly, verification, organization or presentation of the contents, was established as a basic condition to be entitled to copyright protection.

"Art. 1.

(1) Contracting Parties shall protect any database that represents a substantial investment in the collection, assembly, verification, organization or presentation of the contents of the database".[64]

That is, the protection depended on the new contributions which a database could present as compared to other works with similar content and format.

But, what did the words "substantial investment" mean? Maybe the supply of hundreds of data items for the building of the base? A financial investment? Who would be, in that case, the copyright holder: the person investing his money in the project or the creator and designer of the work?.

According to the Proposal,

"Art. 2.

[...]

(4) 'substantial investment' means any qualitative or quantitatively significant investment of human, financial, technical or other resources in the collection, assembly verification, organization or presentation of the contents of the database".[65]

But, is there any sense in establishing a criterion in which the financial contribution means as much as the content contribution? What kind of originality or novelty feature adds the financial investment to the database regarding other required investments? What would happen, then, if a database would have the same contents of an existing work, but in a different format? Would the new work be protected under copyright?

---

[64]   Cfr. WIPO ed., Basic proposal for the substantive provisions of the treaty on intellectual property in respect of databases to be considered by the diplomatic conference, 13.

[65]   *Id.*, 17.

b) The right holder was the maker of the database,[66] "the natural or legal person or persons with control and responsibility for the undertaking of a substantial investment making a database".[67]

This way a tangible reality was put forward – the creation of a database frequently responded to an entrepreneurial initiative – and the proposal opted for protecting the person promoting the creation with a similar right to that of authors.

However, the fact that there could be several and different substantial investments would allow, according to the Proposal, the existence of several potential persons entitled to the same database, as could be inferred from the plural used in the text when referring to the "natural or legal person or persons" which may make a substantial investment in the database.

Does this mean, then, that the same text was enforcing a *de facto* contractual assignment of the right to exploit a database to prevent the existence of several right holders? Or is it to be understood, on the other hand, that the treaty provided for the existence of several copyright holders simultaneously?

c) The protection of the work was guaranteed regardless of its format, allowing the protection of databases not printed on paper (i.e., those recorded on diskettes, CD-ROMs, CD-Is, or those transmitted over the Internet).

d) The maker was entitled to authorize or prohibit the extraction and use of the database contents, and in the case of its use, to do it through any on-line form of transmission.

"Art. 2.

(2) 'extraction' means the permanent or temporary transfer of all or a substantial part of the contents of a database to another medium by any means or in any form.

[…]

---

[66] The term "*maker*" means "manufacturer" and it connotes more a commercial sense than "creator." However, this meaning is applied when "Maker" is in capital letters and refers to "God, the Creator."

Cfr. STYLES, PARKER and HÜLSKAMP eds., *The Oxford Dictionary. Spanish-English/ English-Spanish*, Oxford University Press (Great Britain 1994) 1318.

[67] Cfr. WIPO ed., Basic proposal for the substantive provisions of the treaty on intellectual property in respect of databases to be considered by the diplomatic conference, 15.

(6) 'utilization' means the making available to the public of all or a substantial part of the contents of a database by any means, including by the distribution of copies, by renting, or by on-line availability or other forms of transmission, including making the same available to the public from a place and at a time individually chosen by each member of the public".[68]

Should both concepts be understood therefore as new copyright powers?

e) Finally, the duration of the protection provided was 25 years or 15 years, leaving the choice of one or the other term to national laws; it was also taken into account the fact that, in case of making substantial changes in the contents of the database, the final result would have its own term of protection.

> "The determination of the proper duration of any form of intellectual property protection is bound to depend on many factors, including the nature of the subject matter protected, the prevailing economic and technical circumstances and the interests of right holders, users and society at large. In the case of databases, the need for protection in the first instance is connected to the ability of makers of databases to recover the investment they make in a database. The economic life-span of different databases varies depending on their content and the structure of the marketplace. For dynamic databases that are constantly changed and developed, a shorter term of protection could be justified. New versions may be protected under the proposed Treaty and old versions rapidly become outdated and useless. In the case of static databases, such as encyclopedic, historical and cartographic databases, protection may be needed for a longer period of time. Indeed, the recovery of the heavy investments required by the production of such databases may justify or even need a longer term of protection. For practical reasons, it would be advisable to adopt a single term of protection for all types of databases."[69]

Did this mean that each new contribution to the work, or each new investment, would involve the beginning of a new term? Would not it be necessary to be more explicit about when an investment was significant enough to calculate a new term of protection?

---

[68] *Id.*, 19.

[69] *Id.*, 30.

Although, at the last minute, this Proposal was rejected because it did not obtain enough votes to be part of the texts approved in 1996, it must be recognized its value as an innovative and practical project for the following reasons:

i) The very fact of the acceptance of a specific category for databases due to the singular nature of these works, instead of assimilating them to compilations, was an appropriate and rigorous provision.

ii) The option of the substantial investment criterion, despite comparing concepts of different nature, emphasized that the reasons why a database must be protected were multiple and could not be limited to the selection and arrangement of its contents.

iii) According to this, the text reflected the fact that in order to create a database, the work of one person was not enough, but rather that many people had to make their contribution to the work.

iv) At the same time, the application of a limited term of protection and the definition of the "utilization" and "extraction" concepts, almost as economic interests of the author, was more according to the real life-span of these creations and with the basic operations that are usually performed with their contents.[70]

On September 17 to 19, 1997 the Berne Union members met in Geneva, for an information meeting on intellectual property in respect of databases, to study national and regional laws on the matter. In the meeting, the possibility of establishing a *sui generis* protection system for these works was discussed again, but the opinion of the countries that requested more time to study the issue in detail prevailed.

The participants focused on: the possibility of offering a certain protection to non-original databases, but containing valuable information; the need for free and unrestricted access to the information in the scientific, educational and security fields; and the search for a system balancing the rights and interests of the owner with the rights and interests of the public.

This demonstrates that, although this document was not incorporated into the Protocol to the Berne Convention of 1996, its contents are still today a subject of study in the WIPO for a future incorporation into the treaties system.

---

[70] Cfr. "Reunión de Información de la OMPI sobre la propiedad intelectual en materia de bases de datos", *Boletín de Derecho de Autor*, no. 1, UNESCO (Paris 1998) 21-25.

2.2.2. Reintroducing the Contents of the GATT Agreement and the Inclusion of the Right to Make Available to the Public

Despite the rejection of the proposal of the specific treaty in respect of databases, a new draft was presented in Geneva including other issues related to the protection of artistic and literary works, and also dealing with certain aspects of digital communication and multimedia resulting from the strong development of the NITs during the last years:

> "The Contracting Parties,
>
> Desiring to develop and maintain the protection of the rights of authors in their literary and artistic works in a manner as effective and uniform as possible,
>
> Recognizing the need to introduce new international rules and clarify the interpretation of certain existing rules in order to provide adequate solutions to the questions raised by new economic, social, cultural and technological developments,
>
> Recognizing the profound impact of the development and convergence of information and communication technologies on the creation and use of literary and artistic works [...]".[71]

Some of the ideas included in the Basic Proposal for the substantive provisions of the Treaty on Certain Questions Concerning the Protection of Literary and Artistic Works, which eventually were introduced into the Protocol to the Berne Convention, are:

a) The application of the concept of "published work" to the dissemination or communication of creations to the public through interactive means, allowing the access of the user at a time and from a place he or she wishes.

b) The inclusion in the content of the right of communication to the public of the interactive digital dissemination of a work "made available to the public" at a time and from a place chosen by them; that is, the inclusion of the on-demand communication.

c) A request to the signatory States to make unlawful, with regard to the electronic management of author's rights, the following acts:

---

[71] Cfr. WIPO ed., Basic proposal for the substantive provisions of the treaty on intellectual property in respect of databases to be considered by the diplomatic conference, 9.

    i) To remove or alter any electronic rights management information required to identify the work, the author of the work, the owner of any right in the work and any numbers or codes that represent such information.

    ii) The unauthorized distribution, import for distribution, or communication to the public of copies of works from which such information has been removed or in which it has been altered.

The signing of the Protocol, on December 2 to 20, 1996, implied, among other provisions, the reintroduction of the content of the GATT Agreement regarding computer programs and databases, and the copyright protection of digital or electronic dissemination:

a) The Copyright Treaty assimilated computer programs to literary works in exactly identical terms to the ones used in 1994, although broadening the protection to any format in which the software may have been made:

> "Art. 4. Computer programs are protected as literary works within the meaning of Article 2 of the Berne Convention. Such protection applies to computer programs in any form."[72]

In that same text, and following the same criterion, the protection of databases was established according to the selection or arrangement of their contents and under the name of collections.

> "Art. 5.
>
> Collections of data or other material, in any form, which by reason of the selection or arrangement of their contents constitute intellectual creations, are protected as such. This protection does not extend to the data or the material themselves and is without prejudice to any rights subsisting in the data or material contained in the collection."[73]

b) Through the same WIPO Copyright Treaty the right of communication to the public covered the digital transmission on-demand as a specific right recognized to copyright holders.

---

[72] *Id.*, 4.

[73] *Id.*

"Art. 8.

[...] Authors of literary and artistic works shall enjoy the exclusive right of authorizing any communication to the public of their works, by wired or wireless means, including the making available to the public of their works in such a way that members of the public may access these works from a place and at a time individually chosen by them."[74]

On the other hand, the WIPO Performance and Phonograms Treaty adopted a similar provision regarding performers and producers of phonograms:

"Art. 10.

Performers shall enjoy the exclusive right of authorizing the making available to the public of their performances fixed in phonograms, by wire or wireless means, in such a way that members of the public may access them from a place and at a time individually chosen by them."[75]

"Art. 14.

Producers of phonograms shall enjoy the exclusive right of authorizing the making available to the public of their phonograms, by wire or wireless means, in such a way that members of the public may access them from a place and at a time individually chosen by them."[76]

With the broadening of the right of communication to the public, WIPO introduced the copyright protection of digital communication.

However, as it only covers on-line communication – "from a place and at a time individually chosen by the users" – the content of such right could be interpreted in the strict sense of the term, understanding that the legal protection is limited to point-to-point digital transmission, that is, to the transmission between a transmitter and a given public, whose members access to the content transmitted at a time individually chosen by them, and not simultaneously with its general transmission – such as it happens in the public communication through conventional means.

But, should the text be interpreted in this sense? Does it provide complete protection for digital communication?

---

[74] *Id.*

[75] Cfr. OMPI ed., Tratado de la OMPI sobre Interpretación o Ejecución y Fonogramas, 8.

[76] *Id.*, 10.

The fact is that Article 8 of the Copyright Treaty is, in certain respects, vague, and requires an interpretation according to the provisional *Proposal* preceding the treaties, and jurisprudence:

i) The idea of the communication to the public existing at that time was reaffirmed, which is understood in the broad sense of the term as including the transmission by wire and wireless means, covering from cable transmissions to digital communications, with no further specifications required.

As LIPSZYC says, when summarizing the doctrine on this right, "the communication to the public of a work means any act by which a large number of people may have access to all or part of it, in its original form or changed, by other means different to the distribution of copies [...]. The right of communication to the public covers all direct ('live') or indirect communication (by means of 'fixations', such as records, tapes and magnetic strips or otherwise, films, video copies, etc., or by means of a dissemination agent, as broadcasting – including satellite communications – and cable distribution)."[77]

The right of communication to the public is, therefore, contrasted to the right of distribution – in reference to an offer to the public of the copies of a work through commercial channels, that is, through sale[78] – and a category including communication forms so specific and different such as the exhibition, representation, public performance, projection, public exhibition, broadcasting or cable distribution.

ii) The "making available to the public" of a work is established as a new form of communication to the public in which the members of the public may access the different creations from a place and at a time individually chosen by them.

As it is set out in the Treaty Proposal, this provision, an initiative of the Delegation of the European Union,[79] is an attempt to demonstrate that interactive on-demand communications are covered by the right of communication to the public.

"10.11. One of the main objectives of the second part of Article 10" – this was the number assigned to the right of communication to the public in the first

---

[77] Cfr. LIPSZYC, *op. cit.*, 183-184.

[78] Cfr. WIPO ed., WIPO glossary of terms of the law of copyright and neighboring rights, 83.

[79] Cfr. GOLDSMITH, "Les nouveaux traités de l'OMPI et l'action législative européenne sur le droit d'auteur et les droits voisins", *Legipresse*, no. 139-II, Victoires (Paris 1997) 28.

draft Treaty – "is to make it clear that interactive on-demand acts of communication are within the scope of the provision. This is done by confirming that the relevant acts of communication include cases where members of the public may have access to the works from different places and at different times. The element of individual choice implies the interactive nature of such access." [80]

Nevertheless, it is not possible to infer this idea from the literal wording of the article, since on-demand communication not only implies the individual access to available content in a network, but also the prior request of one such work – an act which seems not to have been considered in the text.

The dissemination of contents over the Internet adequately illustrates this subtle difference: each member of the public may access the on-line contents from the place and at the time they wish, but this does not mean there is an actual request for an on-demand dissemination.

That is why, *strictu sensu*, this new public communication form refers to on-line digital dissemination – which allows its compliance – and not the on-demand and interactive digital dissemination, since, as anyone can see, other media, like television o radio, also allow the public to access a given content at a given time and from the place they wish. That is, conventional means also disseminate their programs and each member of the public decides when to access that broadcasting by turning on their receivers. Obviously, said access is only possible in the presence of receiver devices in a given place. But this is not an exclusive feature of conventional and analog broadcasting, but rather, it also happens with digital technology.

On the other hand, the on-demand – point-to-point – digital transmission implies an act of individual communication, in which the receiver is specifically known, what seems to move away this right even more from the so-called communication to the public, whose main feature is that they are broadcasts intended for an indeterminate number of individuals.

Precisely, and as it will be seen below, the recognition in these Treaties of a right of distribution, capable to cover property transfers like rental, allows to categorize on-demand transmissions in the content of this right, since, after all, this

---

[80] Cfr. WIPO ed., Basic proposal for the substantive provisions of the treaty on intellectual property in respect of databases to be considered by the diplomatic conference, 44. Cfr. GOLDSMITH, *op. cit.*, 28.

practice is only a temporary assignment of a work in exchange for a given consideration.

2.2.3. Other Principles Established

Apart from the specific provisions on copyright for multimedia, both treaties presented other ideas which encouraged the updating of their legal principles:

a) Authors are granted a right of distribution, which consists of making available to the public the copies of their works through sale or other transfer of ownership.

b) Authors of cinematographic works and works embodied in phonograms are granted the right of rental.

c) The recognition of the moral rights of performers, by means of the right to be identified as such, and the right to be opposed to any distortion, mutilation or other alteration of their performance.

d) The recognition of the rights of performers to authorize or prohibit the broadcasting and communication to the public of their unrecorded (non-embodied) performances, together with the right to authorize or not the act of recording (embodying or fixation) itself.

e) Performers are granted the right of reproduction.

Furthermore, authors of computer programs are entitled to the right of rental, unless the program itself is not the object of the rental, but the underlying hardware:

"Art. 7. WIPO Copyright Treaty.

1) Authors of:

i) computer programs; [...]

shall enjoy the exclusive right of authorizing commercial rental to the public of the originals or copies of their works.

2) Paragraph 1) shall not apply:

i) in the case of computer programs, where the program itself is not the essential object of the rental; [...]".[81]

---

[81]   Cfr. OMPI ed., Tratado de la OMPI sobre Derecho de Autor, 5 and 7.

On the other hand, the contracting parties shall provide in their legislations effective legal remedies to safeguard in practice the inviolability of the rights of the authors in digital communication:

"Art. 12. WIPO Copyright Treaty.

1) Contracting Parties shall provide adequate and effective legal remedies against any person knowingly performing any of the following acts knowing, or as regards civil remedies having reasonable grounds to know, that it will induce, enable, facilitate or conceal an infringement of any right covered by this Treaty or the Berne Convention:

i) to remove or alter any electronic rights management information without authority;

ii) to distribute, import for distribution, broadcast or communicate to the public, without authority, works or copies of works knowing that electronic rights management information has been removed or altered without authority.

2) As used in this Article, "rights management information" means information which identifies the work, the author of the work, the owner of any right in the work, or information about the terms and conditions of use of the work, and any numbers or codes that represent such information, whenever one of these items is attached to a copy of a work or appears in connection with the communication of a work to the public."[82]

3. Toward a Global Solution for Multimedia Copyrights

Even if it is essential to study separately the new contents covered by copyright in the two texts mentioned above, this is not enough when trying to get a global vision as how its protection materializes in the international area.

It is true that with this analysis it is possible to glimpse the guidelines that copyright has given to its current and future regulation, and also as regards multimedia works – actual purpose of this research. However, these provisions should be incorporated into the consolidated set of supranational rules to obtain a global, and not only partial solution, to the questions raised.

---

[82] *Id.*

That is why, in this section we shall review the copyright protection included in international treaties, pointing out a way of applying its content to digital and multimedia communications.

3.1. Basic Principles of the Berne System Applied to the Digital Communication Field

Any attempt to explain how to protect intellectual property in supranational texts requires an inescapable first reference to the Berne Convention of 1886.

Although the Convention does not constitute the only international treaty on the matter, its long-standing application, its importance when it was approved and its later significance have turned it into the backbone of the public international system of this right, as was indicated in section 1 of this chapter.

For that reason, it is advisable to devote some time to the analysis of the three principles mentioned which organize this century-old legal system, yet still valid today,[83] to understand its relevance and meaning in the current digital age:

a) The principle of national treatment, by which any work from a country signatory of the Convention shall be entitled to be protected in the rest of the countries which adhered to it, with the same safeguards offered by their legislations to their nationals.

This way a unified environment for the circulation of works is consolidated, although with national legal differences, in which creations can be disseminated with the guarantee that the Law of each signatory country will accord them a treatment no less favorable than it accords to its own authors.

"Art. 2.

6) The works mentioned in this Article shall enjoy protection in all countries of the Union. This protection shall operate for the benefit of author and his successors in tittle."

"Art. 5.

1) Authors shall enjoy, in respect of works for which they are protected under this Convention, in countries of the Union other than the country of origin,

---

[83] The validity of the three basic principles of the Berne Convention became once again obvious in the content of the GATT Agreement of 1994. Cfr. GATT., *op. cit.*, 384.

the rights which their respective laws do now or may hereafter grant to their nationals".[84]

b) The principle of independence of protection, by which the Berne system turns into a flexible structure, asserting the fact that a work lacking legal protection in its country of origin does not prevent it from being protected in the countries which adhere to the Convention, provided that it has been published in one of them.

"Art. 3.

1) The protection of this Convention shall apply to:

a) authors who are nationals of one of the countries of the Union, for their works, whether published or not;

b) authors who are not nationals of one of the countries of the Union, for their works first published in one of those countries, or simultaneously in a country outside the Union and in a country of the Union."[85]

"Art. 5.

2) [...] such enjoyment and such exercise shall be independent of the existence of protection in the country of origin of the work. Consequently, apart from the provisions of this Convention, the extent of protection, as well as the means of redress afforded to the author to protect his rights, shall be governed exclusively by the laws of the country where protection is claimed."[86]

c) The principle of automatic protection,[87] by which the protection of authors and their works would not be subject to any formality, excluding *de jure* the need to register the works in an office created for this purpose – or any similar process – for the existence of adequate legal safeguards for the protection of a work.

---

[84] Cfr. OMPI, Convenio de Berna para la Protección de las Obras Literarias y Artísticas http://www.wipo.org/spa/iplex/wo-ber01.htm (Geneva 1999).

[85] *Id.*

[86] *Id.*

[87] The third principle of protection was not established, as was the case with the other two, in the original text of the Berne Convention of 1886, but in the Berlin revision of 1908. Cfr. LIPSZYC, *op. cit.*, 633.

"Art. 5.

2) The enjoyment and the exercise of these rights shall not be subject to any formality."[88]

The validity of these principles, unquestioned for more than a century, has been called into question as a result of the appearance of multimedia works and digital technology, just as it happens, for example, with the worldwide simultaneous communication of the contents available on the Internet.

Initially there is no objection to the validity of these three principles concerning multimedia works which are disseminated on tangible discrete media – that is, on diskettes, CD-ROMs or CD-Is – since they are applied just as it is done with books, disks or videotapes, just to mention a few works of a more conventional nature. However, with the emergence of digital technology, the process of creation does not result in the expression of a work through a physical medium, but rather intangibility is a new mode of expression.

i) On the application of the principles of national treatment and automatic protection for works disseminated on-line there is no problem questioning its validity, since, precisely, both ideas favor the reciprocity of the protection between countries and the fast application of the current legislation.

In this sense, any work introduced in the Net from a country belonging to the Berne Union will enjoy in the rest of the countries of the Union, where it is possible to access the same, an identical protection to the one guaranteed to the national authors for their works disseminated over the Internet.

ii) However, there are major problems when it comes to interpret the principle of independence of protection.[89]

Due to the features of the Net itself, any work introduced in the World Wide Web (WWW) is available everywhere in the world, provided the necessary technological conditions to access them, in such a way that its dissemination is made simultaneously in the countries adhered to the Berne Convention and in those countries that have not subscribed this agreement.

---

[88] Cfr. OMPI ed., Convenio de Berna para la Protección de las Obras Literarias y Artísticas.

[89] *Vid.* KEREVER, "Propiedad intelectual. Determinación de la ley aplicable a las transmisiones digitalizadas", *Boletín de Derecho de Autor*, no. 2, UNESCO (Paris 1996) 11 et seq.

In this way, and according to the principle mentioned, the works of authors from countries outside the Berne Union will enjoy protection within the Union, regardless of whether they wanted or not to seek said protection. Should, then, the principle of independence of protection remain unchanged?

Such as it is defined in the WIPO Glossary, a published work is "any work made available to the public"[90] regardless of its mode of dissemination, thus confirming the applicability of the protection granted by the principle of independence of protection of the works disseminated over the Internet.

Nevertheless, and taking into account the particular features of this technical system, that allows simultaneous global dissemination, would not it be more natural to consider the application of this principle to the Internet not according to the publication of the work, but to the access on the part of public to it? Would not it be fulfilled thus, in a more precise way, in what countries it should be understood that the work is published and, consequently, in what countries the principle of independence of protection should be applied?

Although the author of a Web page knows beforehand the global reach of the Net – which would also mean his desire for a worldwide dissemination of his work – not all the pages available through this system have this worldwide vocation, therefore to grant these works a simultaneous protection in all the countries of the Berne Union would exceed the intention of contents exclusively aimed at Internet surfers in smaller geographical areas.[91]

3.2. Protection of Copyright Owners and Related or Neighboring Rights

As regards the application of the copyright structure to multimedia works, we have now to define who are entitled to this right, who will not strictly be the original authors or creators, but would collaborate to carry out the creative task.

On the other hand, and as a precaution, it is advisable to remember that ownership rights and authorship of the work are different terms, since, through an assignment agreement, any person can be the owner of a given work without having participated at all in its creation.

---

[90]   Cfr. WIPO ed., WIPO glossary of terms of the law of copyright and neighboring rights, 205-206.

[91]   In the preparatory sessions of the protocol to the Berne Convention of 1996, it was proposed the establishment of a new right of public performance whose content would cover both the direct presentation of the works, and their display on a screen – which would allow its application to the Internet.

3.2.1. The Multimedia Author

The Paris Revision of the Berne Convention of 1971 defines an author as the person whose name appears on the work in the usual fashion for each type of work.

It is, obviously, an incomplete definition with no clues on its possible interpretation, which only repeats the term "author" without offering external reference points to its understanding. But, according to STEWART, the different legal traditions that existed regarding copyright made it difficult in the past to define more exactly the contents of this concept, by bringing the right of author face to face with the right of reproduction, or copyright, as explained in Chapter II.[92]

However, despite this fact, the author can be easily recognizable, as it is possible to identify an author even in the case of multimedia works.

For this, we need to establish:

a) A first distinction between multimedia creations using preexisting works and multimedia creations whose elements are new.

b) A second distinction between the author and the prospective assignees of his rights – although this paragraph is not important within international treaties, since there is no rule offering a legal framework for said assignees.

Once it is verified that a given work complies with the compulsory requirement of originality – this understood, according to LIPSZYC, as the expression "of what is peculiar to an author [...], a mark of his personality"[93] – which turns it into a work worthy of protection, there are no major obstacles to attribute to it its own author, regardless of the fact that he may have used or not preexisting works owned by third parties.

However, and apart from the fact that the author being a natural or legal person, the complexity of the process of the multimedia creation usually involves several persons in the creative process. Therefore, and considering the multimedia work as a general category, we must distinguish between:

a) The original developer of the idea.

---

[92] Cfr. STEWART, *op. cit.*, 113.

[93] Cfr. LIPSZYC, *op. cit.*, 65 and cfr. COLOMBET, *Grandes principios del derecho de autor y los derechos conexos en el mundo. Estudio de derecho comparado*, 3ª ed., UNESCO/CINDOC (Madrid 1997) 14-16.

b) The producer, the person investing the money required to implement the idea.[94]

c) The creator of the content, a figure which could be or not the author of a preexisting work to be included into the multimedia production, in which case it shall have to comply with the following aspects:

 – The formalization of a contract by which the owner of the copyright on the preexisting work undertakes to assign his work to a third party for its use in a multimedia product – provided that the work has not been exclusively assigned before to another person.

 – The payment of royalties, as dividends for the exploitation and use of such work.

 – The verification that such preexisting work is not in the public domain, in which case it would not be necessary a contract to use it or the payment of royalties.

d) The engineer in charge of assembling the elements and contents of the multimedia production.

e) The general organizer of the process, who can be the producer himself or any other person.

The legal relationship between these five figures shall be defined by private contracts, which could be under the provisions of the employment legislation and whose content will be decided by the parties in compliance with national legislations. The relationship established, and the contents included in the work, will determine the final qualification of the creation of a work: as collective, in collaboration, autonomous or derivative work, and the author category.

The Berne Convention, which establishes the works protected in the Public International Law, defines an author as:

i) Authors of books, pamphlets, lectures, addresses, sermons, dramatic or dramatico-musical works.

ii) Authors of musical compositions with or without words.

iii) Authors of cinematographic works, or assimilated works made by a process analogous to cinematography, that is, audiovisual works in general, when

---

[94] About the authorship of creations produced by computers, *vid.* DREIER, "Authorship and new technologies from the viewpoint of civil law traditions", *IIC: International Review of Industrial Property and Copyright Law*, vol. XXVI, VCH (Germany 1995).

their maker has his or her headquarters or habitual residence in a country of the Union.

iv) Authors of photographic works.

v) Authors of maps, illustrations, sketches and three-dimensional works relative to geography, topography, architecture or science, which may appear in the multimedia production. [95]

On the other hand, the protection granted by this Convention shall only apply to:

"Art. 3.

1) [...]

a) authors who are nationals of one of the countries of the Union, for their works, whether published or not;

b) authors who are not nationals of one of the countries of the Union, for their works first published in one of those countries, or simultaneously in a country outside the Union and in a country of the Union.

2. Authors who are not nationals of one of the countries of the Union, but who have their habitual residence in one of them shall, for the purposes of this Convention, be assimilated to nationals of that country."[96]

Thus, the fact that supranational texts do not mention the multimedia author – in his or her different possible figures – does not mean that he or she is not protected, since as the works are artistic, scientific or literary, their creators will be assimilated to those described in the above paragraphs. Therefore, the enumeration of the Berne Convention is a *numerus apertus* and not a limitation of the creative personalities to be protected under the provisions of international treaties.

On the other hand, this idea was also included in the GATT Agreement of 1994, and in the Protocol to the Berne Convention of 1996 in the analysis for the protection of the authors of computer programs and databases: without making a specific reference to the authors of these works, it is understood that their copyrights are protected since their creations have been included in said texts.

---

[95] Cfr. OMPI ed., Convenio de Berna para la Protección de las Obras Literarias y Artísticas.

[96] *Id.*

3.2.2. Individuals Related to the Author: Internet Providers and Integrated Services Digital Network Providers (ISDN)

But, as already said, there are several natural or legal persons, involved in the creation of conventional and multimedia works, who could be considered right holders yet not authors. That is why they are called holders of related or neighboring rights.

These rights were recognized for the first time in the Rome Convention of 1961. This was due on the one hand to the proliferation of expression and communication means and the resulting increase of people involved in the process of creation, publication or distribution of artistic works; and on the other to the claim that these experts for the recognition of their contribution as essential for the final result of the work.[97]

Since then, the holders of related or neighboring rights were:

a) The performers, who were granted total control on the broadcasting and communication to the public of their live performances; on their fixation or recording in a tangible medium; on the reproduction and/or replay of such fixations, if they were originally made without their consent, or with some different purpose to the initially stated and for which they had given their previous consent.

b) The producers of phonograms, who were granted the right to authorize or prohibit the direct or indirect reproduction of their phonograms.

c) Broadcasting organizations, who were granted the right to authorize or prohibit the rebroadcasting of their transmissions; the fixation of them in a tangible supporting medium; as well as their reproduction and communication when done in premises before a ticket-paying public.[98]

This determination of ownership and rights would be completed with the recognition of the rights of the satellite broadcasting organizations and the right of distribution in the Brussels Convention of 1974, and, finally, in the GATT Agreement of 1994, and in the Performance of Phonograms Treaty of 1996.[99]

---

[97] Cfr. NORDEMANN, VINCK, HERTIN and MEYER, *op. cit.*, 338-339 and LIPSZYC, *op. cit.*, 811-812.

[98] Cfr. NORDEMANN, VINCK, HERTIN and MEYER, *op. cit.*, 353-408, cfr. LIPSZYC, *op. cit.*, 853 and NORDEMANN, VINCK, HERTIN and MEYER, *op. cit.*, 438-441.

[99] The rights of performers broaden with the recognition of their moral rights and the inclusion of the right of rental and making available to the public of a work; the rights of the producers

That is why these three figures – apart from the figures specifically recognized by the national legislations – are the possible holders of related or neighboring rights in multimedia works. For this, a creation of this type must include:

i) A musical work, with or without lyrics, sang or instrumental; live or recorded, or obtained from the public transmission made by a broadcasting organization.

ii) Images, with or without sound, obtained from a broadcasting organization transmission; live, or prerecorded.

But in the digital communication field it should also be included, among the holders of related and neighboring rights, the figure of the Internet technical and content provider. This is a coherent proposal since, as in broadcasting organizations, some Internet providers create contents and store them for their distribution.

For this purpose the assimilation to broadcasting organizations or conventional cable companies does not seem possible, since the nature of their signal – digital and interactive – has different features. Consequently, Internet and ISDN providers could only claim the recognition of these rights if they had been the creators of the contents, since the mere technical service of dissemination through networks is not comparable with any creative work.

Nevertheless, today there is no provision for this in the international treaties; therefore, the protection of the rights of these organizations only seem possible by assimilating them to broadcasting organizations, in spite of the differences existing between them.[100]

3.3. Protection of the Subject Matter of Copyright

3.3.1. Novelty and Fixation in a Tangible Medium, Two Requirements Applied to On-line Creations

According to the doctrine of copyright the novelty of the creation and its recording or "fixation" in a tangible medium are the two essential conditions for a work to

---

of phonograms, only with the rights of rental and making available to the public; and the rights of broadcasting organizations, with the rights of fixation, reproduction and communication to the public.

[100] *Vid.* OMAN, "El imperativo de la responsabilidad compartida en Internet", *Boletín de Derecho de Autor*, no. 2, UNESCO (Paris 1998) 28-37.

enjoy the protection offered by this right, since these features allow to distinguish one work from another, emphasizing the defining features of each.

a) The value of the novelty lies in the fact that it gives the work a different and new nature regarding other productions more or less similar, in other words, a given work has its own personality.

> "As regards copyright, the novelty lies in the creative and individualized expression – or representative form – of the work, whatever is the minimum of this creation and individuality. There is no protected work if this minimum does not exist [...]: which expresses the author particularities, his own mark of personality."[101]

b) The fixation in a material medium demands that the creation has to be something more than a simple thought of the author fixed in a tangible medium. Thus the initial idea and its final result are related, but are different concepts:

> "From the very beginning, it was generally accepted that copyright only protected formal creations and not the ideas contained in the work. Ideas are not works and, therefore, their use is free. It is not possible to protect or have an intellectual property in an idea even if it is original.
>
> Copyright is intended to protect and regulate the use of the representative form, the embodiment of its development in specific works suitable for their reproduction, representation, performance, exhibition, broadcasting, etc., according to the specific category they belong to.
>
> Only the tangible form in which the idea is communicated is protected and not the idea itself, whether it is expressed in simple terms or in a work. Copyright protects the formal expression of the development of the thought, granting the creator economic exclusive rights and copyrights in the publication, diffusion and reproduction of the work."[102]

The Berne Convention also points this out by stating: "It shall, however, be a matter for legislation in the countries of the Union to prescribe that works in general or any specified categories of works shall not be protected unless they have been fixed in some material form."[103]

---

[101] Cfr. LIPSZYC, *op. cit.*, 66 and cfr. COLOMBET, *op. cit.*, 12-15.

[102] Cfr. LIPSZYC, *op. cit.*, 62, WIPO ed., *Introduction to Intellectual Property. Theory and practice*, 6 and COLOMBET, *op. cit.*, 9-10.

[103] Cfr. OMPI ed., Convenio de Berna para la Protección de las Obras Literarias y Artísticas.

As regards multimedia works, it seems clear that the fulfillment of the novelty requirement does not present greater difficulties than those faced also by creations that are more conventional. Furthermore, the possibility of including preexisting works or elements in a multimedia production does not prevent the shaping of original creations, like the public existence of some given data does not limit the novelty and specific contribution which can take place when it comes to their collection and arrangement in a database.[104]

However, complying with the requirement of fixation on a material medium is not so simple when applied to certain creations: while the utilization of CD-ROMs, CD-Is or diskettes conveys the idea of a conventional fixation of the work they contain, what happens with works which are not expressed by means of a tangible material? Could it be possible to understand the incorporation into and the diffusion of a work in the Net as its fixation in a physical medium? And its file in a content provider or in the hardware of any computer?

The basic operation of digital technology, which requires the conversion into bytes of any work to be spread, always seems to involve the immaterial nature of the content transmitted, and thus the fulfillment of said requirement would be questioned. However, although the multimedia work cannot be directly perceived through the senses that does not mean that it is more complex than sound and television broadcasting, or the distribution of audiovisual signals by cable, which also share that immaterial feature.

In contrast, and though it has to be recognized that the tangibility of on-line creations is apparently low, it should be borne in mind that both digital and analog distribution require:

a) The initial fixation, before its communication, of the content embodied in any type of medium – computer, CD or the like – from which it could be incorporated into the Net.

b) Its later fixation, for its reception by the human senses, in any type of medium, from which the work can be perceived.

For that reason, and given that double storage requirement, it is only possible to speak of the immaterial nature of these creations just as being part of their communication process and not as an unalterable feature of this type of works.

---

[104] "Under copyright, the term *creation* does not have the usual meaning of producing something out from nothing and the novelty of the work does not have to be absolute." Cfr. STEWART, *op. cit.*, 66.

3.3.2. The multimedia work as a general category

But, apart from the exceptions of computer programs and databases already seen, multimedia works have not been considered a specific copyright category by supranational texts regulating it, maybe – among other things – due to the lack of a statute for these creations.

This does not prevent multimedia work from being afforded a general protection under the international copyright system. Such protection is provided by the application of the Berne Convention of 1971 to literary, scientific or artistic works:

"Art. 2. Berne Convention.

1) The expression "literary and artistic works" shall include every production in the literary, scientific and artistic domain, whatever may be the mode or form of its expression, such as books, pamphlets and other writings; lectures, addresses, sermons and other works of the same nature; dramatic or dramatico-musical works; choreographic works and entertainments in dumb show; musical compositions with or without words; cinematographic works to which are assimilated works expressed by a process analogous to cinematography; works of drawing, painting, architecture, sculpture, engraving and lithography; photographic works to which are assimilated works expressed by a process analogous to photography; works of applied art; illustrations, maps, plans, sketches and three-dimensional works relative to geography, topography, architecture or science."[105]

On the other hand, the Convention of 1967 which created WIPO, uses similar terms:

"Art. 2. Convention establishing WIPO.

8) 'Intellectual property' shall include the rights relating to: literary, artistic and scientific works; performances of performing artists, phonograms, and broadcasts; inventions in all fields of human endeavor; scientific discoveries; industrial designs; trademarks, service marks, and commercial names and designations; protection against unfair competition, and all other rights resulting from intellectual activity in the industrial, scientific, literary or artistic fields."[106]

---

[105] Cfr. OMPI ed., Convenio de Berna para la Protección de las Obras Literarias y Artísticas.

[106] Cfr. OMPI ed., Convenio que establece la Organización Mundial de la Propiedad Intelectual, http://www.wipo.org/spa/iplex/wo-wip01.htm (Geneva 1999).

While this way of protection, through the incorporation into a more general category, is far from being the most suitable effective protection for the rights of their authors, multimedia creations are comparable to other works that, although not mentioned in the treaties, should not remain unprotected.

Obviously, the legal texts, and in particular the treaties mentioned, cannot cover all the alternatives resulting from the artistic, literary or scientific creative reality; that is why, generalizations are used to protect all existing and future creations at the time of their signing. This is the reason why it is asserted that these compendiums have a *numerus apertus* nature[107] making unnecessary – although advisable – the constant updating of the works protected by them.

From all this we can deduce that the protection of multimedia works fixed in computer programs and databases also covers:

a) The protection of Web pages according to the general criteria applied to literary, artistic or scientific works, and regardless of the purpose and specific features of each page.[108]

b) The protection of CD-ROMs and CD-Is, with multimedia contents, according to the same criteria.

3.3.3. Incorporation of Pre-existing Elements

Many multimedia creations, specifically protected or not, include preexisting elements or works, requiring contractual negotiations for their use and exploitation to be part of a new work.

The negotiation will have to be carried out between the author of the new creation and the author of the preexisting element, or between the respective right holders – should the original creators have assigned part or all of their rights of exploitation and the copyrights existing on the work are still in effect because its protection period is unexpired.

For this purpose it will be necessary to negotiate the inclusion of the following works because they are protected by the Berne Convention and its Protocol of 1996:

a) Texts, of any nature, considered literary, scientific and artistic works.[109]

---

[107] Cfr. STEWART, *op. cit.*, 69.

[108] *Vid.* EVANS, "Whose web site is it anyway?", *Internet World*, September issue, Mecklermedia (Westport 1997) 46 and subsequent pages.

[109] Cfr. OMPI ed., Convenio de Berna para la Protección de las Obras Literarias y Artísticas.

b) Graphics considered literary, scientific and artistic works.[110]

c) Sounds considered musical compositions with or without words.[111]

d) Images – still or motion pictures – whether they be photographs, audiovisual or cinematographic works.[112]

e) Databases, according to the selection and arrangement of their content.[113]

f) Computer programs, according to their assimilation to literary works.[114]

g) Other multimedia works.

h) Any combination of the above being a literary, artistic or scientific work.

Even so, not all the inclusions of preexisting works require the authority or consent of its original author or right holder. International treaties mention a number of works that do not require authority for their exploitation by third parties:

"Art. 10.

1) It shall be permissible to make quotations from a work which has already been lawfully made available to the public, provided that their making is compatible with fair practice, and their extent does not exceed that justified by the purpose, including quotations from newspaper articles and periodicals in the form of press summaries."[115]

Specifically, the Berne Convention provides for:

a) Quotations of literary works, provided that their source and the name of the author are mentioned.

b) The reproduction of part of artistic or literary works for the purpose of teaching, or research, also mentioning their source and the name of the author.

"Art. 10.

2) It shall be a matter for legislation in the countries of the Union, and for special agreements existing or to be concluded between them, to

---

[110] *Id.*

[111] *Id.*

[112] *Id.*

[113] Cfr. OMPI ed., Tratado de la OMPI sobre Derecho de Autor, 4 .

[114] *Id.*

[115] *Id.*

permit the utilization, to the extent justified by the purpose, of literary or artistic works by way of illustration in publications, broadcasts or sound or visual recordings for teaching, provided such utilization is compatible with fair practice."[116]

c) The reproduction of articles on current topics whose rights are not expressly reserved, although the source and name of the author must always be clearly indicated.

"Art. 10 bis.

1) It shall be a matter for legislation in the countries of the Union to permit the reproduction by the press, the broadcasting or the communication to the public by wire of articles published in newspapers or periodicals on current economic, political or religious topics, and of broadcast works of the same character, in cases in which the reproduction, broadcasting or such communication thereof is not expressly reserved. Nevertheless, the source must always be clearly indicated; the legal consequences of a breach of this obligation shall be determined by the legislation of the country where protection is claimed."[117]

This restriction is based on the lack of novelty assumed in the work of reporters, since the articles on current topics are written using a specific language and style, which does not have personal creativity features. However, it shall be a matter for legislation in the countries to permit the reproduction by the press, the broadcasting or the communication to the public of articles or news broadcast by radio or television, provided that:

i) National legislation expressly authorizes it.

ii) They are articles on current topics.

iii) They refer to economic, political or religious topics.

iv) They have been previously published or broadcast.

v) Their utilization has not been expressly prohibited by its owner.

---

[116] *Id.*

[117] Cfr. LIPSZYC, *op. cit.*, 694, cfr. NORDEMANN, VINCK, HERTIN and MEYER, *op. cit.*, 623 and FEDERACIÓN INTERNACIONAL DE PERIODISTAS, *Derecho de autor. Un manual para periodistas*, FIP (Brussels 1988) 8.

Also *vid.* JACKOBSEN, "El derecho de autor en los medios de comunicación", *Boletín de derecho de autor*, vol. XXXIII, no. 1, UNESCO (Paris 1999) 3-19.

d) The reproduction of literary and artistic works required to report current events.

> "Art. 10.
>
> 2) It shall also be a matter for legislation in the countries of the Union to determine the conditions under which, for the purpose of reporting current events by means of photography, cinematography, broadcasting or communication to the public by wire, literary or artistic works seen or heard in the course of the event may, to the extent justified by the informatory purpose, be reproduced and made available to the public."[118]

e) The reproduction of any element when included into a work created by the author for its private use.

Obviously, and as already said, in addition to these five options it should be considered the use of works existing in the public domain, and therefore of free access, although such situation could be determined by the terms of protection established in each national legislation.

3.3.4. Links in Web pages and Protection of Domain Names

Apart from the controversy arising from the protection of works on the Internet, Web pages cast some doubts on the legal system required to protect domain names – that is, the address of a page in the Net – and on the lawful nature of the inclusion of links – also called *hyperlinks* – to other pages without the consent of their author or assignee:

a) The question of the protection of domain names must be dealt with according to the legal framework established by the Domain Names System (DNS), which organizes the diffusion over the Net giving each page a domain name (for example, www.ompi.org) and an Internet Protocol number (IP) – both assigned by the Internet Corporation for Assigned Names and Numbers (ICANN) – so that users can identify and access a given page.

While most of the domain names were registered, at the beginning of the Net, in good faith, the growth of the commercial communication and electronic commerce prompted, eventually, the continuous confrontation between the legal owners of domain names and those pretending to use them – infringing the rights of the

---

[118] Cfr. OMPI ed., Convenio de Berna para la Protección de las Obras Literarias y Artísticas.

former – in order to benefit from the popularity of the name of a given company or organization.

Contrary to expectation, this legal conflict would not be settled by a copyright approach – since an Internet address is not a type of creation to be used – but by the jurisprudence and regulation of international law relating to trademarks – since this is the right allowing to register an Internet address as a creation and property of a specific natural or legal person.

In this regard, WIPO, in its Report relating to Internet Domain Names,[119] has defined three conditions which can give rise to abusive name registration: to be identical or misleadingly similar to a third party trademark; that its owner does not have legitimate rights or interests in that domain name; or that it has been previously registered and is being used in bad faith.

b) On the other hand, the fact that certain Web pages provide the user with links to other pages available in the Net, gives rise to the problem whether it is necessary to have the authority of their authors or right holders to do so.

According to the above paragraphs, and since this is a connection between domain names and IPs, copyright would be *a priori* out of the question. However, it is true that a link between Web addresses establishes a relationship between the contents of different owners, likewise the author of a scientific paper establishes, by means of quotations and footnotes, links to the ideas and works of other researchers.

Therefore, in this case resorting to the right of quotation seems logical, since jurisprudence considers it a legitimate use of the work of an author, for which his express consent is not required:

"Art. 10. Berne Convention.

1) It shall be permissible to make quotations from a work which has already been lawfully made available to the public, provided that their making is compatible with fair practice, and their extent does not exceed that justified by the purpose, including quotations from newspaper articles and periodicals in the form of press summaries."

---

[119] Cfr. OMPI ed., Informes 1 y 2 relativos a los Nombres de Dominio, http://ecommerce.wipo.int/domains/process/esp/wipo1.html (Geneva 1999) and http://wipo2.wipo.int/domains/process2/esp/wipo2.html (Geneva 2002).

3.4. Protection of the Content of Copyright

The origin of copyright – as set out in Chapter II – gave rise to three different approaches based on the main aspects of this right: the economic features, from the economic view of copyright; the moral features, in the German personal approach; and both types of features, in the personal-economic view.

Today, this third option seems to prevail on the copyright regulatory texts, as it can be seen in the national legislations and supranational treaties.

3.4.1. The Moral Rights of the Multimedia Author

The moral rights of the authors were first recognized in the Rome Revision of the Berne Convention of 1928. Although at that time some national legislations – for example, from Bulgaria, Switzerland, Romania, Italy, Poland, Czechoslovakia and Finland – already included these rights, there was a need to establish some international rules in this regard to guarantee authors an appropriate protection of an important part of the content of their rights. This was intended to prevent some nations to resort to other rules, such as the laws relating to unfair competition or libel, in order to produce similar effects.[120]

The development of these rights, and their incorporation to the treaties and legislations on the subject, offer a current configuration summarized in 1980 by the WIPO Glossary:

> "These rights include the right to decide the publication of the work; the right to claim the authorship of the work (to have the name of the author and the name of the work mentioned in connection to the use of the work); the right to prohibit the mentioning of the name of the author if he wishes to remain anonymous; the right to choose a pseudonym in connection with the use of the work; the right to object to any unauthorized alteration or mutilation of said work and to any other derogatory action in relation to said work; the right to withdraw the work from the public use and compensating any damages caused to the persons previously authorized to use the work.
>
> Most copyright laws recognize moral rights as an inalienable part of copyright, different from 'economic rights'. Some legislations even grant moral rights to performers when there is a distortion of their performances

---

[120]   Cfr. LIPSZYC, *op. cit.*, 641 and STEWART, *op. cit.*, 120.

and guarantee them the right to claim the mentioning of their name in connection with their performances".[121]

Since these are inalienable and untransferable rights that cannot be waived,[122] the moral rights of the multimedia author are not different from those enjoyed by other authors of more conventional works, since their content cannot be arbitrarily recognized according to the person to whom they belong.

In this particular case, the interactive capability of some multimedia works – especially those which the public can access on-line – and the technical skill of some copyright offenders, facilitates even more the alteration, distortion, destruction or removal of their content, actions which obviously threaten the essence of the moral principles of this right.

Therefore, based on the Berne Convention, the multimedia author is basically entitled to two moral rights: the right to claim authorship of his work and the right to object to its alteration:

"Art. 6 bis.

Independently of the author economic rights, and even after the transfer of said rights, the author shall have the right to claim authorship of the work and to object to any distortion, mutilation or other modification of, or other derogatory action in relation to, the said work, which would be prejudicial to his honor or reputation."[123]

---

[121] Cfr. WIPO ed., WIPO Glossary of Terms of the Law of Copyright and Neighboring Rights, 96 and 161.

For other opinions, COLOMBET, *op. cit.*, 39-95, LIPSZYC, *op. cit.*, 45-53 and STEWART, *op. cit.*, 59-75.

[122] As a legal right included in the Universal Declaration of Human Rights of 1948, copyright has the inherent features of this legal category.

"Art. 27. Universal Declaration of Human Rights of 1948.

2) Every person has the right to the protection of the moral and material interests resulting from any scientific, literary or artistic production of which he is the author."

Cfr. DURÁN LALAGUNA coord., *Manual de Derechos Humanos* (Granada 1993) 81-92, 94, 109 and 225; and VERDOOT, *Declaración Universal de los Derechos del Hombre. Nacimiento y significación*, Biblioteca Mensajero (Bilbao 1969) 246-251.

[123] Cfr. OMPI ed., Convenio de Berna para la Protección de las Obras Literarias y Artísticas.

By virtue of the Protocol to the Berne Convention of 1996, these two rights have also been granted to the holders of related and neighboring rights which, paradoxically until then, only enjoyed the protection of their economic rights. Nevertheless, the protection is only granted to natural persons – that is, to performers – and not to legal persons – that is, broadcasting organizations.

"Art. 5.

1) Independently of a performer's economic rights, and even after the transfer of those rights, the performer shall, as regards his live aural performances or performances fixed in phonograms, have the right to claim to be identified as the performer of his performances, except where omission is dictated by the manner of the use of the performance, and to object to any distortion, mutilation or other modification of his performances that would be prejudicial to his reputation."[124]

This settled the legal loophole existing since the Rome Convention of 1961, which recognized the economic aspect of related or neighboring rights, leaving aside their more personal aspects.

3.4.2. Economic Rights of the Multimedia Author

The so-called economic rights, developed in parallel with the economic view of copyright, include the right to undertake and authorize or prohibit the following acts: the reproduction of the work; its translation, its public performance and recitation; broadcasting, public communication and distribution; adaptation; and rental.

Their protection as author's rights is expressed as follows:

a) The right of reproduction is the right of authorizing or prohibiting the reproduction of copies of a work, or its mere reproduction by any means.

"The right to exploit the work in its original or transformed form, by its material fixation in any medium, and by any process allowing its communication and the obtaining of one or several copies of all or part of it."[125]

---

[124] Cfr. OMPI ed., *Tratado de la OMPI sobre Interpretación o Ejecución y Fonogramas*, 6.

[125] Cfr. STEWART, *op. cit.*, 179.

This right can only be restricted by national legislations when "it does not come into conflict with a normal exploitation of the work and does not unreasonably prejudice the legitimate interests of the author."[126]

As regards its impact on the multimedia work, the right of reproduction can be affected by the features of digital technology, that allows a large quantity of copies in a short time and similar in quality to the original work.

On the other hand, and in relation to technological development, how should this right be understood when in order to enjoy a work it must be reproduced (copied)? That is, what happens when, in order to use a computer program, CD-ROM or database, it must be previously reproduced on a computer screen or stored it in its hard disk?

Logic leads us to think that the reproduction of a work, in this sense, must be authorized and considered a lawful act, which is required to use a work and, therefore, authorized by the author or right holder through the same distribution of his creations.

b) The right of translation is the expression of written or oral works in other language than the one used in the original version. According to WIPO, the translation "must reproduce accurately and truthfully both its content and style."[127]

The right of translation can be granted to translators in recognition of their capability "to create by means of another language,"[128] without prejudice to the rights of the author of the translated work. Thus, a translation shall always require due authorization, since the right to translate a work is another right of its original creator.

Therefore, a multimedia author may also authorize or prohibit this practice regarding computer programs, databases and other multimedia productions, if these are translated for their distribution or communication outside the country of origin.

c) The right of public performance by which a creation is presented before a quantitatively and qualitatively undetermined public – home representations excluded – and which is owned by the holder of the copyright of the work.[129]

---

[126] *Id.*, 222-227 and 695; and cfr. STEWART, *op. cit.*, 122.

[127] Cfr. WIPO ed., WIPO glossary of terms of the law of copyright and neighboring rights, 259.

[128] *Id.*

[129] *Id.*, 209.

On the other hand, the right of recitation is linked to this right, defined by WIPO in the following terms:

"The oral presentation of a literary right in front of an audience, and by means of any technical device, such as a microphone, phonogram, broadcasting, etc."[130]

Both rights make sense in the multimedia field through the ephemeral or permanent incorporation of this type of performances or recitations into digital creations. Such performances or recitations could have taken place in the past, or can be included as they happen, like in live concerts, performances or similar events over the Internet.

d) The right of broadcasting is the right to authorize or prohibit the broadcasting or rebroadcasting, by wire or wireless means; among which satellite broadcasting is included.[131]

This right includes, therefore, the digital broadcasting by radio, as well as the digital broadcasting by satellite, covering works transmitted through such technical channels.

e) The right of communication to the public implies a general transmission, not restricted to "specific individuals that are members of private groups,"[132] and it is a broad concept including, among other features, the already mentioned "make available to the public."

f) The right of distribution, which allows "the making available of the copy of a work to the general public or to part of it," by using sales commercial channels.

However, under the Brussels Convention Relating to the Distribution of Program-Carrying Signals Transmitted by Satellite of 1974, the acts of distribution shall have two meanings:

i) Distribution is the operation by which a cable provider transmits derived signals to the general public from a satellite or any other broadcasting mean.

---

[130] *Id.*, 217.

[131] *Id.*, 27 and LIPSZYC, *op. cit.*, 187-188.

[132] *Id.*, 42.

ii) Distribution will also mean the making available to the public of copies of a work for its sale or transfer of ownership, according to the Protocol to the Berne Convention of 1996.

The acts of sale and marketing of multimedia products are, therefore, legally protected regardless of their format – off-line or on-line – and of the distribution channel used – conventional sale or electronic commerce.

g) The right of adaptation, arrangement and alteration of the work, is defined as:

"The modification of a preexisting work from one category to another, such as the screen adaptations of novels or musical works."[133]

This concept includes the alteration of the work, keeping it in the same original category, for its exploitation by other means, like rewriting a novel for young people.[134]

Precisely, since it is an economic right, the wrong exercise of this right could cause the infringement of the moral rights of the author, for example, if the original meaning of the work is violated or if its content is distorted.

On the other hand, the right of adaptation or transformation has been claimed in connection with the creation of higher versions of a given software program, as well as with the constant transformation undergone by Web pages.

The fact is that the evolution of the content of this right has turned it, according to LIPSZYC, into "the right of the author to exploit his work by authorizing the creation of derivative works of it," including revisions, updates, abridgements, condensations or musical arrangements, among others.[135]

h) The right of rental, considered by some legal systems to be a part of the general right of distribution,[136] is the transfer to the public, for a certain time, of the copy of a work for a consideration.

---

[133] *Id.*, 3.

[134] *Id.*

[135] Cfr. LIPSZYC, *op. cit.*, 211-212.

[136] Cfr. WIPO ed., Basic Proposal for the Substantive Provisions of the Treaty on Certain Questions Concerning the Protection of Literary and Artistic Works, 34-41.

First included in the GATT Agreement of 1994, and then reaffirmed in the Protocol to the Berne Convention of 1996, it covers cinematographic works, works fixed in phonograms and computer programs:

"Art. 11.

In respect of at least computer programs and cinematographic works, a Member shall provide authors and their successors in title the right to authorize or to prohibit the commercial rental to the public of originals or copies of their copyrighted works. [...] In respect of computer programs, this obligation does not apply to rentals where the program itself is not the essential object of the rental."[137]

"Art. 7.

(1) Authors of:

(i) computer programs, (...) shall enjoy the exclusive right of authorizing commercial rental to the public of the originals or copies of their works.

(2) Paragraph 1) shall not apply:

(i) in the case of computer programs, where the program itself is not the essential object of the rental; [...]".[138]

3.4.3. Moral and Economic Rights of Related or Neighboring Rights Holders

As related or neighboring rights holders, performers, as well as producers of phonograms and broadcasting organizations, have been granted moral and economic rights progressively.

The first recognition took place in the Rome Convention of 1961, followed by the Geneva Convention of 1971, the GATT Agreement of 1994, and the Protocol to the Berne Convention of 1996.

This Protocol recognized comprehensively both types of rights in the Performance and Phonograms Treaty:

a) Performers have:

---

[137] Cfr. GATT ed, *op. cit.*, 387.

[138] *Id.*

    i) the following moral rights: to claim to be identified as the performer of his performances, except when this omission is due to the way in which the performance is used, and to object to any distortion, mutilation or other modification of his performances prejudicial to his reputation.

    ii) the following economic rights of: broadcasting, communication to the public, reproduction, fixation, distribution, rental, and making available to the public.[139]

In the digital field, the recognition of the right of making available to the public of their performances is very important, since it puts related or neighboring rights holders on a level with copyright holders, protecting the dissemination of their works via Internet or ISDN just as the author of such creations is protected:

"Art. 10.

Performers shall enjoy the exclusive right of authorizing the making available to the public of their performances fixed in phonograms, by wire or wireless means, in such a way that members of the public may access them from a place and at a time individually chosen by them."[140]

b) The producers of phonograms have:

    i) the following economic rights of: reproduction, distribution, rental and making available to the public.[141]

As above, this right is recognized in connection with the digital communication of the works they have produced:

"Art. 14.

Producers of phonograms shall enjoy the exclusive right of authorizing the making available to the public of their phonograms, by wire or wireless means, in such a way that members of the public may access them from a place and at a time individually chosen by them."[142]

---

[139] Cfr. OMPI ed., Tratado de la OMPI sobre Interpretación o Ejecución y Fonogramas, 6-8.

[140] *Id.*

[141] *Id.*, 9-10.

[142] *Id.*, 10.

Performers and producers of phonograms are granted the right of remuneration for broadcasting and communicating to the public their works, when this transmission is made by digital technology and for a consideration:

"Art. 15.

1) Performers and producers of phonograms shall enjoy the right to a single equitable remuneration for the direct or indirect use of phonograms published for commercial purposes for broadcasting or for any communication to the public.

[...]

4) For the purposes of this Article, phonograms made available to the public by wire or wireless means in such a way that members of the public may access them from a place and at a time individually chosen by them shall be considered as if they had been published for commercial purposes."[143]

Thus, in order to be lawful, the common practice of musical diffusion over the Internet, through WAV and MP3 files is conditional on the authorization of their performers and producers.[144]

c) On the other hand, broadcasting organizations, under the Rome Convention of 1961, and the GATT Agreement of 1994, have been granted:

  i) the following economic rights: to authorize or prohibit the fixation, reproduction and communication to the public of their broadcastings.

"Art. 13.

Broadcasting organizations shall enjoy the right to authorize or prohibit:

[...]

b) the fixation on a material base of their broadcasts;

c) the reproduction:

  i) of the fixations of their broadcasts made without their consent;

---

[143] *Id.*, 10.

[144] *Vid.*, DE LA HORADADA, http://www.internet.ad/mp3/intro.html (Spain 1999).

ii) of the fixations, made in accordance with the provisions of art. 15 of their broadcasts, if the reproduction is made for purposes different from those referred to in those provisions."[145]

"Art. 14.

[...]

3) Broadcasting organizations shall have the right to prohibit the following when undertaken without their authorization: the fixation, the reproduction of fixations, and the rebroadcasting by wireless means of broadcasts, as well as the communication to the public of television broadcasts of the same [...]."[146]

Even though, in this case, the right to making available to the public has not been specified, as it happens in the case of performers and producers of phonograms, the extent of the concepts of broadcasting and communication to the public make it possible to apply them to the digital dissemination by wire or wireless means.

Obviously, there is an omission in the treaties system because cable providers and Internet or ISDN content providers are not included among the organizations contributing to the communication of artistic works. But, there are two ways in which their rights could be protected: by assimilating them to broadcasting organizations and, therefore, through an extensive application of the treaties mentioned, or by specifically including them in future texts.

3.5. Other Applicable Legal Principles

3.5.1. Term of Protection

The regulation of the term of protection of copyright works was initially introduced in the Berlin Revision of the Berne Convention of 1908, which established the life of the author and fifty years after his death – although at that time the signatory countries of the text could still apply a shorter term of protection, if they wanted to.

In the Rome Revision of 1928, that same term was limited to 25 years for cinematographic works, putting them on a level with the protection granted to photographic works – since both creations were obtained by analogous processes.

---

[145] Cfr. LIPSZYC, *op. cit.*, 403-404.

[146] Cfr. PUTNAM ed., *op. cit.*, 388.

Subsequently, in the Stockholm Convention of 1967, this term would be extended, for films, up to fifty years after the death of the last person that national legislations would consider as one of the authors, putting its protection on a level with the general protection granted to literary, artistic or scientific works.

Almost thirty years later, in the Protocol to the Berne Convention, the protection granted to performers and producers of phonograms, was of 50 years from the date of the fixation of their performances; and broadcasting organizations were granted twenty years of protection after their broadcastings.

a) Since it is a singular work, composed of different expressive elements, a multimedia creation enjoys a term of protection similar to the one granted to any other type of artistic, literary or scientific creation, which is established in the life of the author and fifty years after his death, the calculation of the term shall begin on the first of January of the year following the death of the author, although the protection becomes effective right away.

That is what the Berne Convention and the GATT Agreement of 1994 established:

"Art. 7.

1) The term of protection granted by this Convention shall be the life of the author and fifty years after his death.

[...]

5) The term of protection subsequent to the death of the author and the terms provided by paragraphs (2), (3) and (4) shall run from the date of death or of the event referred to in those paragraphs, but such terms shall always be deemed to begin on the first of January of the year following the death or such event."[147]

"Art. 12.

Whenever the term of protection of a work, other than a photographic work or a work of applied art, is calculated on a basis other than the life of a natural person, such term shall be no less than fifty years from the end of the calendar year of authorized publication, or, failing such authorized publication within fifty years from the making of the work, fifty years from the end of the calendar year of making."[148]

---

[147] PUTNAM ed., *op. cit.*, 387.

[148] Cfr. OMPI ed., Convenio de Berna para la Protección de las Obras Literarias y Artísticas.

Exceptions to this general rule are the cases of pseudonym or anonymous works, whose terms of protection shall expire fifty years after the work has been lawfully made available to the public. However, when the pseudonym adopted by the author leaves no doubt as to his identity, or the author discloses his or her identity, the term of protection applicable shall be the general rule, which shall always be deemed to begin on the first of January of the year following the death of the author.[149]

On the other hand, in the case of a multimedia work made in collaboration, the term of protection shall be calculated from the death of the last surviving member of the team – being this rule under the provisions each national legislation applies to these types of works.[150]

b) With regard to multimedia works, one must be aware of the term of protection of software and databases, since both works have been specifically regulated:

In both cases their term of protection is the same term granted to multimedia works as a whole, since the GATT Agreement as well as the Protocol to the Berne Convention do not specify different terms to those mentioned above. However, the application of such a long term of protection seems unreasonable for creations whose useful life is considerably shorter, unless their contents are renewed or their capabilities increased – in the case of software – resulting in the creation of higher versions of the original work which would deserve new terms of protection.

As compared to such a long term, and as indicated in 2.1.2. of this chapter, patent rights offer a more reasonable and suitable solution by fixing the duration of the protection in twenty years from its filing.[151]

c) In the case of multimedia works including elements or contents previously created, there are two different and simultaneous terms of protection: the term of protection applied to the multimedia work and the term of protection of the preexisting material, from the very moment of its fixation, publication, reproduction or communication, regardless of its inclusion into a new work.

---

[149] *Id.*

[150] *Id.*

[151] Cfr. WIPO ed., *Introduction to Intellectual Property.* Theory and practice, 8.

In the case of the latter the term of copyright protection of some elements of a given multimedia production may have expired and fallen into the public domain, allowing, therefore, its free use.

As a general rule, and regarding the rights of performers and producers of phonograms, the term of protection expires fifty years after the death of the author, according to the Berne Convention of 1971; term which was ratified in the Protocol to the Berne Convention of 1996:

"Art. 17.

1) The term of protection to be granted to performers under this Treaty shall last, at least, until the end of a period of 50 years computed from the end of the year in which the performance was fixed in a phonogram.

2) The term of protection to be granted to producers of phonograms under this Treaty shall last, at least, until the end of a period of 50 years computed from the end of the year in which the phonogram was published, or failing such publication within 50 years from fixation of the phonogram, 50 years from the end of the year in which the fixation was made."[152]

Exceptions to this terms of protection are:

  i) cinematographic works, since the term of protection can be computed from the moment the work has been made available to the public.

  ii) photographic works, whose term of protection shall be a matter for legislation in the countries of the Union, however, this term shall last at least until the end of a period of twenty-five years.[153]

d) On the other hand, and as regards works in the public domain, whose use is free, its communication to the public is unlawful in countries where the term of protection has not expired, unless the right holders give their express authorization.[154]

This provision, based on the idea that works are always protected in each country through national legislations – that is, in compliance with the principle of national treatment – poses a serious problem for on-line dissemination over the Internet, since the global nature of the Net would make it necessary to know in

---

[152] Cfr. OMPI ed., Tratado de la OMPI sobre Interpretación o Ejecución y Fonogramas, 16.

[153] Cfr. OMPI ed., Convenio de Berna para la Protección de las Obras Literarias y Artísticas.

[154] Cfr. LIPSZYC, *op. cit.*, 259-260.

which countries the term of protection of a work is still in force in order to limit its diffusion in that country.

3.5.2. Fulfillment of Certain Formalities for the Protection of a Work

It is worthy of mention that none of the legal safeguards offered by copyright, as seen in previous pages, may be invoked by a multimedia author if he does not comply with the formal requirements needed to obtain an effective legal protection.

While during the 18th and 19th century some of the most important national legal systems enforced the registration of the work in an *ad hoc* register, in 1886, the Berne Convention established the automatic protection of works without any formality and as soon as the original idea was fixed in a physical medium.

"Art. 5.

2) The enjoyment and the exercise of these rights shall not be subject to any formality."[155]

Thus, this lacking in formalities became one of the most important principles of the international copyright system. However, since 1952, the criterion changed and the ideas of the Anglo-Saxon legal tradition – which required registration of the work – were adopted.

In that same year the Universal Copyright Convention was held in Geneva,[156] one of whose provisions required that any work to be protected under copyright, would have to contain the copyright symbol (©) together with the date of the first publication and the name of the holder or proprietor of the right:

"Art. 3.

1) Any Contracting State which, under its domestic law, requires as a condition of copyright, compliance with formalities such as deposit, registration, notice, notarial certificates, payment of fees or manufacture or publication in that Contracting State, shall regard these requirements as satisfied with respect to all works protected in accordance with this Convention and first published outside its territory and the author of which is not one of its nationals, if from the time of the first publication all the copies of the work published with the authority of the author or other copyright proprietor bear the symbol

---

[155] Cfr. OMPI ed., Convenio de Berna para la Protección de las Obras Literarias y Artísticas.

[156] About its origin, cfr. LIPSZYC, *op. cit.*, 744-751 and BOGSCH, *op. cit.*, 24.

© accompanied by the name of the copyright proprietor and the year of first publication placed in such manner and location as to give reasonable notice of claim of copyright."[157]

Nineteen years later, and in the framework of the Convention for the Protection of Producers against Unauthorized Reproduction of their Phonograms of 1971, was enacted a provision already included in the Rome Convention, which had taken place ten years before: to bear the ℗ symbol – for producer – in phonograms and similar works, together with the year of publication and the name of the producer, as a safeguard of the rights of producers:

"Art. 5.

If, as a condition of protecting the producers of phonograms, a Contracting State, under its domestic law, requires compliance with formalities, these shall be considered as fulfilled if all the authorized duplicates of the phonogram distributed to the public or their containers bear a notice consisting of the symbol ℗, accompanied by the year date of the first publication, placed in such manner as to give reasonable notice of claim of protection; and, if the duplicates or their containers do not identify the producer, his successor in title or the exclusive licensee (by carrying his name, trademark or other appropriate designation), the notice shall also include the name of the producer, his successor in title or the exclusive licensee."[158]

Both symbols have been increasingly included in most of the published works circulating in the world, being its presence sufficient condition to obtain legal protection in those countries whose legislation require the compliance with any formality.

3.5.3. Proposals for an Effective Legal Protection of Copyrights: Legal Proceedings and Arbitration as Ways to Solve Disputes

But the legal recognition of copyright under the Berne system, and under the rest of the international treaties, not only aim to protect the author, but also to create an

---

[157] Cfr. BOGSCH, *op. cit.*, 24.

[158] Cfr. OMPI ed., Convenio para la Protección de Productores de Fonogramas contra la Reproducción No Autorizada de sus Fonogramas, http://www.ompi.org/spa/iplex/wo-pho01.htm (Geneva 1999).

effective and real system of protection, in which any breach of the moral and economic rights of creators, and related and neighboring rights holders, is punished by the law.

Therefore, while bearing in mind the need to protect the moral rights of the author, the violation of his economic rights usually has important consequences both in his finances and in the macroeconomic figures of a country. So much so that the members of the Berne system have included in their treaties some provisions to encourage the countries to undertake "different antipiracy legal actions."[159]

Thus, the Berne Convention of 1971 both prohibited unlawful copies and provided for the seizure of such works in the countries where a work enjoyed legal protection, including the works coming from a country where the work was not protected and was introduced within some of the countries of the system:

"Art. 16.

1) Infringing copies of a work shall be liable to seizure in any country of the Union where the work enjoys legal protection.

2) The provisions of the preceding paragraph shall also apply to reproductions coming from a country where the work is not protected, or has ceased to be protected.

3) The seizure shall take place in accordance with the legislation of each country."[160]

Logically the digital and multimedia technological evolution opened up new fields for the commission of crimes against copyright, since today there is a wide range of works in the market, easily reproducible and with an appreciable improvement in their quality, as well as a wider diffusion potential. This is why copyright should prevent, in the digital field:

a) The unlawful reproduction of works contained in off-line media, particularly in CD-ROM and CD-I formats.

b) The infringement of copyright in works available on-line, materialized in:
 – Their commercial and home unlawful reproduction.

---

[159] The first research about the economic influence of copyright was conducted in the United States in 1959. Taking as a reference data of 1954, it was pointed out that the contribution of this right to the Gross Domestic Product (GDP) was around 2%. Cfr. LIPSZYC, *op. cit.*, 57-59.

[160] Cfr. OMPI ed., Convenio de Berna para la Protección de las Obras Literarias y Artísticas.

- Their diffusion through different means of communication to the public.
- The alteration of their content and information regarding the author.
- The electronic management of the corresponding intellectual property rights.

The Protocol to the Berne Convention of 1996, in its Copyright Treaty, pointed it out in the following terms:

"Art. 12.

1) Contracting Parties shall provide adequate and effective legal remedies against any person knowingly performing any of the following acts knowing, or with respect to civil remedies having reasonable grounds to know, that it will induce, enable, facilitate or conceal an infringement of any right covered by this Treaty or the Berne Convention:

  i) to remove or alter any electronic rights management information without authority;

  ii) to distribute, import for distribution, broadcast or communicate to the public, without authority, works or copies of works knowing that electronic rights management information has been removed or altered without authority.

2) As used in this Article, 'rights management information' means information which identifies the work, the author of the work, the owner of any right in the work, or information about the terms and conditions of use of the work, and any numbers or codes that represent such information, when any of these items of information is attached to a copy of a work or appears in connection with the communication of a work to the public."[161]

Today the prevention and punishment of crimes against copyright is made through two consolidated legal solutions: turning either to courts or to arbitration as a private option to solve disputes.

i) As it is well-known, an ordinary proceeding starts by filing a timely demand before a court according to the Procedural Law of the national legislation of each country.

---

[161] *Id.*

In this sense, copyright protection has been secured by means of civil law, criminal law and unfair competition law, used, respectively, to obtain damage recovery, to punish and deter offenders, and to protect the entrepreneurial competition.

For instance, the Geneva Convention for the Protection of Producers against Unauthorized Reproduction of their Phonograms of 1971, specified the last two options as methods against piracy crimes, excluding bootlegging, which today, are punished by the law today:

"Art. 3.

The means by which this Convention is implemented shall be a matter for the domestic law of each Contracting State and shall include one or more of the following: protection by means of the grant of a copyright or other specific right; protection by means of the law relating to unfair competition; protection by means of penal sanctions." [162]

Precisely, since we are dealing with unlawful acts taking place worldwide, it is worth bearing in mind that international courts are responsible for exerting an effective copyright protection.

The Berne Convention refers in its articles to the application of national laws, establishing that "the seizure shall take place in accordance with the legislation of each country"[163] and recognizes the right of each nation to exert, through the provisions they consider appropriate, the control or prohibition of the "circulation, representation" and "exhibition of any work or production."[164]

However, in case an injured party cannot find satisfactory and sufficient legal protection before the ordinary courts of his country, he will be entitled to request protection for his rights before the Human Rights European Court – provided he is a national of a country which has subscribed the European Convention for the Protection of Human Rights of 1950, and the crime has been committed in that country.

That is so since, although the European Convention of Human Rights does not explicitly include copyright as a right to be protected, the Jurisprudence of the Strasbourg Court has confirmed its inclusion in the Text with the following cases: *De Geïllustreerde Pers vs. Holland* – which never reached the Court, because it

---

[162] Cfr. NORDEMANN, VINCK, HERTIN and MEYER, *op. cit.*, 444.

[163] Cfr. OMPI ed., Convenio de Berna para la Protección de las Obras Literarias y Artísticas.

[164] *Id.*

was solved through a report of the Committee of Ministers – (1976), *Chappel vs. United Kingdom* (1989), *News Verlags vs. Austria* (2000) and *Krone Verlag vs. Austria* (2002).[165]

ii) Concerning arbitration, an alternative option to the ordinary legal process, it allows the settlement of disputes *inter partes* in less time and at a lower cost for the parties involved.[166]

Arbitration, in part unknown to the general public, bases its efficacy on the voluntary compliance of both parties with the decision taken by the arbiters of the dispute – always in odd number – which is called arbitral award.

Previously, and if desired, it is possible to attempt the settlement of the dispute through a mediation process, consisting of securing an *inter partes* agreement, not as a result of a demand, but as a peaceful solution reached freely and voluntarily by the parties, thanks to a mediator or legal advisor.

Both options, arbitration in particular, are significant in the case of intellectual property disputes, due to the huge financial damage that the infringement of a copyright can represent – which is clear, specially, in the information industry and multimedia fields -; so this is one of the reasons why the parties involved want to put an end to the dispute as soon as possible.[167]

For that reason, in 1993 WIPO created an Arbitration Center, which a year later would start to solve disputes related to this special properties category. In his introductory speech, Francis Gurry, in charge of the Center, pointed out that the reasons for its creation were the same ones that usually induce the parties involved to choose this option:

---

[165] Cfr. "Chappell Case. Judgment of 30 March 1989", *Publications of the European Court of Human Rights* (Germany 1989) 4-39, MARTINUS NIJHOFF ed., "De Geïllustreerde Pers Case", *Yearbook of the European Convention of Human Rights*, volumes 1973 and 1977, pages 124-151 and 640-642, and "News Verlags Case" and "Krone Verlag Case", in EUROPEAN COURT OF HUMAN RIGHTS, http://hudoc.echr.coe.int/hudoc (Strasbourg 2002), cases 31457/96 and 34315/96 respectively.

Instead, the International Covenant on Economic, Social and Cultural Rights of 1966, expressly recognized this right. In this regard, cfr. DURÁN LALAGUNA, *op. cit.*, 94 and 109.

[166] *Vid.* AA VV, Colloque mondial sur l'arbitrage des litiges de propriété intellectuelle, OMPI (Geneva 1994).

[167] About this particular, *vid. Nemec and Others vs. Slovakia*, in EUROPEAN COURT OF HUMAN RIGHTS, Web page mentioned, case 48672/99, decision issued on 2001.

- The slow pace of ordinary legal proceedings.
- The legal loopholes on copyright existing in the legal systems in many countries, due to the lack of synchronization between law development and technological evolution.
- The huge financial losses deriving from an expensive and slow legal process, during which the work in dispute can still be exploited.[168]

The arbitration proceeding commences when the claimant transmits a request for arbitration to the WIPO headquarters, which is immediately notified to the respondent who, from then on, will have thirty days to answer. The respondent shall submit to the Arbitration Center a copy of his answer to the claimant and a copy thereof shall at the same time be transmitted by that party to the claimant.

Once it is received in the WIPO headquarters, the parties agree on the number of arbitrators of the tribunal. Where the parties have not agreed on the number of arbitrators, the tribunal shall consist of a sole arbitrator, except where the Center in its discretion determines that, in view of all the circumstances of the case, a Tribunal composed of three members is appropriate.

Within 45 days after the commencement of the arbitration, the tribunal shall be established or completed. Once it is established, the claimant shall have thirty days to formalize his claim, which the Center shall notify to the respondent, who shall, within thirty days communicate his statement of defense.

The arbitration should, wherever reasonably possible, be heard and the proceedings declared closed within not more than nine months after either the delivery of the Statement of Defense or the establishment of the Tribunal, whichever event occurs later. The final award should, wherever reasonably possible, be made within three months thereafter.

If the proceedings are not declared closed within the period of time specified, the Tribunal shall send the Center a status report on the arbitration, and it shall send a further status report to the Center, at the end of each ensuing monthly period during which the proceedings have not been declared closed.

If once the decision is taken, and the arbitral award is made, should the parties consider that the tribunal's final decision is not clear, they shall have thirty days to file a complaint.[169]

---

[168] Cfr. AA VV, Colloque mondial sur l'arbitrage des litiges de propriété intellectuelle, OMPI (Geneva 1994) 301-307.

[169] Apart from the customary mediation and arbitration proceedings, WIPO added two new proceedings: expedited arbitration and a procedure combining mediation and arbitration.

The WIPO On-Line Arbitration Center was established to offer its services for the resolution of domain names disputes and other issues related to the commerce of intellectual property. [170]

3.6. The Technological Solution as an Alternative to Law for the Protection of Multimedia Works

However, despite all the legal efforts to ensure copyright protection which are carried out through the Berne system, or the legislation of each country, it is clear that Law cannot offer an absolute practical solution against the commission of crimes in this field.

The constant practice of unlawful copies, some CDs rental shops, bootlegging, or the customary practice of offering registered commercial software free of charge when purchasing a computer – just to mention a few examples – prove the inadequacy of the different legal systems in putting an end to an activity whose extent and variety of cases exceed the legal limits, ignoring law enforcement and the punishing content of the laws.

For that reason, resorting to technical devices of protection and to electronic rights and copies management, should be common practice within the multimedia industry, as has been indicated by WIPO in the different meetings established for that purpose.

In this sense, current provisions for the technical protection of copyright include the manufacturing of locking systems that, at the same time, allow software management and commercialization,[171] bearing in mind these five elements:

a) Data transmission confidentiality.

b) The possibility of verification or authentication of the interested parties.

c) The integrity and inalterability of the content.

d) The confirmation of the commercial transaction and the assignment of a copyright.

e) Transaction date and time entries in a registry.

---

[170]   About this subject, cfr. OMPI ed., http://arbiter.wipo.int/arbitration/ny-convention/text.html (Geneva 1999).

[171]   *Vid.* RODRIGUES, "Impacto de la tecnología digital en el ejercicio y gestión colectiva de los derechos conexos, en el marco de la Convención de Roma", *Boletín de Derecho de Autor*, no. 4, UNESCO (Paris 1997) 16-24, and KOOPS, *The crypto controversy. A key conflict in the Information Society*, Kluwer Law International (Holland 1999).

The basic operation of these systems is similar to the One-stop Shops or "one window" models, whose precedent is the Copyright Licensing Agency's Rapid Clearance System (CLARCS), and which was introduced for the first time to make photocopies of books, magazines or newspapers with the authorization of their authors, at prices fixed by the owner of the copyright.

The system has two databases: one, containing the works, its terms and conditions of use and royalties; and another one, containing registered users; in short, it is a simple system of double entry establishing conditions and prices for the use of each work – copying types.

In this sense, One-stop Shops contain a list of the works available, together with the name of the copyright holder, the amount of money specified as royalties and the system of payment managed and performed through the same window. Thus, the person interested in lawfully using a particular work only needs to go to one of these windows, to request the creation he wishes and pay the corresponding rights.

For this, he receives a digital key identifying each work, containing the title, the name of the author, and possible methods of assignment and use. Among these systems, we would like to point out:

a) The Imprimatur system of the European Commission, allowing authors to obtain, by means of a computer, a digitized number for each of his works which will be applied to every copy of an original creation.

The number, which will be assigned by a distributor created for that purpose – Unique Number Issuer – will be obtained through a company which will charge a certain amount of money to the authors for these services.

Thus, once the work is protected with an identification number, it will be offered to a distributor of digital works, for addition to the database and it is made available to the public, stating all the information on the rights and terms and conditions to use the work.

In this way, if someone wishes to use a work, he only has to pay to the distributor of the work the specified charge, a percentage of which will go to the author.

b) The Copymart system, designed by the University of Kyoto, Japan, consists of two database systems: one is an on-line database, containing the complete catalogue of accessible creations, which will operate on a subscription-basis; and the other is a copy system – called Copy Market – where the user will be able to select the work he wishes to copy, paying a charge in order to copy the work.

c) Different systems established in the United States, due to the extent of the American communication industry. Among them, stands out the Broadcast Music Inc. system. In 1997, the company that manages the rights of performers made available to the public an experimental catalog of works over the Internet, which users could access and request the delivery of a given work, registering automatically the number of persons accessing each work, as well as the date and time of its dissemination.

Other two outstanding systems, within the American industry, are the Work's Net Project and the Serial Copying Management Systems (SCMS): the first one allows composers and publishers to obtain a digital identifier for their works – the International Standard Works Code -; the second one, offers an on-line recordings distribution service, which indicates the terms and conditions of use, as well as the number of copies authorized. Both share similar features with the International Recording Code Standard (IRCS).[172]

---

[172] Other systems are: *New Media Licence Scheme* and *Copyright Xpress*, from Australia; *Sabam*, from Belgium; *Ivy*, from Canada; *Kopiosto*, from Finland; *Sesam*, from France; *Clearingstelle Multimedia*, from Germany; *CopySwede,* from Sweden; *Multimedia Copyright Clearing Centre*, from Switzerland; and *Media Image Resource Alliance* or *Authors' Registra*, from the United States.

The Development of Community Copyright Principles through the Regulation of Multimedia Works in the Information Society

The multimedia work was included for the first time in the international system of treaties on copyright in the 1990s. The first works in this regard, sponsored by WIPO in 1978, resulted eventually in the GATT Agreement of 1994 and in the Protocol to the Berne Convention of 1996. Both granted protection to computer programs and databases, and a new right of "making available to the public" was created as an economic right of the author covering the digital transmission of his creations.

In both cases the resemblance of its result is amazing and, as it has already been noted in Chapter III, this coincidence was not arbitrary. Prior to the GATT Uruguay Round, WIPO worked with a group of experts of UNESCO to adapt copyright to the NITs and, since many member countries of the World Trade Organization (WTO) were also members of the Berne Convention, the interaction between both organizations seemed logic.

The proposals presented by the delegation of experts from the European Union (hereinafter, EU) had the greatest impact. The important role the delegation played when writing both texts was based on two main reasons: first, the fact that the same delegation spoke before both organizations on behalf of a high number of countries; second, the influence of the studies which the EU had been developing since 1989 – when the *Green Paper on Copyright and the Challenge of Technology* was published – dealing with the relations between intellectual property and the NITs.

But, even though the role of the Community in the negotiations of the GATT had an effect on the final agreement, its importance was diminished by the greater interest which the EU had in issues related to the audiovisual policy, which also were subject of the conversations of the Uruguay Round; therefore, its involvement was more evident during the previous discussions of the Protocol to the Berne Convention.

Essentially the EU supported an innovative copyright regulation focused on the recognition of a right in favor of the makers of databases, based on their contribution in selecting and collecting their content.

The first steps regarding this issue had been taken in 1993, when the EU supported the passing of an *ad hoc* legislation; nevertheless, its materialization would only take place in 1996, when the Directive on legal protection for databases was approved including this *sui generis* right.[1] But, was it regulated in a different way from WIPO's failed proposal? What does this right involve for Community agencies? Do the same doubts arise as those which arose in the Geneva proposal? And, how was this concept coordinated with the right of the author of a database?

Said directive was the fifth legislative initiative within the copyright field. Its predecessors had been the Directives on the protection of computer programs (1991), on the rights of rental and lending (1992), on the harmonization of the term of protection (1993) and on the satellite broadcasting rights and distribution by cable (1993).[2]

For enacting these directives the EU relied on previous works and studies about copyright, among which stands out the above mentioned *Green Paper on Copyrights and the Challenge of Technology* of 1989, considered the starting point of the Community policy on this matter. However, the actual source of this policy must be looked for in the Court of Justice of the European Communities (hereinafter, ECJ) case-law and in the reports which the Community developed on cultural policy at the end of the 1970s:

In 1966 the decision in the *Consten and Grundig Verkaufs GmbH vs. the European Communities*[3] case recognized the incorporation of intellectual properties in the Rome Treaty, as well as the application to these creations of the regulatory principles of the Community market. Consequently, the free movement of the goods protected by copyright, or by other rights of similar nature, could not be restricted by means of the imposition of specific national tariffs on their imports or exports.

However, the cultural treatment given to copyright superseded the basically commercial approach that it had been given to that date.

---

[1]   *Vid.* EUROPEAN PARLIAMENT and COUNCIL Directive on the Legal Protection of Databases, (96/9/EC), March 11, 1996.

[2]   The reference of all these legal texts appears in the bibliography of this work.

[3]   *Vid.* Cases 56 and 58/64 [1966], COUR DE JUSTICE DES COMMUNAUTÉS EUROPÉENNES, *Recueil de la Jurisprudence de la Cour*, vol. XII (Luxembourg 1966) 429-559.

But from the 1980s this double point of view was completed with the proposals made through the audiovisual policy and the Information Society, whose aim was to provide fresh impetus to the shaping of the legal framework established until then. But, how did copyright materialize regarding both perspectives? Which was their contribution? And, in which of them, specifically, does the regulation of multimedia works fit?

With this convergence of approaches as a background, the Community copyright pursued three major objectives: firstly, to reach the legislative harmonization between the Member States in order to increase the creation and commercialization of these goods; secondly, to build a comprehensive legal framework in keeping with the law of the main international treaties; [4] and thirdly, to achieve a certain synchronism between technological development and its own evolution.

In practice, and since the first Community directive adopted in 1991, these three objectives were materialized in the formulation of a quasi-doctrine on copyright and related rights, with the peculiarity that their inspiring principles came from ideas already included in the international treaty system and national laws. This way, while disregarding all reference to the media and to creations of a more conventional nature, the EU legislation focuses basically on the NITs and multimedia works.

In anticipation of the agreements of the treaty system and reflecting their evolution – such as in the proposal of a directive on copyrights and the Information Society – the Community legislation has always offered a comprehensive and detailed answer analyzing the causes, consequences and limits of the rights established.

Consequently, the Community copyright is not a closed concept, but rather it is a developing notion which will be completed with the legislation on digital broadcasting, including measures of control for collecting societies or with the harmonization of the moral rights of the author, for example. However, which have been the principal ways of regulation to date? What has been said about computer programs? What has been said about databases? Or, what does copyright in the digital era mean for the EU?

---

[4] The EU Council proposal for the ratification of the Protocol to the Berne Convention by the Member States, was adopted on March 16, 2000.

  Cf. Proposal for a Council Decision on the approval, on behalf of the European Community, of the WIPO Copyright Treaty and the WIPO Performances and Phonograms Treaty (98/C 165/08) COM (1998) 249 final-98/1141 (AVC), submitted on April 27, 1998, http://europa.eu.int/eur-lex/es/com/dat/1998/es_598PC0249.html (Brussels 1999).

In the following pages there is an analysis on the perspective adopted by the EU regarding this legal concept, emphasizing its protection of the multimedia work and in its closer aspects to the digital dissemination. For this, and after a study of its precedents and legislative causes, its evolution and current content are described, emphasizing the specific features of the Community regulation distinguishing it from other national laws.

1. Antecedents

Beyond the economic objectives of the original EEC, different treaties subsequently signed incorporated new political, social and cultural goals. Precisely, thanks to a series of actions in favor of cultural diffusion – inconceivable when the Rome Treaty was signed – copyright would become a specific subject of the Community regulation. And although the incorporation of this right into the normative policies only took place explicitly upon the signing of the Mäastricht Treaty, in 1992,[5] the studies from four points of view would be significant for its regulation.[6]

1.1. An Approach to the Origins of the Community Regulation on Copyrights

1.1.1. Intellectual Property in the Free Market Game

From a strictly economic view, copyright already represented in 1995 a contribution of around 4 to 7% to the Gross Domestic Product (GDP) from each Member State, with an approximate value of 250,000 million ECUs.[7] Hence, the economic interest of its study and subsequent regulation.

Logically the first copyright measures, or rather intellectual property measures, were included within the Community priority to create a free commerce area without tariff barriers between the member countries of the new union.

Creative works were submitted, therefore, to the interaction of the free market established in the Rome Treaty, thus becoming one of the multiple types of goods affected by the most basic rules of Community trade: the lack of tax barriers

---

[5] *Vid.*, among others, PÉREZ BUSTAMANTE y CONDE, *La Unión Política Europea. 1969-1999*, Dykinson (Madrid 1999).

[6] Cf. EDELMAN, "Reflexiones sobre el derecho de autor y su evolución en la Comunidad Europea", *Boletín de Derecho de Autor*, no. 4, UNESCO (Paris 1993) 12.

[7] *Id.*, 10.

between member countries; the struggle against the consolidation of a dominant position of a given company in the market; and the free circulation of goods, services, persons and capitals.

"Art. 3.

For the purposes set out in Article 2, the activities of the Community shall include, as provided in this Treaty and in accordance with the timetable set out therein:

    a) the prohibition, as between Member States, of customs duties and quantitative restrictions on the import and export of goods, and of all other measures having equivalent effect.

       [...]

    c) an internal market characterized by the abolition, as between Member States, of obstacles to the free movement of goods, persons, services and capital.

       [...]

    (g) a system ensuring that competition in the internal market is not distorted.

    (h) the approximation of the laws of Member States to the extent required for the functioning of the common market;

       [...]."

"Art. 23.

1) The Community shall be based upon a customs union which shall cover all trade in goods and which shall involve the prohibition between Member States of customs duties on imports and exports and of all charges having equivalent effect, and the adoption of a common customs tariff in their relations with third countries."

"Art. 49.

Within the framework of the provisions set out below, restrictions on freedom to provide services within the Community shall be prohibited in respect of nationals of Member States who are established in a State of the Community other than that of the person for whom the services are intended."

"Art. 50.

Services shall be considered to be 'services' within the meaning of this Treaty where they are normally provided for remuneration, in so far as they are not governed by the provisions relating to freedom of movement for goods, capital and persons."[8]

Nevertheless, from the very beginning the practical application of these three ideas has posed different problems regarding each particular circumstance, requiring to impose limits and exceptions to these rules, or their interpretation by the Court of Justice of the European Communities (hereinafter, ECJ).

In short, caselaw has affirmed the incorporation of intellectual property into the Rome Treaty together with a possible limitation for the free circulation of intellectual property based on the protection of the intellectual property rights recognized in each Member State and on the protection of artistic heritage.

Thus, the specific reference made by the Treaty about industrial property as an obstacle to the free trade of goods and services was also transferred to the intellectual property system and, by extension, to copyright.

"Art. 30.

The provisions of Articles 28 and 29 shall not preclude prohibitions or restrictions on imports, exports or goods in transit justified on grounds of public morality, public policy or public security; the protection of health and life of humans, animals or plants; the protection of national treasures possessing artistic, historic or archaeological value; or the protection of industrial and commercial property. Such prohibitions or restrictions shall not, however, constitute a means of arbitrary discrimination or a disguised restriction on trade between Member States."[9]

In 1971 the ECJ both recognizes, through the *Deutsche Gramophon vs. Meter* case, the incorporation of this right in the former Article 36 of the Rome Treaty – current Article 30 – and reminds that, although the Treaty should not hinder the safeguard of rights which are the specific subject of the industrial and commercial property, the restriction of these rights is possible.

---

[8] Cf. ALONSO GARCÍA ed., *Tratado de Amsterdam y versiones consolidadas de los Tratados de la Unión Europea y de la Comunidad Europea*, Civitas (Madrid 1998) 239 and 252.

[9] *Id.*, 241-242.

"4) A related or neighboring right to copyright may, just as in the case of an industrial or commercial property right, be affected by the provisions of Article 36 of the Treaty."[10]

In fact, the ECJ reinforced this way the provisions of Article 82 of the Treaty, whose content refers to the so-called abuses of dominant position in the market:

"Art. 82.

Any abuse by one or more undertakings of a dominant position within the common market or in a substantial part of it shall be prohibited as incompatible with the common market in so far as it may affect trade between Member States.

Such abuse may, in particular, consist in:

a) directly or indirectly imposing unfair purchase or selling prices or other unfair trading conditions;

b) limiting production, markets or technical development to the prejudice of consumers;

c) applying dissimilar conditions to equivalent transactions with other trading parties, thereby placing them at a competitive disadvantage;

d) making the conclusion of contracts subject to acceptance by the other parties of supplementary obligations which, by their nature or according to commercial usage, have no connection with the subject of such contracts."[11]

As GROVES, MARTINO, MISKIN, and RICHARDS state, "the differences between the laws on copyright of the Member States of the EC often are a barrier to

---

[10] Cf. Deutsche Grammophon Gesellschft mbH vs.Metro-SB-Großmärkte GmbH &Co. KG, C 78/70 [1971], in COUR DE JUSTICE DES COMMUNAUTÉS EUROPÉENNES, Recueil de la Jurisprudence de la Cour, vol. XVII (Luxembourg 1971) 487-514.

[11] Cf. ALONSO GARCÍA ed, *op. cit.*, 265.
    Vid., also, the *Radio Telefis Eireann (RTE) and Independent Television Publications Ltd (ITP) vs European Communities Commission*, known as the *Magill* case, in CELEX LEXIS database, cases C-241/92 P and C-242/91 P, 691J0241, and Decision 89/205/EEC, December 21, 1988.

commerce,"[12] therefore it was necessary to prevent the consolidation of such economic monopolies; nevertheless, this did not mean losing their specific identity features.

In this sense, five years before, the ECJ had already sanctioned the abusive use of national laws on copyright for being a barrier to free commerce, such as was stated in the decision of the *Grundig-Verkaufs GmbH vs. the Commission of the European Communities* case. Such decision stated the possible incompatibility of certain entrepreneurial agreements with the basic principles of the commercial policy of the Community.

> "[...] An agreement between a producer and a reseller intended to apply national barriers to commerce between Member States may be against the most fundamental objectives of the Community." [13]

1.1.2. "The Rights of the "Cultural Worker"

Since 1974 new working fields appeared in the Community which tend to the incorporation of objectives foreign to a mere commercial policy.

One of its greatest exponent will be the cultural field which, as an industry, presents the challenge of promoting the trade of cultural assets.

Contrary to expectations, this impulse was not only an economic objective, but also the realization of the desire of the Community to keep the identity features of each country and of the search of an European common identity.[14]

Nevertheless, "just as the cultural sector is not equivalent to culture, the Community action over this sector is not a cultural policy"[15] in the strict sense of the word, but rather an approximation to the social and economic problems of the undertakings and cultural workers. Precisely the improvement of the working

---

[12] Cf. GROVES, MARTINO, RICHARDS and MINKIN, *Intellectual Property and the Internal Market of the European Community*, Graham & Trotman (London 1993) 80.

[13] Cf. Cases 56 and 58/64 [1966], COUR DE JUSTICE DES COMMUNAUTÉS EUROPÉENNES, *Recueil de la Jurisprudence de la Cour*, vol. XII (Luxembourg 1966) 429-559.

[14] On November 22, 1977 the Commission dealt, for the first time and clearly, with the Community cultural issue, proposing to the Council of Ministers to start a community action on this sector.
Cf. GRÉGOIRE, "L'action communautaire dans le secteur culturel", *Revue du Marché Commun*, no. 217, Editions Techniques et Economiques (Paris 1998) 3.

[15] *Id.*, 3.

conditions of the cultural worker will be one of the main concerns of the Commission, which are also materialized in the recognition of copyright as a socio-working right of the creator and not as a right exclusively bound to property doctrines.

> "If the right of exploitation of his work belongs to the author, this is not only because he is the owner of such work (as others are owners, for example, of real property), but rather because the work is the fruit of his labor and because said work must give to who performs it the adequate means." [16]

The first areas of action were the protection of the works of art and photography, and the resale rights – *droit de suite* – for the benefit of the author of an original work of art:[17] the Commission mentioned then the lack of synchronism between the timetable of technological advances and the development of legislation, which had caused the increase of criminal piracy practices against the fair exploitation of books, phonograms and motion pictures.

With this purpose during 1982, a proposal for two directives was considered to indirectly and directly regulate copyrights. The first directive, an indirect measure, was intended to assign financial resources for the subsidy of concerts and dramatic works; the second directive, a direct measure, was intended to regulate the copyright term of protection which, at that time, ranged between fifty and eighty years according to the national laws.[18]

In 1984 the representatives of the Member States undertook the first real legal action, although only through a resolution. The text pretends to encourage the action of governments against audiovisual piracy, even though it does not propose a concrete method for this. It was only a commitment to ratify as soon as possible the international agreements on copyright and related rights, and to tighten up criminal sanctions which the laws imposed to the violators of the aforementioned rights.

---

[16] *Id.*, 7.

[17] Cf. COMMISSION DES COMMUNAUTÉS EUROPÉENES, "Le renforcement de l'action communautaire dans le secteur culturel, *Bulletin des Communautés Européennes,* suplemento 6/82, Office des Publications des Communautés Européennes (Luxembourg 1983) 18.
    Vid. EUROPEAN PARLIAMENT and COUNCIL Directive 2001/84/CE of 27 September 2001, on the resale right for the benefit of the author of an original work of art., in http://europa.eu.int/comm/internal_market/en/intprop/docs/index.htm (Brussels 2002).

[18] *Id.*, 19.

The audiovisual industry was then a booming sector having a strong impact on the Community and world economy, hence the need to establish a protective regulation for a growing market.

The European Commission, as explained in the *Green Paper on Copyrights and The Challenge of Technology* of 1985, was working with figures which spoke of a 70% penetration of cassette recorders in the German, French and British households, together with near 286-million units of blank tapes sold in all the Community. [19]

1.1.3. Integrating an Audiovisual Sector with an Importance of its Own

The new audiovisual media represented to culture opportunities and risks which the Commission had to channel adequately. Their proposal for the 1988-1992 period consisted, among other measures, in writing an "audiovisual charter" including the rights of audiovisual creators, not only in connection with their freedom of expression and creation, but also with their copyrights.

On the other hand, the search of a consensus in the community with regard to printed editions eventually resulted in a communication of the Commission entitled *Books and Reading: Cultural Challenges for Europe* (1989) which stated:

"I. The creation as a starting point of books.

1. Any action regarding books shall necessarily take into account their authors and translators, who are the very source of the creation. The mission of the Community is to ensure, also as far as intellectual workers are concerned, according to the provisions of article 117 of the EEC Treaty 'the improvement of living and working conditions in order to equalize them by means of progress' [...].

2. Copyright allows authors to take advantage of the fruit of their intellectual activity, while it acts as an incentive to the production of literary works since it protects authors [...]".[20]

---

[19]   Cf. Resolution of the representatives of the Governments of the Member States of 24 July 1984, on measures to combat audio-visual pirating, 84/C 204/01, *Official Journal of the European Communities* of August 3, 1984, 16/vol. 01, Office of Official Publications of the European Communities (Luxembourg 1984) 194-195.
    Cf. COUNCIL, *Green Paper on Copyright and the Challenge of Technology,* 110-111.

[20]   Cf. COUNCIL Books and Reading: A Cultural Challenge for Europe, COM (89) 258 final (Brussels 1989) 2.

In 1989, the Green Paper on Copyrights and the Challenge of Technology was published, which today it is still considered the basic starting point of the works of the Community on this right.

The eruption of audiovisual and computer technologies had caused specific problems related to the industry of the sector: piracy, the private reproduction of audiovisual and sound materials, distribution and rights of rental – phonograms and videograms in particular –, and the protection of computer programs and databases.[21] In Italy the losses of the record industry, due to piracy, were estimated in 25-million dollars in 1984, and in Portugal, market share of pirated videos reached in 1985 around 75 percent or 80 percent of the market.

Clearly the audiovisual sector demanded a substantive law for the protection of authors, producers and distributors economic interests, providing for the establishment of effective methods of action, as well as for the reinforcement of the system of sanctions.[22] In this sense, the Community actions in the audiovisual field had to attain two basic objectives:

a) The recognition of copyright and related rights in those areas and countries in which they did not exist, that is, their regulation in relation with producers of motion pictures, phonograms and videos; performers and radio and television companies; and cable providers.

b) The punishment of piracy as a crime together with the imposition of civil and penal sanctions in the event of infringement of the law. Among them, imprisonment should be included in the case of felonies or repeated offenses.[23]

In February 1990 the Commission Communication on the community audiovisual policy[24] chose as a high-priority objective the creation of a common legal framework for the development of the sector, even though the same Communication revealed that the Community lacked a global approach on the topic due to a severe

---

[21]   Cf. COUNCIL *Green Paper on Copyright and the Challenge of Technology,* 15.

[22]   *Id.,* 46.

[23]   *Id.,* 87-89.

[24]   *Vid.,* COMMISSION OF EUROPEAN COMMUNITIES Communication of the Commission to the Council and Parliament on Audiovisual Policy, COM (90) 78 final, February 28, 1990, in COMMISSION OF EUROPEAN COMMUNITIES, *European Community audio-visual policy. Collection of Legislative and Policy Texts,* Office of Official Publications of the European Communities (Brussels-Luxembourg 1990).

normative fragmentation. However, the suggestion does not go unheeded and in 1993 the regulation of broadcasting by satellite and distribution by cable is proposed as a first step for the consolidation of a community policy on audiovisual copyright.[25]

The Directive, adopted in September 1993, had been preceded in 1992 by a similar directive concerning the regulation of the rights of rental and lending in the phonographic and cinematographic industry; but, in fact, the actual cause of Community concern was the arrival of the Compact Disc (CD), whose rental was already a consolidated entrepreneurial sector.[26]

To put an end to this, both rights were recognized by the Directive to authors, performers, phonogram producers and producers of the first fixation of a motion picture – regarding the original and its copies. [27]

On the other hand, transborder and national transmissions, through satellite broadcasting and distribution by cable, were regulated a year later in order to stop their "legal insecurity."[28] That legislation established "minimal rules to make and guarantee the free transborder satellite distribution of programs, as well as the full and simultaneous distribution by cable of the broadcastings of other Member States, mainly on a contractual basis."[29] This way two new rights were recognized in favor of authors, performers, producers of phonograms and broadcasting organizations:

a) A right of broadcasting, as an exclusive right to authorize the communication to the public of their works by satellite.

b) A right of distribution by cable.[30]

---

[25] *Id.*, 48.

[26] Cf. EUROPEAN COMMISSION *Green Paper on copyright and the challenge of technology,* 155-157.

[27] Cf. COUNCIL Directive on rental right and lending right and on certain rights related to copyright in the field of intellectual property (92/100/CEE), November 19, 1992, 246/63.

[28] Cf. COUNCIL Directive on the coordination of certain rules concerning copyright and related rights applicable to satellite broadcasting and cable retransmission (93/83/EEC), September 27, 1993, 248/15.

[29] *Id.*, 248/18.

[30] *Id.*, 248/19-248/20.

1.2. The Protection of Computer Programs as Literary Works: First Step for the Protection of Multimedia (1991)

1.2.1. Objectives of the Regulation

The *Green Paper on Copyrights and the Challenge of Technology* of 1989, includes the first specific mention to computer programs, whose protection is related to the legal framework of the audiovisual sector. At that time piracy affects these works, partly due to the manufacture of personal computers and to the differences existing on whether copyright was the most adequate protection for them.

The chapter of the *Green Paper* devoted to this issue, defined the term computer program for the first time: from an utilitarian point of view, software is "a set of instructions allowing a data-processing machine – that is, a computer – to perform its functions."

The text also offers a first approach to other basic concepts of the computing field, anticipating some issues which would eventually be scarcely relevant in the final draft of the Directive:

a) The difference between "package" and "software," in which the first one is the computer program with the basic documentation on its use; and the second one, is the "package" together with the design material used – even though, curiously enough, the term "package" seems a more general term than "software" and, maybe, the reversal of terms and meanings would be advisable.

b) The difference between "operating systems" and "application programs": the former control the internal operation of the computer; and the latter perform the tasks requested by the user, being working tools strictly speaking.

c) The difference between "source code" and "object or machine code," in which the program is expressed in binary digits, having been translated by a specific compiler.

d) The different presentations and media in which computer programs are embodied: paper strips, punched cards, magnetic discs and tapes, optical discs and integrated circuits.

Compared to copyright, patents seem to offer an alternative protection. However, this system presents certain drawbacks in practice, since it is understood that computer programs can only be protected under this right insofar as they involve an "invention from a technical point of view,"[31] generating a modification on the matter in which they are fixed or on the energy of their physical environment, such as it is required by some of the most relevant national laws.[32]

The Commission, which had been committed since 1985 to present a proposal for the legal protection of computer programs, thus mentions three principles inspiring the future document:

a) The support of the protection of software under copyright, against those holding that intellectual property is a method for the creation of monopolies.

b) The incentive of policies favoring the protection of computer programs by means of patents rights and contracts between provider and user.

c) The study of the possible protection under copyright for the access or interface protocols – allowing programs and appliances interoperability – since its monopoly would seriously affect the computer industry if it could not develop compatible products.

In 1991, the Commission reveals the conclusions of the public poll on the issue, which have been arisen in the *Green Paper*.[33] The conclusions reflect the opinions of different members of the computer industry who, basically, expect: the compatibility of access and interface protocols with other parts of computer programs; and the application, for the purpose of the acts limited by copyright, of the criteria established by the Berne Convention.

Previously, in a meeting with the members of the industry, the need to issue a directive for the protection of computer programs had already been established. Thus, the idea of building a protection system by creating a *sui generis* right, focused on the previously conceivable protection of the investor or maker, was abandoned.[34]

The first text of the future directive was approved by the Commission on December 1988, hence the announcement in the *Follow-up to the Green Paper* of

---

[31] Cf. COMMISSION *Green Paper on copyright and the challenge of technology,* 176.

[32] About the legal situation of software in the Member States of the EU in that time, *Id.,* 178.

[33] *Vid.,* COMMISSION OF EUROPEAN COMMUNITIES Follow-up to the Green Paper. Working program of the Commission in the field of copyright and neighboring rights, COM (90) 584 final, January 18, 1991 (Brussels 1991).

[34] Cf. JONGEN and MEIJBOOM eds., *op. cit.,* 2.

a prompt regulation in this regard was based on solid grounds. In October 18, 1989 the text was approved by the Economic and Social Committee and nine months later, by the Parliament. In the same month, but in 1990 – and also on the 18th – the Commission modified the text, including the amendments made by the Parliament, and approved its final proposal. Eventually the Directive on the legal protection of computer programs was adopted on May 14, 1991, after the approval by the Council – which had adopted its Common Position on December 1990.[35]

The Directive includes in its preliminary recitals a justification of its *raison d'être*, stating two causes as main grounds:

i) A financial reason, typical of the most traditional Community policy, based on the high financial investment of human and technical resources required for the creation of software.

ii) A legal reason, based on the need to obtain an identical, uniform and complete protection of these works in all Member States of the Community.

In addition, and echoing the contents of the *Green Paper*, a set of general guidelines on the ideas defining its content was also included:

a) The broadening of the object of protection, considering that the term computer program shall include all programs, regardless of the material they are fixed on[36]

b) The elimination of the qualitative or aesthetic criteria of a computer program as an element to determine whether it is an original work.

c) The compliance of the national legislation of each Member State to permit "all elements of hardware and software to work with other hardware and software," that is, their interoperability.[37]

But, is not this measure contrary to the essence of copyright? How can a right protecting a creator compel him to disclose part of the creative process of his work in order to share it with others?

---

[35] The Council met about 12 times since April 1989 to December 1990. On December 13 it reached a Common Position about the Directive text, which it transmitted to the Commission, and the Commission to the Parliament, on January 1991. *Id.*, 22.

[36] The Commission Proposal indicated that the term included "the expression (by any form, language, scientific representation system or code) of a set of instructions, whose purpose is to make a computer run a specific task or function." Cf. CZARNOTA and HART, *op. cit.*, 8.

[37] Interoperability is defined as the "ability to exchange and share data." *Id.*

d) The limitation of the protection to the expression of a computer program, excluding the underlying ideas and principles.

e) The understanding that copyright does not hinder the unauthorized reproduction of a work when this operation is technically necessary for the use of that program.

f) The establishment of measures similar to the ones of the Berne Convention regarding the term of protection.

g) The authorization of the protection of computer programs by other alternative legal channels.

1.2.2. Requirements for Protection: Interpretation of the Concepts of Originality and Formal Expression of a Work

As would happen in 1994 with the GATT Agreement and in 1996 with the Protocol to the Berne Convention, the Directive opted for establishing a basic protection for computer programs through its assimilation with literary works, being this one the first supranational text to follow this path. Prior to the EU regulation, only the legislation of the United Kingdom had provided for a similar solution in the group of Member States, as a result of the *Thrustcode vs. W. W. Computing Ltd* case of 1956; the *Copyright (Computer Software) Amendment Act* of 1985; and the *Copyright (Computer Programs) Regulations*:[38]

> "Art. 1.
>
> 1. In accordance with the provisions of this Directive, Member States shall protect computer programs, by copyright, as literary works within the meaning of the Berne Convention for the Protection of Literary and Artistic works [...]".[39]

Among other interesting issues aroused by this kind of protection, two of them should be taken into account, as had already been noted in the *Green Paper* and whose practical effectiveness of assimilation depends upon: how shall the originality criterion in computer programs be applied and how to protect not only their formal expression, but also the ideas and algorithms which generate them.

---

[38] Cf. GROVES, MARTINO, MINSKIN and RICHARDS, *op. cit.*, 82, HART and FAZZANI, *Intellectual Property Law*, Macmillan Law Masters (London 1997) 133 and JONGEN and MEIJBOOM, *op. cit.*, 9.

[39] *Id.*, 122/44.

a) As for the determination of the originality condition in computer programs, several doubts appear: is it possible to speak of the originality of a program in the same sense of a musical composition or novel? Or is not it logical that some computer programs repeat certain sequential structures, just as books repeat certain syntactic constructions and words?

As the *Green Paper* stated, the most consolidated doctrine on copyright had always understood originality as the result of a creator's brainwork and not as the achievement of a given aesthetic or qualitative status, although in practice that status allows the differentiation of creations, since it is not possible to protect the ideas *per se*, but rather the way of expressing them.

However, the characteristics of a computer language imply a certain paradox: firstly, some software applications have instruction sequences very related, even if their result is apparently disparate; secondly, there are in the market similar computer products, whose programming sequences differ notably.

Therefore, how to articulate an originality notion comprising these situations?

The software creation and development process itself questioned this basic principle of copyright, to which the case-law of the national courts of some Member States had added new interpretations of this criterion:

i) In 1985, the German Supreme Court demands in the *Inkasso Case* that computer programs should represent original and creative individual achievements over the average to obtain the protection of copyright, with which the percentage of software eligible for protection can be reduced to 15% of the market.[40]

ii) In 1986 the French Cassation Court rectifies the decision of a Parisian court on the *Atari Case* and offers this protection to a computer game by the simple fact of being new – original – apart from the value of its aesthetic merits.[41]

All these elements formed the basis for the use in the *Green Paper* of the same criterion used for the protection of topographies of semiconductor products, whose originality was determined according to the final result and not to each of their elements considered individually.

---

[40] *Südwestdeutsche Inkasso KG vs. Bappert and Burker Computer GmbH* (Federal Supreme Court, 1985). Cf. COMMISSION *Green Paper on Copyright and the Challenge of Technology,* 187 and 202.

[41] *Atari vs Sidam* (French Cassation Court, 1986). *Id.*

"The topography of a semiconductor product shall be protected provided it is the result of its creator's own intellectual effort and is not commonplace in the semiconductor industry. Where the topography of a semiconductor product consists of elements that are commonplace in the semiconductor industry, it shall be protected only to the extent that the combination of such elements, taken as a whole, fulfills the abovementioned conditions."[42]

Finally, when the Directive initiates its *iter legis*, the opinion of the Parliament includes an amendment defining the originality concept as "the result of the creative effort of the author",[43] regardless of whether it secures certain parameters in its result.

Thus, in the final text of the Directive it becomes evident that the Commission reaffirms a concept of originality similar to the one traditionally formulated by doctrine and basic principles of copyright. Any reference to the qualitative criteria or aesthetic merits of the program is excluded, which would have introduced an almost revolutionary idea in the copyright field.[44] This way, the originality notion as a result of a creative personal effort, differentiated and differentiable is consolidated, yet without going into more specific details.

"Art. 1.

[...]

3. A computer program shall be protected if it is original in the sense it is the result of its creator's own intellectual effort. No other criterion should be used to grant the protection."[45]

b) As for the protection of ideas insofar as they have been formally expressed and embodied, the *Green Paper* had already established that the type of media used to fix a computer program would not determine its protection; and had accepted its

---

[42] Directive 87/54/CEE, *EC Official Journal,* L 24, January 27, 1987. *Id.,* 188 and 204.

[43] The Economic and Social Committee had already announced that originality would be one of the most significant issues to be dealt with in the new Directive, as it stated in its opinion of October 1989.

[44] Cf. CZARNOTA and HART, *op. cit.,* 14 and 16. Cf. COUNCIL, Directive on the legal protection of computer programs (91/250/CEE), May 14, 1991, 122/42.

[45] *Id.,* 122/44.

expression through paper, a magnetic tape, optical or magnetic discs, and even "in the form of a series of electrical charges in a chip."[46]

Nevertheless, this text did not mention the application of the rule offering protection only to those works embodied in a formal medium, since it was understood that the matter had already been generously dealt with in a doctrine which had always rejected the protection of the ideas *per se*.

But, should computer programs receive a different treatment? Why the ideas originating a certain computer application would have to be protected when the ideas giving rise to scientific works are not? Could it be that the ideas giving rise to a software program are always exclusive?

The opinion of the Parliament had clearly expressed that the ideas and original principles of a computer program should be excluded from the protection granted by copyright, as interfaces are:

> "Secondly, the so-called 'idea-expression dichotomy,' an essential thing in the laws on copyright – the ideas are not protected, but the form in which these are expressed – raises important issues in connection with software. A program consists of a series of commands and instructions, and it is only possible to protect the ideas, insofar as it is possible to hinder their use."[47]

This was ratified by the Commission upon publishing the Revised Proposal in October 1990.[48] Therefore, in the 'whereas' clauses of the Directive this point of view is confirmed and it is indicated that the formal expression of the software differs from the principles and ideas applied in its language of creation.

Therefore, it is established that:

 i) The ideas and principles that underlie any element of a computer program, including those which underlie its interfaces, are not protected by copyright.

 ii) The ideas contained in the logic, algorithms and programming languages shall enjoy this right.[49]

---

[46]   Cf. COMMISSION *Green Paper on copyright and the challenge of technology*, 189.

[47]   Cf. GROVES, MARTINO, MINSKIN and RICHARDS, *op. cit.*, 82.

[48]   Cf. CZARNOTA and HART, *op. cit.*, 16-18.

[49]   Cf. COUNCIL Directive on legal protection of computer programs, 122/43.

"Art. 1.

[…]

2. The protection provided for in the Directive shall be applied to any form of expression of a computer program. The ideas and principles which underlie any element of a computer program, including those which underlie its interfaces, shall not be protected by copyright in accordance with this Directive."[50]

1.2.3. Computer Authorship and Right Holders

When it comes to defining the beneficiary of a copyright on a computer program, the Directive starts up from a real situation in which the author of it does not have necessarily to be its owner. Certainly, there are assignment agreements in which the author waives the ownership of the program in exchange for a given consideration. For that reason, the Directive starts its Article 2 underlining this basic difference:

"Art. 2. Authorship of computer programs.

1. The author of a computer program shall be the natural person or group of natural persons who has created the program or, where the legislation of the Member State permits, the legal person designated as the right holder by that legislation."[51]

This first approach to computer authorship is inevitably based on the traditional concept of author which, *a priori*, does not recognize legal persons the possibility to hold the authorship of a work, therefore only natural persons can enjoy said privilege.

However, as has already been said, when a work is sold there is not only an author's assignment of rights in favor of the brand or undertaking who sells his work, but also there appears a new natural or legal person who thanks to copyright will turn into the right holder of related or neighboring rights. This way, it is recognized that most creative initiatives have to be attributed to an undertaking, brand or a corporation other than a sole corporation, and a clear distinction between

---

[50] *Id.*, 122/44. This provision was included in the Proposal for a Directive by the Commission and the Council, suggested by the Parliament.
Cf. GROVES, MARTINO, MINSKIN and RICHARDS, *op. cit.*, 84.

[51] Cf. COUNCIL Directive on legal protection of computer programs, 122/44.

author and right holder – two compatible figures, but not always the same – must be made.

For this reason, the Directive does not speak exclusively of authors, individuals or right holders, but of beneficiaries of the protection:

"Art. 3. Beneficiaries of protection.

Protection shall be granted to all natural or legal persons eligible under national copyright legislation as applied to literary works."[52]

Logically, with such a broad definition, the concept of the employee is not excluded. In this case, the employer will be entitled to the economic rights on the program created by an employee in the execution of his duties, unless both parties sign an opposite agreement. Even so, the employee will still have moral rights on the work.[53]

"Art. 2.

[...]

3. Where a computer program is created by an employee in the execution of his duties or following the instructions given by his employer, the employer exclusively shall be entitled to exercise all economic rights in the program so created, unless otherwise provided by contract."[54]

Due to the complexity of the creative tasks, the Directive contemplates that a computer program could be created by several natural persons. That is why it refers to software as a joint work – when the exclusive rights are hold by all –, and as collective work – when the principles of each national legislation define the ownership of a work.[55]

"Art. 2.

1. [...] Where collective works are recognized by the legislation of a Member State, the person considered by the legislation of the Member State to have created the work shall be deemed to be its author;

---

[52]   *Id.*

[53]   Cf. CZARNOTA and HART, *op. cit.*, 14.

[54]   *Id.*

[55]   Cf. COUNCIL Directive on legal protection of computer programs, 122/44.

2. In respect of a computer program created by a group of natural persons jointly, the exclusive rights shall be owned jointly."

However, the Directive is vague when it comes to explaining this issue, how is a joint work distinguished from a collective work, or from a work made in collaboration? Have these terms similar meanings? Or is it, on the other hand, a matter of slight differences between kind and species? Should they be interpreted, therefore, according to the provisions of the laws of each Member State?

In addition, the text does not take into account other two matters of interest that had been mentioned in the *Green Paper*: the authorship of programs generated by computers and how to enjoy moral rights in a work created by several authors:

As outlined in the *Green Paper*, "[…] in the future, computer programs will be increasingly created with the aid of a programmed computer,"[56] which does not exclude the need of an author who, however, will make almost no contribution to the work. From this point of view, from the mutual person-machine demand, the Commission tends to favor the recognition of the right of ownership to the computer user, since it understands that a computer is "[…] basically a tool"[57] and it is the user who transmits the instructions so that it can perform accordingly.

Nevertheless, the Directive does not provide a specific answer for this issue, therefore a few doubts remain unanswered: Is this, then, the appropriate system to choose? Or should the legislation of each Member State decide this question?

On the other hand, and regarding the exercise of moral rights on joint works, it is usually considered that these rights always belong to the original creator of the program, even in the case of collective works in which all co-authors will share them or will dispose of them according to each particular contribution, and to the specific type of work.

However, to define this issue with precision is obviously difficult and, therefore, the Commission suggests in its *Green Paper* the contractual assignment of these rights in favor of the employer, of the person who orders the work or the assignee of the economic rights.

Logically, the idea, such as the Commission itself eventually recognized, is ridiculous, since the law has always considered moral rights as legal rights that cannot be transmitted. Probably that was the reason why the Council discarded this idea and did not mention it in the Directive.

---

[56]   Cf. COMMISSION Green Paper on Copyright and the challenge of technology, 196.

[57]   *Id.*, 198.

1.2.4. Exceptions to the Exercise of Economic Rights: The Obligatory Authorization of the Acts Required for the Functioning of Software

In accordance with the rights usually recognized to authors, the Directive bases its content on those rights which, due to the computer program nature, can be exercised. Thus, the author or right holder of the work is entitled to authorize or prohibit:

a) The permanent or temporary reproduction of a program, in part or in whole, by any means and in any form.

"Art. 4.

[...]

a) the permanent or temporary reproduction of a computer program by any means and in any form, in part or in whole."[58]

b) the translation, adaptation, arrangement and any other alteration of a computer program and the reproduction of the results thereof.

"Art. 4.

[...]

b) the translation, adaptation, arrangement and any other alteration of a computer program and the reproduction of the results thereof, without prejudice to the rights of the person who alters the program."[59]

This way, the right holder reserves from its inception the right to make higher versions of a certain program, or to authorize another person to make them. In addition, this right allows to change the coding used and, in general, to make any other transformation to the program, as well as to change the ownership on the result of these actions.

c) The sale and lending of the original computer program and its lawful copies.

"Art. 4.

[...]

c) any form of distribution to the public, including the rental, of the original computer program or of copies thereof."[60]

---

[58] Cf. COUNCIL Directive on legal protection of computer programs, 122/44.

[59] *Id.*

[60] *Id.* and 122/43.

Therefore, the principle of exhaustion of rights[61] is applied, by which the first sale in the EU of a copy of a program by the right holder shall exhaust the distribution right within the Community of that copy, with the exception of the right to control further rental of the program or a copy thereof.

However, and regarding the protection of these rights, the peculiarities in the functioning of computer programs and their utilitarian nature have hindered the consolidation of a copyright absolute and without exceptions. Like the international treaty system and national laws oppose to this exclusivity a series of compulsory licenses of use, the Directive authorizes software users to perform certain acts, even without the consent of the right holder. These exceptions rely on two causes:

- The need to perform certain restricted acts when they are essential for the legitimate user to use the program.

- The need to obtain the information necessary to achieve the interoperability of a program with other software applications.

The amended proposal for the Directive, published by the Commission in October 1990, would establish the following principles:

a) The author or right holder shall not prevent a legitimate user from reproducing the computer program in order to load or run it.

b) A back-up copy must be authorized if this is necessary for its use.

c) The authorization of the right holder shall not be required when the legitimate user makes the necessary corrections for its regular use.

d) The study of a program shall not be prevented, provided that the user does not apply unlawful methods violating copyright.

e) The user is entitled to take the necessary steps to create an interoperable program, including the use of reverse engineering and the translation of the object code to other type of language.

---

[61] The principle of exhaustion of rights was stated by the ECJ in the *Coditel vs.Ciné Vog* case. Cf. C-62/79 [1980] ECR 881 and [1981] 2 CMLR 362 in DOWNING, *EC Information Technology Law*, John Wiley & Sons (Great Britain 1995) 25-26 and GUY and LEIGH, *The EEC and Intellectual Property*, Sweet & Maxwell (London 1981) 114 and 128, and C 155/73, [1974] ECR in PORTER, *Beyond the Berne Convention. Copyright, broadcasting and the single market*, John Libbey (United Kingdom 1991) 29.

In 1989 the *Green Paper* stated what has been considered obvious: "The authorized use of a program under a license agreement implies an implicit authorization to reproduce, adapt and translate it, without which the program cannot be used for its intended purpose."[62] Such acts, until then considered restricted in relation with conventional works, are considered now essential in order to use the product purchased.

In fact, its need was obvious under certain circumstances: when a user or purchaser must unload a copy in the hard drive of a computer; when in order to run it a translation through the appropriate decoder is required, transforming the source code into object code, being the latter transformed into recognizable elements by any human being; and when the program must be adapted to the specific needs of the user and this has been established in a contract.[63]

Finally, all this will be included in the Directive, exempting the user from obtaining an authorization from the author:

i) To reproduce, translate, adapt, arrange or alter a program when this is necessary for its use.

"Art. 5.

1. In the absence of specific contractual provisions, the acts referred to in Article 4(a) and (b) do not require authorization by the right holder where they are necessary for the use of the computer program by the acquirer, including for error correction."[64]

ii) To make a back-up copy, under the same circumstances.

"Art. 5.

[…]

2. The making of a back-up copy by a person having a right to use the computer program may not be prevented by contract in so far as it is necessary for that use."[65]

---

[62] Cf. COUNCIL Green Paper on Copyright and the Challenge of Technology, 190.

[63] *Id.*, 192.

[64] *Id.*, 122/44.

[65] *Id.*, 122/44 and 122/45, and

iii) Observe, study and test the program in order to determine the principles and ideas used in its creation, provided that these acts are made during the loading, displaying, transmitting or storing the program.

"Art. 5.

[…]

3. A person having a right to use a copy of a computer program is entitled to observe, study or test the functioning of the program in order to determine the ideas and principles which underlie any element of the program if he does so while performing any of the acts of loading, displaying, running, transmitting or storing the program which he is entitled to perform."[66]

iv) Reproduce and translate a code where both acts are indispensable to achieve the interoperability of the program with other programs independently created, provided that the following conditions are met:

"Art. 6.

[…]

a) these acts are performed by the licensee or by another person having a right to use a copy of a program, or on their behalf by a person authorized to do so.

b) the information necessary to achieve interoperability has not previously been readily available to the persons referred to in subparagraph (a); and

c) these acts are confined to the parts of the original program which are necessary to achieve interoperability."[67]

According to these requirements the Directive prohibits: the use of the information obtained for other purpose different from the one mentioned; its communication to third parties, when this is not necessary to achieve interoperability; and its use for the creation and commercialization of similar programs.[68]

---

[66] COUNCIL Green Paper on Copyright and the Challenge of Technology, 193. *Id.*

[67] *Id.*, 122/45,

[68] GROVES, MARTINO, MISKIN and RICHARDS, *op. cit.* 82, and 86-87, and KROKER, "The Computer Directive and the Balance of Rights", *European Intellectual Property Review*, no. 5, Sweet & Maxwell (London 1997) 249. Cf. COUNCIL Directive on Legal Protection of Computer Programs, 122/45.

Moreover, according to the Directive, Member States shall provide, in accordance with their national laws, appropriate remedies against a person performing any of the following acts: any act of putting into circulation a copy of a computer program knowing, or having reason to believe, that it is an infringing copy; the possession, for commercial purposes, of a copy of a computer program knowing, or having reason to believe, that it is an infringing copy; and any act of putting into circulation, or the possession for commercial purposes of, any means the sole intended purpose of which is to facilitate the unauthorized removal or circumvention of any technical device which may have been applied to protect a computer program.

Nevertheless, can this implied consent be invoked under any circumstances as has been previously mentioned? Would it be more reasonable to obtain an express permit from the right holder when it is impossible to use a program without performing some of the acts listed above?

In this regard, it is conceivable that not all computer programs must be adapted to optimize their operation; sometimes, especially when their use is not intended for corporate purposes, a computer program is used without requiring any change in its content or structure. Furthermore, usually a person who needs to make an adaptation in order to make a software work for the purposes it was acquired, orders the creation of an *ad hoc* program to meet his requirements.

On the other hand, the loading and running of a program does not always require its previous reproduction, since sometimes it is possible to load and run a program from the diskette or CD-ROM delivered to the user. This seems to be based on Article 4 of the Directive where the authorization of the author is only required insofar as these acts need such reproduction, therefore it may be deduced that this is not always necessary.

But, is it possible to control the acts performed by a user? For example, is it possible to recognize which of the copies of a program is a back-up copy and which is an unlawful copy? How can an author be aware of the execution of these acts? Would it be enough to include a technical device, preventing the reproduction of the program more than once? However, is an author entitled to control the use of an acquired copy? And finally, why focus specifically on the restriction of the reproduction of a program when the author himself has to do this to assign his work to an undertaking to commercialize it?

1.2.5. Is the Term of Protection Appropriate?

The last issue dealt with by the Directive was the term of protection to be granted to these works, according to the opinion of the Economic and Social Committee.[69]

The Commission pointed out in the *Green Paper* two main opposing views regarding this matter: one supporting a term of protection during the life of the author and fifty years after his death; and the other, following the French example of 1985, supporting a shorter term based on the mere utilitarian features of software, its short life and the limited economic investment required – though the latter is not always true.

It was, in short, the restoration of copyright under the Berne Convention against the introduction of innovations in its principles:

The supporters of the second option considered copyright similar to patent rights and utility patents, and that software should not be granted a longer term than the one granted to other types of functional and industrial contributions; as regards the arguments of the supporters of a longer term, they were based on the fact that other works protected by copyright also have a short life, which has not resulted in the reduction of their term of protection.[70]

But should the Council have favored the first criterion it would have meant that computer programs have the typical features of other technical, industrial and commercial creations, whose protection could have been granted through other legal provisions, to the detriment of copyright.

"Art. 9.

1. The provisions of this Directive shall be without prejudice to any other legal provisions such as those concerning patent rights, trademarks, unfair competition, trade secrets, protection of semi-conductor products or the law of contract [...]".[71]

That is why, eventually, and in keeping with the provisions of the Berne Convention, the term of protection was established for the life of the author and fifty years after his death.

Provisions were also made for particular cases: works performed by several authors together, where the term of protection is calculated from the death of the

---

[69] Cf. CZARNOTA and HART, *op. cit.*, 14.

[70] Cf. COUNCIL Green Paper on Copyright and the Challenge of Technology, 194.

[71] Cf. COUNCIL Directive on Legal Protection of Computer Programs, 122/45.

last surviving co-author; and anonymous or pseudonymous works, and those performed by a legal person, where the term of protection starts from the time that the computer program is first made available to the public.

"Art. 8.

1. Protection shall be granted for the life of the author and for fifty years after his death or after the death of the last surviving author; where the computer program is an anonymous or pseudonymous work, or where [...] a legal person is designated as the author by national legislation [...], the term of protection shall be fifty years from the time that the computer program is first lawfully made available to the public [...]".[72]

In any case, the term of protection shall be deemed to begin on the first of January of the year following the death of the author or the making available to the public of the work.

Subsequently, and with the adoption of the Directive of 1993 harmonizing the term of protection of copyright and certain related rights, the protection would be broadened to seventy years *post mortem auctoris*, which implies a direct contradiction with the useful life of these works.

"Art. 1.

1. The rights of an author of a literary or artistic work within the meaning of Article 2 of the Berne Convention shall run for the life of the author and for 70 years after his death, irrespective of the date when the work is lawfully made available to the public.

2. In the case of a work of joint authorship the term referred to in paragraph 1 shall be calculated from the death of the last surviving author.

3. In the case of anonymous or pseudonymous works, the term of protection shall run for seventy years after the work is lawfully made available to the public. However, when the pseudonym adopted by the author leaves no doubt as to his identity, or if the author discloses his identity during the period referred to in the first sentence, the term of protection applicable shall be that laid down in paragraph 1.

[...].

---

[72] *Id.*

6. In the case of works for which the term of protection is not calculated from the death of the author or authors and which have not been lawfully made available to the public within seventy years from their creation, the protection shall terminate."[73]

But, is not computing industry developing faster than conventional creations? Does not the permanence of artistic and literary works contrast with the ephemeral nature of a computer work? On account of this, would not it be necessary to establish a different term of protection for each type of work?

2. Regulation of Multimedia Works and Digital Technology

2.1. Copyright in the Legal Framework of the Information Society

With the adoption of the Directive of 1991 on the legal protection of computer programs, copyright was included definitely within the audiovisual policy of the Community, although this approach is more than questionable. Since then, and after the adoption in 1992 and 1993 of the Directives on rental and lending rights, and on satellite broadcasting and distribution by cable, the actions of the Community on the audiovisual sector would barely consider again intellectual property.

However, this was not due to a lack of interest, but rather because these policies were considered insufficient then to cover a series of problems directly connected with the NITs and the project of the Community regarding the Information Society.

The idea of creating an Information Society was first formulated in the *White Book on Growth, Competitiveness and Employment. The Challenges and Ways Forward Into the 21st Century*, published at the end of 1993, which was supported by Jacques Delors. Nevertheless, since 1979 the Commission was pondering this idea:

"The European society of today is in fact already an Information Society, in which scientific and intellectual activities, commercial transactions and day-to-day life rely on a clever information network.

---

[73] Cf. COUNCIL Directive Harmonizing the Term of Protection of Copyright and Certain Related Rights, 290/11.

The new family of electronic technologies transforms the way in which this information network works, reducing costs considerably, changing the working habits in companies and industries, and offering the citizens a wide range of new or improved products and social services."[74]

A year later, on July 1994, the communication *Europe's Way to the Information Society* introduced the protection of intellectual property rights among the key issues of the legal framework of the new European society. Its reference, however, was simple and based on three very specific points: the need to revise the measures related to the right of reproduction and related rights; the development of the proposal for a directive in connection with the legal protection of databases – whose first studies dated from 1993; and the announcement of the proposal for a directive on private reproduction, which eventually was not formulated.[75]

The Information Society was the point of contact of the three approaches that had been proposed at that stage regarding copyright: its commercial implications, its contribution to the cultural dissemination and its repercussion in the audio-visual industry.[76]

In addition, the document put forward the next new *Green Paper*, regarding copyright and its role in the Information Society, in the line of the *Green Paper* which in 1989 had set the first principles of the actions of the Community.

The *Green Paper on Copyright and Related Rights in the Information Society* was published in July 1995. This Paper considered the *status quaestionis* of intellectual property and introduced the subjects in which the Community would concentrate its future efforts: digital transmission, dissemination and broadcasting; rights management; and multimedia works technical identification and protection systems.

Soon after, in May 1996, the Council underlined as one of the favorable conditions for the development of a multimedia content industry, the adoption of

---

[74] Cf. Council La Société Européenne face aux nouvelles technologies de l'information. Une réponse communautaire, COM (79) 650, 23 novembre 1979, in ALABAU, European Union and its telecommunication policy. En el camino hacia la Sociedad de la Información, Fundación Airtel Móvil-Miján (Ávila 1998) 285-286, and *vid.* Europe's Way to the Information Society. Action Plan, COM (94) 347 final, July 19, 1994, Office of Publications of the European Communities (Luxembourg 1994).

[75] *Id.,* 8.

[76] For more information on this issue, see the bibliography of this work.

practical approaches as regards the commercialization of rights. This way new management methods were proposed, more appropriate to current transborder transmissions.[77]

The main actions are taken in three fields:

a) The promotion of quality European multimedia contents.

b) The adoption of new approaches regarding the commercialization of copyrights and related rights.

c) The encouragement and exchange of entrepreneurial methods with positive results.

The promotion of multimedia contents pursuant to the exploitation of the European cultural heritage, entrepreneurial services, geographical information and scientific, technical and medical information. Furthermore, the use of multilingual interactive multimedia is encouraged to obtain large economic benefits and to protect cultural identity and linguistic diversity.

The first outcome of these two initiatives was the adoption in 1996 of the Directive on legal protection of databases, and the adoption on May 22, 2001 of a new Directive harmonizing certain aspects of copyright and related rights in the Information Society.

Even though the regulation on databases can be qualified as innovative since it proposes the introduction of the new *sui generis* right in favor of the makers of these creations, the proposed regulation on copyrights in the Information Society echoes basically the content of the Protocol to the Berne Convention of 1996, since it provides for the right to make available to the public as a way to regulate interactive digital dissemination – although this did not prevent the introduction of some other more original issues.

In general, both initiatives meet the expectations of the Community to harmonize the legislation of Member States, since some of them have no provisions in this regard, or else the national differences in their content prevent considerably the establishment of a common normative zone.

"Whereas certain differences in the legal protection of computer programs offered by the laws of the Member States have direct and negative effects on the

---

[77] Cf. CONSEJO, Resolución relativa a las nuevas prioridades políticas en materia de Sociedad de la Información, de 21 de noviembre de 1996, Diario Oficial de las Comunidades Europeas, no. C 376, de 12 de diciembre de 1996, http://europa.eu.int/eur-lex/lif/dat/1996/es_396Y1212. 01.html (Bruselas 1999).

functioning of the common market as regards computer programs and such differences could become greater as Member States introduce new legislation on this subject;

Whereas existing differences having such effects need to be removed and new ones prevented from arising, while differences not adversely affecting the functioning of the common market to a substantial degree need not be removed or prevented from arising."

"(4) Whereas copyright protection for databases exists in varying forms in the Member States according to legislation or case-law, and whereas, if differences in legislation in the scope and conditions of protection remain between the Member States, such unharmonized intellectual property rights can have the effect of preventing the free movement of goods or services within the Community. "

"(5) Whereas, without harmonization at Community level, legislative activities at national level which have already been initiated in a number of Member States in order to respond to the technological challenges might result in significant differences in protection and thereby in restrictions on the free movement of services and products incorporating, or based on, intellectual property, leading to a re-fragmentation of the internal market and legislative inconsistency. The impact of such legislative differences and uncertainties will become more significant with the further development of the information society, which has already greatly increased transborder exploitation of intellectual property. This development will and should further increase. Significant legal differences and uncertainties in protection may hinder economies of scale for new products and services containing copyright and related rights."[78]

In fact, as it has already been mentioned, the influence between EU and WIPO proposals had been reciprocal.

---

[78] Respectively, cf. Council Directive on legal protection of computer programs, 122/42, PARLIAMENT and COUNCIL Directive on the Legal Protection of Databases, 77/20, and PARLIAMENT and COUNCIL Directive 2001/29/EC, May 22, 2001, On the Harmonization of Certain Aspects of Copyright and Related Rights in the Information Society, in http//europa.eu.int/comm/internal_,market/en/intprop/index.htm (Brussels 2002)

2.2. The Protection of Databases regarding Content Selection and Arrangement: Creation of a *Sui Generis* Right in Favor of Maker (1996)

2.2.1. Objectives of the Regulation

Although the regulation of the Community regarding databases only started in 1996, the need to deal with this issue had already been mentioned in the *Green Paper on Copyright and the challenge of technology* of 1989. Two years before a communication of the Commission had pointed out the great interest aroused by databases in an information market increasingly wide and international, since most of the valuable knowledge would be collected in this type of works. In fact, in 1985 the worldwide database business generated around five billion dollars, even though the four-fifths of this figure represented the United States market.[79]

Although the abovementioned *Green Paper* stated that few people thought that this was of minor importance – in comparison with the repercussion of audio-visual works, for example – the Commission could not avoid their mention and therefore devoted a chapter of the *Green Paper* to data banks, focusing on three matters:

a) The possible restrictions on the incorporation into data banks of works protected, in whole or in part, by copyright, since such incorporation requires the consent of their authors or right holders.

b) The classification of the retrieval of information as a restricted act, taking into account that a distinction should be made between their on-screen display – which would be equivalent to the mere reading of the material – and their printing – which would imply a real act of reproduction.

c) The definition of the most appropriate protection measure for this type of products, which not only prompted the debate on copyright as an effective way for the protection of these creations, but also the possibility of establishing a *sui generis* right protecting the maker of a database.

The answers to the consultation of the Commission, laid down in the *Follow-up to the Green Paper*, were presented in two sessions, which took place on April 26, and 27, 1990. During these sessions, members of the industrial sectors involved in

---

[79] *Id.*, 207. About this subject, *vid.* PÁEZ, "Derecho comunitario y nuevas tecnologías: Libro Verde y Directivas de Bases de Datos, *Informática y Derecho. Revista Iberoamericana de Derecho Informático*, UNED, no. 19/22 (Spain 1998) 97.

the making of databases put forward some issues that the Commission had not raised before:

   i) The existence of a generalized trend to use the term database instead of data bank, hence a certain uniformity in the use of one or other was required; furthermore, in order to define a work as such the study of its structure based on two parameters has to be made: the process of data collection, arrangement and storing; and the digitization and computer processing of the data contained.

   ii) The convenience to grant copyright protection together with additional legal protection measures.

   iii) The definition of a database not as a compilation, but as a literary work in its broader sense.

   iv) The establishment of the first ownership of copyright in favor of the database creator.

   v) The lawful incorporation of works protected by copyright without the consent of their right holders, and not considering these acts as unlawful.

   vi) The determination of said restricted acts, such as the displaying, entering, loading, transmitting, storing and on-line loading of the database.

   vii) The compliance with the provisions of the Berne Convention in those issues which could come up in the future, for which there are not other types of solutions.

The outcome was a first agreement when it comes to point out copyright as the most appropriate measure of protection, at the same time that was discarded the possible formulation of a *sui generis* right offering legal coverage to the makers of databases.[80]

Without doubt, authors had a special interest in keeping their legal status against possible new holders of a right of similar features, in addition to the desire of consolidating a system that placed their economic interests in an exclusive position. Why then, is there fear in granting rights in favor of producers and investors? Or how is it possible to explain without that commercial vision the claim of their

---

[80]   Cf. *vid.*, COUNCIL OF EUROPEAN COMMUNITIES Follow-up to the Green Paper. Working program of the Commission in the field of copyright and neighboring rights, COM (90) 584 final, 17.01.91 (Brussels 1991).

right to include works protected by copyright without the right holder authorization?

Finally, the official text of the Directive offered a neutral justification of its content. As it is usual in the EU legislation, a point of contact was draw with the economic practices defined as basic objectives of the EEC, among which it emphasizes the creation of a market in which the free movement of goods and services is not prevented.

> "(2) Whereas such differences in the legal protection of databases offered by the legislation of the Member States have direct negative effects on the functioning of the internal market as regards databases and in particular on the freedom of natural and legal persons to provide on-line database goods and services on the basis of harmonized legal arrangements throughout the Community; whereas such differences could well become more pronounced as Member States introduce new legislation in this field, which is now taking on an increasingly international dimension;
>
> (3) Whereas existing differences distorting the functioning of the internal market need to be removed and new ones prevented from arising, while differences not adversely affecting the functioning of the internal market or the development of an information market within the Community need not be removed or prevented from arising."[81]

However, this is not the only purpose of the new Directive, since in its preliminary recitals there are also other different economic and legal goals:

a) The aspiration to confirm copyright as the appropriate legal measure for the protection of these works, settling this way the debate on possible alternative protection measures.

b) The need to create a stable legal framework for databases, with a view to generate a greater dynamism in the information market.

c) The opportunity to grant certain rights to those making some type of human, technical or economic investment in the making of a database, as long as this investment is substantial.

---

[81] Cf. EUROPEAN PARLIAMENT and COUNCIL Directive on the Legal Protection of Databases, 77/20.

2.2.2. Requirements for the Protection and Definition of Authorship

Although the most original contribution of the Directive is the creation of a *sui generis* right in favor of the makers of databases, its comprehension and distinction requires the previous study of the type of protection granted to databases by copyright. This way it will be possible to discern the similarities and differences that could be established between both concepts.

a) In the first place, the Directive refers to the concept of author; proceeding then to dealing with it applying the classic principles of national laws, international treaties and doctrine, and repeating the terms already used in 1991 when it comes to establish the authorship of computer programs.

The author is, therefore, the creator of the database, both if he is only one natural person or a group, or a legal person, where the legislation of each member State so permits.

"Art. 4.

1. The author of a database shall be the natural person or group of natural persons who created the base or, where the legislation of the Member States so permits, the legal person designated as the right holder by that legislation."[82]

In the event of a collective work, the rights are granted to the right holder under whose initiative it was made; however, if the work has been created jointly, the rights will be owned by all co-authors.

"Art. 4.

[...]

2. Where collective works are recognized by the legislation of a Member State, the economic rights shall be owned by the person holding the copyright.

---

[82] Cf. EUROPEAN PARLIAMENT and COUNCIL Directive on the Legal Protection of Databases, 77/25, and COUNCIL Amended Proposal for a Council Directive on the Legal Protection of Databases (93/C 308/01), COM (93) 464 final, http://europa.eu.int/comm/dg15/en/intprop/indprop/922.htm (Brussels 1999).

3. In respect of a database created by a group of natural persons jointly, the exclusive rights shall be owned jointly."[83]

Finally, when the work is prepared within the scope of his employment, that is, the creation of an employee, the right holder is always the employer, unless otherwise agreed and when national laws so permits.

b) Secondly, the Directive refers to the object of protection, defining which are the works to be protected and under which circumstances they shall be protected.

The Directive gives copyright protection to the "databases which, by reason of the selection or arrangement of their contents, constitute the author's own intellectual creation,"[84] so the originality requirement is assessed according to both parameters since the author's own intellectual creation feature lies in them:

"(15) Whereas the criteria used to determine whether a database should be protected by copyright should be limited to the fact that the selection or the arrangement of the contents of the database is the author's own intellectual creation; whereas such protection should cover the structure of the database."[85]

"Art. 3.

1. In accordance with this Directive, databases which, by reason of the selection or arrangement of their contents, constitute the author's own intellectual creation shall be protected as such by copyright. No other criteria shall be applied to determine their eligibility for that protection."[86]

However, how is it possible to determine if the selection or arrangement of a database contents is original enough so that the author can obtain copyright protection? Are there multiple ways of establishing, for example, the arrangement of the data of a telephone directory? Or does this mean that these simpler type of databases cannot be protected?

---

[83] *Ibidem.*

[84] Cf. EUROPEAN PARLIAMENT and COUNCIL Directive on the Legal Protection of Databases, 77/25.

[85] Cf. EUROPEAN PARLIAMENT and COUNCIL Directive on the Legal Protection of Databases, (96/9/EC), March 11, 1996, 77/21.

[86] *Id.*, 77/25.

As Edelman states, "traditionally, originality is the mark of creativity: a work is original when it expresses, in a new way, what has always been said. In short, while any person can speak – something that is common – not everyone has a style. However, when the Commission affirms that originality comes from the creation and that the same creation is determined by means of elections, it takes copyright out of its personal scope to give it a content different from literature and art." [87]

Again, selection, arrangement and originality, such as happened in the Protocol to the Berne Convention, are the indicators of the appropriateness of a work to receive copyright protection. That is why the Directive adds, as a natural consequence, certain restrictions according to this protection:

i) The protection shall refer to the structure of the database and not to its contents, whose protection remains in force through copyright if this has not exhausted its term of protection.[88]

ii) No aesthetic or qualitative criteria should be applied to determine the eligibility of the database for copyright protection.

Nevertheless, in order to establish when a work can be protected by copyright, it was necessary to define what a database was to specify its differences with similar creations such as compilations, collections or fixations of independent works in exclusive products:

"(17) Whereas the term 'database' should be understood to include literary, artistic, musical or other collections of works or collections of other material such as texts, sound, images, numbers, facts, and data; whereas it should cover

---

[87]   Cf. EDELMAN, *op. cit.*, 16. See a thorough opinion in CERINA, "The originality requirement in the protection of databases in Europe and the United States", *IIC: International Review of Industrial Property and Copyright*, no. 5/1993, VCH (Weinheim 1994) 592-597.

[88]   On the other hand, the Council Proposal did not limit the protection to the structure of the work, although it required the compliance of similar parameters:

"14. Whereas the criteria used to determine whether a database should be protected by copyright should be defined to the fact that the selection or the arrangement of the contents of the database is the author's own intellectual creation; whereas such protection should cover the structure of the database."

Cf. COUNCIL Amended Proposal for a Council Directive on the Legal Protection of Databases, (93/C 308/01), COM (93) 464 final.

collections of independent works, data or other materials which are system-atically or methodically arranged and can be individually accessed [...]".[89]

According to this, the following works shall not be considered databases: simple audiovisual, cinematographic, literary or musical fixations; and computer programs used to create databases. Whereas this Directive protects collections, sometimes called 'compilations,' of works, data or other materials.

Would it not be more useful to define which works can be considered databases? Or does a user decide to use a database according to its aesthetics and not to the usefulness of its content?

The provisions of the Directive were not exclusive when it comes to determine the expression of databases being eligible for said protection. That is why, this should be extended to:

– All existing works regardless of their method of creation.

– All existing works regardless the medium in which they may have been embodied, that is, off-line or on-line.

2.2.3. The rights of the author and the term of protection

As for the content given to copyright in databases, their rights shall only be exer-cised "in regard of the expression of the database",[90] as it is logical when the object of the protection is the selection and arrangement of the contents.

In practice, this will imply the granting of the following rights: in the moral field, those rights granted to authors according to the Berne Convention and na-tional laws.

"(28) Whereas the moral rights of the natural person who created the database belong to the author and should be exercised according to the legislation of the Member States and the provisions of the Berne Convention for the Protec-tion of Literary and Artistic Works; whereas such moral rights remain outside the scope of this Directive." [91]

---

[89] Cf. EUROPEAN PARLIAMENT and COUNCIL Directive on the Legal Protection of Databases, 77/21.

[90] EUROPEAN PARLIAMENT and COUNCIL Directive on the Legal Protection of Databases, 77/25.

[91] *Id.*, 77/22.

In the economic field, the right to carry out or authorize the reproduction, distribution, communication, display and representation of the database.

> "Art. 5.
>
> In respect of the expression of the database, which is protectable by copyright, the author of a database shall have the exclusive right to carry out or to authorize:
>
> a) temporary or permanent reproduction by any means and in any form, in whole or in part;
>
> b) translation, adaptation, arrangement and any other alteration;
>
> c) any form of distribution to the public of the database or of copies thereof. The first sale in the Community of a copy of the database by the right holder or with his consent shall exhaust the right to control resale of that copy within the Community;
>
> d) any communication, display or performance to the public;
>
> e) any reproduction, distribution, communication, display or performance to the public of the results of the acts referred to in (b)."[92]

This way the content which covers all possible ways of exploitation is defined, according to the nature of the work, and among which are included the rights related to the possible alterations of the database to make a better use of it.

The author may determine how and who must exploit his work, as well as the control over their means of communication – on-line or off-line – and distribution. In this last case it must be taken into account that the right of distribution of copies fixed in a material medium is exhausted with the first sale within the Community, such as happened with computer programs.

> "(30) Whereas the author's exclusive rights should include the right to determine the way in which his work is exploited and by whom, and in particular to control the distribution of his work to unauthorized persons;
>
> (31) Whereas the copyright protection of databases includes making databases available by means other than the distribution of copies;

---

[92] *Id.*, 77/25.

(32) Whereas Member States are required to ensure that their national provisions are at least materially equivalent in the case of such acts subject to restrictions as are provided for by this Directive;

(33) Whereas the question of exhaustion of the right of distribution does not arise in the case of on-line databases, which come within the field of provision of services; whereas this also applies with regard to a material copy of such a database made by the user of such a service with the consent of the right holder; whereas, unlike CD-ROM or CD-i, where the intellectual property is incorporated in a material medium, namely an item of goods, every on-line service is in fact an act which will have to be subject to authorization where the copyright so provides." [93]

But, since these works can be altered for the benefit of their lawful user, the author shall not be able to prevent the carrying out of certain acts with this purpose:

i) The performance of any of the abovementioned acts when they are required to access and use a database content.

ii) The reproduction for private use, which paradoxically is only authorized in the case of non-electronic databases.

iii) The use for teaching or scientific research, – that is, non-commercial purposes – as long as the source is indicated.

iv) The use for the purposes of public security or administrative or judicial procedure.

v) Other exceptions to copyright authorized under each country national law.[94]

On the other hand, the Directive does not clearly specify the term of protection for this right, therefore it may be deduced that the terms fixed by the Directive harmonizing the term of protection of copyright and certain related rights of 1993 shall apply. The Directive establishes the term of protection for authors as the life of the author and 70 years after his death,[95] taking into account that the calculation starts

---

[93] *Id.*, 77/22.

[94] *Id.*, 77/25.

[95] Cf. COUNCIL Directive Harmonizing The Term of Protection of Copyright and Certain Related Rights, 290/11.

in one or another time according to whom is the author as was the case of computer programs.[96]

2.2.4. Subject, Object and Content of the Sui Generis Right

But the main innovation of the Directive was the introduction of a new right, different from copyright, but having similar features: the *sui generis* right of the maker of databases.

The idea was mentioned for the first time in the *Green Paper* of 1989, and its proposal was based on the verification of two circumstances related to the creation of some of these works: in the first place, that many of the databases contents were not protected by copyright, although their compilation, indexation and making available to the public meant a significant investment in time and effort. Secondly, the fact that a structure and method of selection with no originality does not always tally with some contents lacking of originality.

> "(39) Whereas, in addition to aiming to protect the copyright in the original selection or arrangement of the contents of a database, this Directive seeks to safeguard the position of makers of databases against misappropriation of the results of the financial and professional investment made in obtaining and collection the contents by protecting the whole or substantial parts of a database against certain acts by a user or competitor."

> "(40) Whereas the object of this *sui generis* right is to ensure protection of any investment in obtaining, verifying or presenting the contents of a database for the limited duration of the right; whereas such investment may consist in the deployment of financial resources and/or the expending of time, effort and energy." [97]

Thus, while copyright continues offering protection to the author or creator of a work, the *sui generis* right protects its maker, provided that he had made a substantial quantitative or qualitative investment; that is, a substantial investment in human, technical or financial resources.

---

[96] The Directive makes a certain confusion regarding this issue, since it does not specify which is the copyright term of protection, while it specifies the *sui generis* right term of protection, as will be shown in the following epigraph. About this matter, cf. PATTERSON, *op. cit.*, 135 and CHALTON, "Effect of the E.C. database Directive on U.K. Copyright Law", *European Intellectual Property Review*, no. 6, Sweet & Maxwell (United Kingdom 1997) 87.

[97] Cf European Parliament and Council Directive on legal protection of databases, 77/22.

A maker is a natural or legal person in charge of searching and collecting content. And precisely that content "may be copied and rearranged electronically, without his authorization, in order to produce a database"[98] of identical content using electronic and digital technology.

In order to prevent these acts, the maker shall enjoy the right to authorize or prohibit that said content is extracted and re-utilized, being an essential requirement that his work had involved a substantial investment, evaluated qualitatively or quantitatively.

"Art. 7.

1. Member States shall provide for a right for the maker of a database which shows that there has been qualitatively and/or quantitatively a substantial investment in either the obtaining, verification or presentation of the contents to prevent extraction and/or re-utilization of the whole or of a substantial part, evaluated qualitatively and/or quantitatively, of the contents of that database."[99]

But, there are some issues that remain uncertain: how can it be determined if an investment has been substantial, who could control if this criterion has been satisfied and which is its meaning.

The Directive defines, on the other hand, the acts of extraction and re-utilization, explaining that the latter does not refer exclusively to its new incorporation into another database, but also its communication to the public through the different ways of transmission authorized by copyright:

– Extraction means the permanent or temporary transfer of certain contents of a database to another medium and regardless the means used.

– Re-utilization means making available to the public the contents of a database by distribution, by renting, by on-line or other forms of transmission, excluding public lending.

"Art. 7.

[...]

2. For the purposes of this Chapter:

---

98 *Id.*, 77/22.
99 *Id.*, 77/25.

a) 'extraction' shall mean the permanent or temporary transfer of all or a substantial part of the contents of a database to another medium by any means or in any form;

b) 're-utilization' shall mean any form of making available to the public all or a substantial part of the contents of a database by the distribution of copies, by renting, by on-line or other forms of transmission. The first sale of a copy of a database within the Community by the right holder or with his consent shall exhaust the right to control resale of that copy within the Community.

[…]".[100]

However, there is a series of exceptions to the rights granted to the maker whose restrictions virtually tally with the restrictions usually imposed to copyright:

"(50) Whereas the Member States should be given the option of providing for exceptions to the right to prevent the unauthorized extraction and/or re-utilization of a substantial part of the contents of a database in the case of extraction for private purposes, for the purposes of illustration for teaching or scientific research, or where extraction and/or re-utilization are/is carried out in the interests of public security or for the purposes of an administrative or judicial procedure; whereas such operations must not prejudice the exclusive rights of the maker to exploit the database and their purpose must not be commercial;

(51) Whereas the Member States, where they avail themselves of the option to permit a lawful user of a database to extract a substantial part of the contents for the purposes of illustration for teaching or scientific research, may limit that permission to certain categories of teaching or scientific research institution." [101]

Therefore, it is established that: extraction for private purposes of a non-electronic database; extraction for the purpose of illustration for teaching or scientific research, as long as the source is indicated and to the extent justified by the non-commercial purpose to be achieved; and extraction and re-utilization for the purposes of public security or judicial procedure.

---

[100] *Id.*, 77/26.

[101] *Id.*

"Art. 9.

Member States may stipulate that lawful users of a database, which is made available to the public in whatever manner may, without the authorization of its maker, extract or re-utilize a substantial part of its contents:

a) in the case of extraction for private purposes of the contents of a non-electronic database;

b) in the case of extraction for the purposes of illustration for teaching or scientific research, as long as the source is indicated and to the extent justified by the non-commercial purpose to be achieved;

c) in the case of extraction and/or re-utilization for the purposes of public security or an administrative or judicial procedure."[102]

Furthermore, the user may extract and re-utilize some of the contents when they are not a substantial part of the contents, they are not against the normal exploitation of the work and they do not damage their right holders.

"Art. 8.

1. The maker of a database which is made available to the public in whatever manner may not prevent a lawful user of the database from extracting and/or re-utilizing in substantial parts of its contents, evaluated qualitatively and/or quantitatively, for any purposes whatsoever. Where the lawful user is authorized to extract and/or re-utilize only part of the database, this paragraph shall apply only to that part.

2. A lawful user of a database which is made available to the public in whatever manner may not perform acts which conflict with normal exploitation of the database or unreasonably prejudice the legitimate interests of the maker of the database.

3. A lawful user of a database which is made available to the public in any manner may not cause prejudice to the holder of a copyright or related right in respect of the works or subject-matter contained in the database."[103]

---

[102] *Id.*, 77/26.

[103] *Id.*, 77/26.

On the other hand, the Directive establishes a specific system for the following acts:

- On-line transmission, in which there is no exhaustion of rights regarding the re-utilization of a database, such as established by the ECJ case-law.
- On-screen display, which should be subject to the authorization by the right holder when this implies the transfer of material.

As for the term of protection, it is established in a completely new way: A term of fifteen years calculated from the first of January of the year following the date of completion is established, after which a *sui generis* right is granted.

Nevertheless, in the case of a database that is made available to the public during such period, the term of protection shall be calculated from the first of January of the year following the date when the database was first made available to the public. Thus, a database not only is legally protected since its making, but its term of protection is calculated from a later time.

On the other hand, and if the content of the database is substantially altered and a new investment is made, it will be granted its own term of protection, different from the original one.

"Art. 10.

3. Any substantial change, evaluated qualitatively or quantitatively, to the contents of a database, including any substantial change resulting from the accumulation of successive additions, deletions or alterations, which would result in the database being considered to be a substantial new investment, evaluated qualitatively or quantitatively, shall qualify the database resulting from that investment for its own term of protection."[104]

In fact, the term of protection is one of the particular features of the *sui generis* right that separates it from copyright and establishes it as a different right. So much so that this objective exists that, on a same database, there are two rights whose expiry occurs in different times.

But, is it logical that the Directive did not establish a similar term of protection? Are the contributions of authors and makers made on different contents? And if we accept that their tasks differ, would not it be more adequate to grant a maker a

---

[104] *Id.* In this regard, it must be taken into account that the burden of proof on the time of completion, falls on the maker. *Id.*, 77/24.

similar term of protection to that of the holders of related or neighboring rights, or vice versa?

2.2.5. *Copyright and* Sui Generis *Right, a Complementary Protection?*

From the above analysis, it may be deduced that the intention of the Directive is to make clear the existence of two specific rights. However, Chapter IV of the Directive establishes certain common provisions for both rights which, nevertheless, consist of very general subjects, more related to the conditions of application of the Directive than with the configuration of the features of one of these two concepts.

- a) Member States shall provide appropriate remedies in respect of infringements of the rights provided for in this Directive.
- b) Any other prior legal protection, existing on the data, works or other elements incorporated into the database should remain in force.
- c) Member States shall bring into force the laws, regulations and administrative provisions necessary to comply with this Directive before January 1, 1998.
- d) The application of all the measures adopted in respect of databases created prior to such date and also on those works completed before the same.
- e) The application of the *sui generis* right to those works which were completed not more than fifteen years prior to that date. It shall expire fifteen years from the first of January 1998.
- f) Every three years, Member States shall submit a report on the application of the Directive in their territories. The Commission shall transmit to the European Parliament, the Council and the Economic and Social Committee this report on the application of the Directive.[105]

And although there are certain coincidences between both rights which facilitate the assimilation of their structure, there is no doubt that this is due to the influence of copyright on the *sui generis* right and not to the similarity of their special content.

a) The individual subjects of the law have a different nature.

While copyright is consolidated as a right in favor of the creator of a database, the right of the maker – more focused on a commercial recognition – is understood as

---

[105] *Id.*, 77/27.

a right in favor of the person making an investment in the process of creation and distribution of a database. To be precise, the maker is given credit for his searching and collecting of material, apart from the fact that in such tasks may have existed personal creative processes, understood as features of the author himself.

b) Different criteria for granting protection.

The selection and arrangement of data made by an author shall have originality and must be the result of his creative effort, while the maker shall make a substantial – human, technical or financial – investment when it comes to search and to collect content. In both cases, nevertheless, the criteria set forth are not clearly enough defined to know beforehand where is the limit of their compliance or non-compliance.

c) Their object, on the other hand, is complementary.

Even though there is only one object of protection, both rights are focused on the protection of different parts of the same: copyright protects the structure of a database, while the *sui generis* right protects its content or, rather, the act of collecting it.

d) The protection given by the *sui generis* right is an innovation.

Copyright gives the author of a work the right to reproduce, translate, adapt, rearrange, modify, distribute, communicate, display or perform his or her work. On the other hand, the *sui generis* right of the maker puts forward two new categories: extraction and re-utilization, although the latter is comparable with the typical categories of dissemination.

Further, there is no doubt that re-utilization implies in practice the performance of an act of reproduction for the fixation of the content extracted in a given medium.

e) The term of protection is different.

The term of protection granted to an author is the life of the author and seventy years after his death; however, the term of protection granted to a maker is only fifteen years from the date of completion of the making of the database.

f) Some restrictions imposed to both rights are similar.

The similarities refer to the utilization for private purposes of a non-electronic database; extraction for the purpose of illustration for teaching or scientific research; and extraction and re-utilization for the purposes of public security or a judicial procedure.

In summary, although the *sui generis* right is considered a particular type of legal right, it is similar to copyright and related and neighboring rights. That is why, perhaps it might be appropriate to considered it as such. Said option would secure its addition to the principles and doctrine of intellectual property, telling the substantial differences regarding copyright, but revealing that there is a certain connection between both rights.

Such being the case, do we need to create the legal concept of maker? Could not it be assimilated with the producer? And would not it be possible to apply the existing related rights system?

Precisely, one of the issues not solved by the Directive is the definition of maker. Since the Directive refers to the person who searches and collects the content of a database, the text discards as "maker" an enterprise devoted to the mass production of databases and nearly assimilates the meaning of "maker" to the "editor" or "compiler" of the work.

Edelman said in 1993 and in view of the proposal for a Directive, "there is a significant sliding as for the idea of creation. In fact, traditionally, a creation must lead to make an original 'form' expressing the author's personality. However, in this case, the creation is limited to a selection; which has nothing to do with copyright – a writer, a composer or a sculptor does not conceive his work according to a selection or arrangement of a 'content'."[106]

In this sense, and about the maker, the Directive states:

i) That he has to make a substantial – economic, technical or human – investment in the work to obtain such recognition.

ii) That he is the person who makes the search and collection of the contents.

iii) That his acts also refer to the collection, verification or presentation of their contents.

iv) That subcontractors shall not be considered makers.[107]

---

[106] EDELMAN, *op. cit.*, 16.

[107] *Id.*, 77/22 and 77/23.

That is why it is deduced that one database can have more than a maker if each one makes different types of investments; and the reason why the author can also be the maker, since the Directive does not have any provision preventing this.

Therefore, one creation can have three right holders: the creator of the contents, the author of the database and the maker.

Certainly, their respective rights may be assigned. In fact, if an effective and simple management of said rights is expected, it is advisable their contractual assignment to one person. But, if this assignment does not happen? Would not there be a great number of problems for the use of certain elements of a database? And, taking into account the different rights of authors and makers, is it legally appropriate that they both negotiate this?

It is undeniable that the creation of the *sui generis* right is justified because it is understood as a legal device for the cases in which a database lacks originality in its structure. However, the duplicity and triplicity of rights on a same work generates conflicts concerning their management. That is why, the practical complementarity of the protection of authors and makers is not clear at all.

To this it must be added that: since WIPO did not adopted the proposal for a treaty on the *sui generis* right for the protection of databases, what kind of international effectiveness can have this right when apart from the EU and the U.S.A., most national laws have not incorporated it?

2.3. The Legal-Technical Protection of Copyright in the Information Society (2001)

2.3.1. The Digital Issue within the Community

In 1989 the *Green Paper on Copyright and the challenge of technology* explained the problems derived from the private reproduction of audiovisual materials, focusing on phonograms and videograms, TV and radio broadcasting, and broadcasting by cable.

Through its analysis it was anticipated that the technical advances would soon allow to create other type of material "which shall also cover different types of information, possibly in combination with images and sound, digitally recorded in a certain type of medium,"[108] whose name eventually was multimedia work.

---

[108] Cf. COUNCIL *Green Paper on Copyright and the Challenge of Technology,* 99.

However, the *Green Paper* only made one direct reference to digital technology and focused on the consequences of the right of a user to make a private copy, since the NITs allowed fast and high-quality reproduction of works. Therefore, to protect the works it was suggested to sell technical devices able to stop indiscriminate reproduction. Its objective would be to obtain a certain balance between the rights of the author, the rights of the maker of the recording equipment and the rights of the lawful user. Among the most outstanding systems were *Copycode*, *Macrovision, Solocopy* and *Solocopy Plus*:

> The Copycode system, developed by the Technological Investigation Center of CBS Records, consisted of the codification of the sound recording so that said code would only be perceived by a technical device which, after detecting the code, would stop the recording which was being carried out; the Macrovision system, very similar to the Copycode system, would be devoted to control the unauthorized reproduction of video and television programs; the Solocopy system, created by the Technical Committee of the International Electrotechnical Commission, was based on the incorporation into the source work of a signal which would indicate to the recording device whether the work could be copied or not. This way it would be possible to record from an original to a copy, but not from copy to copy; the Solocopy Plus system, slightly different from the previous one, would be used to make the first copies from analog sources.[109]

But the comprehensive treatment of the digital and multimedia issue started in 1995 with the publication of the *Green Paper on Copyright and Related Rights in the Information Society*. As its title states, for the first time two concepts were merged together in a document whose implications were suggested by the EU since the beginning of the 1980s, and which required the creation of new categories to obtain a certain tuning between this right and the NITs.

During the consultation rounds held with the representatives of the sectors involved, it became evident that copyright had to evolve to adapt itself to the current technological changes. Specifically, the reproduction right, the right of communication to the public and the rental right which would have to be provided with new features.

Digital technology represented a qualitative and quantitative step forward from analog technology. With it the conventional point-to-multipoint communication

---

[109] *Id.*, 139-142.

conception – from a transmitter to several receivers indiscriminately – was abandoned, to give way to point-to-point dissemination – from a transmitter to only one receiver and with a tailor made content.

The key point was that copyright had always evolved within an analog scene, from where any necessary reflection had to be made for the purposes of its digital evolution. To be precise, the undergoing changes in the environment referred to:

i) A new concept of the word author, which no longer could be conceived as exclusively individual, apart from the fact that the owner of a work would frequently be a legal person.

ii) The modification of the criterion of originality in some works which were "adaptations or performances of pre-existing works."[110]

iii) A new concept of first publication, where creation and dissemination were carried out simultaneously through an electronic network.

iv) A new definition of the exclusivity margin that copyright would grant to the creators of digital works.

v) The redefinition of the concept of private use.

vi) The reconsideration of the functioning of the rights management systems, especially in the case of collecting societies.

vii) The commercialization of intangible works, that no longer reached the public through a physical medium.

In fact, it was necessary to "react and adapt, in a proportionate and coherent way, the current legal framework of the new environment."[111]

In the light of this purpose, the new *Green Paper* redefined the *status quaestionis*, underlining the lack of a specific stance of the Commission on the future normative. In fact, there was a widespread opinion on what matters required a special treatment:

a) The application of the legislation of the country of origin in transborder broadcastings, due to the variety of national laws which a global dissemination environment involves.

b) The consideration of the principle of exhaustion of rights in the provision of on-line digital services.

---

[110] *Id.*, 25.

[111] *Id.*, 28.

c) The reflection on the conception of the reproduction right and private copy in the new technological environment.

d) The definition of new legal categories – or the possibility of incorporating them into existing categories – for the digital acts of transmission, dissemination, communication to the public and broadcasting.

e) The reinforcement of the moral right of the author, given the new digital possibilities of modification and alteration of interactive creations.

f) The creation and deployment of technical systems which, while allowing the acquisition and management of rights through "one window," could be used to control the use of works and restrict their reproduction.

Although some of these problems had been partially dealt with in the Directive on the legal protection of databases, the lines to be follow were dealt with in greater detail in the communication *Follow-Up to the Green Paper on Copyrights and Related Rights in the Information Society* in late 1996. It contained the answers offered from different instances to the problems initially explained in the *Green Paper*:

There was consensus when it came to state the basic starting point: any adaptation of copyright to the new technological environment must be done through "coherence with the prevailing concepts and traditions"[112] and taking into account the forthcoming signing of the Protocol to the Berne Convention.

In short, some conclusions were reached on certain issues requiring a new legal framework; on others, the Commission would have to continue working.

The following are some of the decisions adopted:

a) The broadening of the reproduction right to cover certain acts of temporary or ephemeral reproduction.

b) The reduction of the legality offered until then to the private copy, which would only be kept in certain occasions, with the authorization of the right holder and in exchange for a fair remuneration.

c) The introduction of a right of communication to the public protecting on-demand transmissions. This right would be granted to the right holders of an exclusive right of digital reproduction, since on-demand transmission often required an act of reproduction in order to carry it out.

---

[112] *Id.*, 2.

d) The convergence of access control technical systems to works with rights management and acquisition systems.

e) The harmonization of the distribution right, and its exhaustion, regarding all work categories, since it only existed in relation with computer programs and databases. In any case, the rule of its non-exhaustion would be kept for on-line services.

The following are the issues that still were to be solved:

– Digital broadcasting and its different variants, whose development was still incipient. Therefore, it was necessary to wait to know its impact in the phonographic market to determine the need to adopt measures in relation with copyright.

– Digital transmissions across frontiers, in which the Commission wished to apply the legislation of the country of origin, such as had been established in the Directive on copyrights and rights related to copyright applicable in satellite broadcasting and cable retransmission of 1993.

"Art. 1.

[...]

b) The act of communication to the public by satellite occurs solely in the Member State where, under the control and responsibility of the broadcasting organization, the program-carrying signals are introduced into an uninterrupted chain of communication leading to the satellite and down towards the earth."[113]

However, the different sectors involved requested the Commission to confine itself to its advisory role and not to perform a harmonizing task, since they considered that this issue could be solved through contracts and the current International Law.

The definition of the rights and obligations for collecting societies, regarding collection systems, fee calculation, process of supervision and application of competition rules.

---

[113] Cf. COUNCIL Directive on the coordination of certain rules concerning copyright and related rights applicable to satellite broadcasting and cable retransmission (93/83/CEE), September 27, 1993, 248/19.

– The harmonization of moral rights, an issue which the Commission relegated to its longer term objectives.

2.3.2. The New Directive "Iter Legis"

Since the first proposal for a Directive in 1997, it is noticed that the Commission is determined to continue with the regulation and hierarchy lines of objectives pointed out in the *Green Paper* of 1995, and in its subsequent *Follow-up*. Said body submits the first text of the proposal for a Directive on the harmonization of certain aspects of copyright and related rights in the Information Society in April 1997, which was adopted on December 10, 1997.[114]

The Commission organized the content of the document in two clearly differentiated parts: one, containing the preliminary recitals, a summary of the problems requiring the attention of the Community and the definition of possible solutions. The other containing the description of articles completed with an explanation of the same.

The text emphasizes repeatedly the need to create a legal framework for the appropriate protection of creations, for the future promotion of investments in the NIT, making it clear that their development will mean the definite establishment of a competitive Information Society in the Community.

The economic impact of copyright and related rights on the audiovisual and digital area was obvious: the musical recording market value had increased in 1996 to almost 40,000 million dollars (EU 34%); in 1994 the sales volume of the first fifty companies of the audiovisual sector of the Community was worth 40,000 million ecus; and the growth of the databases sector amounted 27% between 1989 and 1994. Among the future prospects was the sale, for 2000, of 25 million digital videodisc players, "which offers to the content industry many opportunities when it comes to develop new markets for movies, music or multimedia."[115]

---

[114] About its content, cf. GÓMEZ SEGADE, "Propuesta de Directiva sobre determinados aspectos de los derechos de autor y los derechos afines en la Sociedad de la Información", en ROGEL coord., *Nuevas tecnologías y propiedad intelectual*, REUS and AISGE (Madrid 1999) 17-38, KELLEHER and MURRAY, *IT Law in the European Union*, Sweet & Maxwell (London 1999) 28-50 and DOHERTY and GRIFFITHS, "The Harmonization of European Union Copyright Law for the Digital Age," *European Intellectual Property Review*, no. 1, Sweet & Maxwell (London 2000) 17 and subsequent pages.

[115] *Id.*, 4-5.

Thus, according to what the *Green Paper* of 1995, and its *Follow-up* stated, "the proposal intends to keep the high level of protection of copyright which is traditional in Europe, establishing at the same time a fair balance between the rights and interests of the different right holder categories, and between the rights and interests of these and those of the users of the material protected." Therefore, a revolution regarding this right is not started, but rather the promotion of its evolution in the new digital environment.[116]

As for the interests of special concern, the Commission focused on the issues mentioned in the *Follow-up to the Green Paper*; that is: the reproduction right, the right of communication to the public – covering the on-demand transmission – the technological information and right management devices, and the distribution right – and the resulting exhaustion of rights.

> "(14) Whereas this Directive should define the scope of the acts covered by the reproduction right with regard to the different beneficiaries; whereas this should be done in conformity with the *acquis communautaire*; whereas a broad definition of these acts is needed to ensure legal certainty within the Internal Market.
>
> (15) Whereas this Directive should harmonize the right applicable to the communication to the public of works, where this has not yet been done by existing Community legislation;
>
> (16) Whereas the legal uncertainty regarding the nature and the level of protection of acts of on-demand transmission of copyright works and subject-matter protected by related rights over networks should be overcome by providing for harmonized protection at Community level; whereas it should provide all right holders recognized by the Directive with an exclusive right to make available to the public copyright works or any other subject-matter by way of interactive on-demand transmissions [...];
>
> [...]
>
> (18) Whereas copyright protection under this Directive includes the exclusive right to control distribution of the work incorporated in a tangible article; whereas the first sale in the Community of the original of a work or copies thereof by the right holder or with his consent exhausts the right to control resale of that object in the Community [...];

---

[116] *Id.*, 10.

(19) Whereas the question of exhaustion does not arise in the case of services and on-line services in particular;

[…]

(30) Whereas technological development will allow right holders to make use of technological measures designed to prevent and inhibit the infringement of any copyright, rights related to copyright or *sui generis* rights provided by law."[117]

In January 1997 the Commission transmits said proposal to the Parliament and the Council. From there, it was transmitted to the Economic and Social Committee that gave its favorable opinion on September 1998. On January 20, 1999, the Committee on Legal Affairs and Citizens's Rights debated the report drawn by R. Barzanti on its behalf and the Parliament gave its opinion on February 10, 1999 in favor of the proposal as amended and, after the introduction of the corresponding amendments, the Commission would publish the new proposal in May 1999.[118]

The Commission accepted in whole or in part 44 of 56 amendments presented to the Directive. Nevertheless, as the same document points out, not all the amendments proposed were of the same type, therefore it was simple to classify and to organize them.

a) As for substantive issues, the Commission accepted a number of parliamentary amendments regarding the lawful exploitation of a work without the consent of the author or right holder:

i) The distinction between private analog copying and private digital copying, linking the exercise of this exception in both cases to fair compensation.

ii) The introduction of a compensation for the right holders in most of the cases in which the Directive provides for a legal exception to the exclusive rights of the author.

iii) The new wording for the exception of reproduction relating to libraries, archives and other teaching, educational or cultural institutions for acts of reproduction (copies) made for archive or conservation purposes.

iv) The extension to all persons with disabilities of the exception previously reserved for visually-impaired or hearing impaired persons.

---

[117] *Id.*, 44-45 and 47.

     v)   The introduction of a new exception concerning parliamentary proceedings and reporting.[119]

b) As for formal issues, a series of suggestions were made on the terms used in the final text of the future Directive:

    i) The incorporation of the adjective "essential" to indicate that the act of reproduction, which must be authorized by the author, must be an integral and essential part of a technological process.

    ii) The introduction of a new exception for broadcasters relating to so-called ephemeral reproductions.

    iii) The introduction of an exception to the right of distribution for authorized acts of reproduction.

    iv) To explicitly forbid circumvention of the technical protection measures or any other acts performed to circumvent said measures.

    v) The setting-up of a permanent Contact Committee, in charge of solving the possible problems derived from the application of the Directive.[120]

c) Finally, the Commission did not accept, for reasons of substance, the following amendments:

    i) The introduction of a right to use certain works when this does not mean any financial damage for the author or right holder. Such right would be permitted by the law, or by the author or owner of the work.

    ii) The introduction of an exception in favor of broadcasters relating to the digital use of their archived productions, for which broadcasters would not need the authorization of the author or right holder.

    iii) The introduction of an exception for the analog use of certain works of the press.

---

[118] Cf. Council Proposal on the Harmonization of Certain Aspects of Copyright and Related Rights in the Information Society, COM (1999) 250 final, May 21, 1999, in (Brussels 1999) 11-13 and 15.

[119] *Id.,* 2-3.

[120] *Id.,* 3.

iv) The reiteration that the exceptions and limitations to the exclusive rights of authors do not prevent the use of technical protection measures.[121]

As a final result, the proposal for a Directive was a first substantive regulatory framework of copyright, in the line of the GATT Agreement of 1994, and the Protocol to the Berne Convention of 1996. However, it is not merely a repetition of some measures adopted in these texts, but it goes beyond proposing a series of principles that, virtually, establish a copyright system.

Then, the Council transmitted a detailed report on December 7, 1999; the report was sent to the Commission that completed its study on March 14, 2000. Examined in May by the Permanent Committee of the Representatives of Member States, it was adopted in May 2001.

2.3.3. Consolidation of the Community Distribution Right

The new Directive mentions, once again, the distribution right.

Its regulation is one of the most recurrent problems to date in the Community policy and the ECJ caselaw, since the exercise of this right relies very closely on the distinction made between goods and services.

As already noted early in this chapter, the ECJ had established in its case-law – *Polydor vs. Harlequin Record Shop*, case 270/80; *Tournier*, case 395/87; *Musik-vertrieb*, cases 55/80 and 57/80; EMI *Electrola vs. Patricia*, case 341/87 – two basic principles for the regulation of this right:

a) Its exhaustion with the first sale within the EU regarding the supply of articles, goods or tangible products; and its non-exhaustion regarding the provision of services, therefore each one of them shall be authorized individually.

b) Its non-application when the work is sold in a country outside the EU. Therefore, the right holder will be able to freely distribute his works, prohibiting the import of similar goods by members of the EU, from countries outside the EU.

In 1991 the Directive on the legal protection of computer programs had already sustained this double perspective, although without specifying the non-exhaustion of this right in the on-line distribution of software, which should be considered as services.

---

[121] *Id.*, 3-4.

"Art. 4.

[...]

> c) any form of distribution to the public, including the rental, of the original computer program or of copies thereof." The first sale in the Community of a copy of a program by the right holder or with his consent shall exhaust the distribution right within the Community of that copy, with the exception of the right to control further rental of the program or a copy thereof." [122]

In 1994 this idea which was demanded by the representatives of the sectors, involved in the provision of services of the Information Society during a hearing with the Commission, as it was stated in the *Green Paper* of 1995, and in its Follow-up of 1996. This document specially emphasizes that this right would not be exhausted when the distribution had been initially made outside the EU:

> "Thus, once copies of works have been put into circulation in one Member State, they may be distributed throughout the Single Market but if copies have been distributed only in non-EU countries, they may not be distributed within the EU without authorization." [123]

The answers to the *Green Paper* left little room for doubt about the position of the industry: the interested parties understood that the provision of services can be made an undefined number of times, so it was necessary to establish specifically the non-application of the principle of exhaustion of rights in the provision of on-line services.

That is why the proposal for a Directive of 1997, and its subsequent revision of 1999, included the creation of a Community distribution right, stating its non-exhaustion in the distribution of works in non-EU countries. Nevertheless, the final Directive (2001) did not include any reference to the provision of on-line services, whose importance is basic in the current trade traffic.

"Art. 4.

1. Member States shall provide for authors, in respect of the original of their

---

[122] Cf. COUNCIL Directive on Legal Protection of Computer Programs, 122/44.

[123] Cf. COUNCIL Follow-up to the Green Paper on Copyright and Related Rights in the Information Society, COM (96) 508 final, November 20, 1996, 18.

works or of copies thereof, the exclusive right to authorize or prohibit any form of distribution to the public by sale or otherwise.

2. The distribution right shall not be exhausted within the Community in respect of the original or copies of the work, except where the first sale or other transfer of ownership in the Community of that object is made by the right holder or with his consent."[124]

With the explicit incorporation of this right, the EU constitutes an exclusive geographical legislation zone characterized by its exhaustion with the first sale of the goods. This way, the EU applies one of the principles of the Protocol to the Berne Convention of 1996.

"Art. 6. Copyright Treaty.

1) Authors of literary and artistic works shall enjoy the exclusive right of authorizing the making available to the public of the original and copies of their works through sale or other transfer of ownership.

2) Nothing in this Treaty shall affect the freedom of Contracting Parties to determine the conditions, if any, under which the exhaustion of the right in paragraph (1) applies after the first sale or other transfer of ownership of the original or a copy of the work with the authorization of the author."[125]

But, is it possible to keep the traditional distinction between goods and services in the new digital environment? Can we correctly speak of intangibility in the case of on-line distribution?

Firstly, the intangibility of the original work to be distributed while providing services must be questioned; that is, does an on-screen display define the intangibility of a work? Or is it a quasi-tangible display?

In order to communicate any work it is necessary to save or store it in some type of tangible medium, as is the case with sound recordings or motion pictures. In the case of on-line services, the work is stored in a computer hard drive, in a diskette, or in an Internet server, which may be considered as the media in which the work is embodied.

---

[124]   Cf. EUROPEAN PARLIAMENT and COUNCIL Directive on the Harmonization of Certain Aspects of Copyright and Related Rights in the Information Society (2001).

[125]   Cf. OMPI ed., Tratado de la OMPI sobre Derecho de Autor, 4.

Therefore, although in an act of distribution there is no delivery of a tangible medium, the work will not be able to be transferred if it is not fixed in a tangible medium. Consequently, the fact of its intangibility must be relativized.

Secondly, the very intangibility of a work leads to the question of the possibility of protecting the provision of services by copyright.

As Lipszyc stated in 1993, while "in the Roman legal conception the fixation of a work in a material medium is not a prerequisite for its protection, save some exceptions," under Anglo-Saxon systems, "the requirement of fixation is still decisive."[126] Therefore, if the exercise of a right will depend on the tangibility or intangibility of the protected work, then the legal tradition of each legislative corpus and its current content should be taken into account.

Apart from this issue, the proposal for the Directive of 1999, already introduced a series of restrictions to the distribution right, similar to those imposed to the reproduction right:

> "3 bis. Where Member States may provide for exceptions to the reproduction right by virtue of paragraphs 2 or 3, they shall likewise provide for exceptions to the distribution right under Article 4, in so far as they are justified by the purpose of the permitted reproduction."[127]

2.3.4. Scope of the Reproduction Right in a Digital Environment

The *Green Paper* of 1995, had set out some of the problems of the evolution to digital technology, among which was the conversion of reproduction into an act available not only to professionals, but also to particular users. The digitization, which was starting in households in those days, contributed to increase the private reproduction of works due to a noticeable quality improvement of copies. In the field of analog technology, the reproduction made by individuals had been compensated with a fee for the media and recording devises used; but this method may disappear in a digital field where the use of technical devices to control the copies may restrict them.

In the *Follow-up of the Green Paper* the representatives of the sectors involved showed their particular perception of the arrival of the digital technology, which

---

[126] Cf. LIPSZYC, *op. cit.*, 42.

[127] Cf. COUNCIL Proposal for a Directive on the Harmonization of Certain Aspects of Copyright and Related Rights in the Information Society, COM (1999) 24.

they considered a threat to their interests and to the laws in force. However, they understood that this legal system could not be abolished abruptly, so it seemed that the payment of a fee would still be the most appropriate means to counteract its negative effects.

Nevertheless, this was not the only doubt raised by the interested parties. The exceptions to the reproduction right were in close connection with this problem, as well as the consideration of the lawful nature of the temporary or ephemeral reproduction. Should digitization, electronic reading and on-line loading be considered acts of reproduction? Was it reasonable to extend the scope of this right again?

Both the first proposal for a Directive, and the Directive of 1999, understand the right as do international agreements. This is the way the final text reflected it:

"Art. 2.

Member States shall provide for the exclusive right to authorize or prohibit direct or indirect, temporary or permanent reproduction by any means and in any form, in whole or in part:

a) for authors, of the original and copies of their works,

b) for performers, of fixations of their performances,

c) for phonogram producers, of their phonograms,

d) for the producers of the first fixations of films, in respect of the original and copies of their films, and

e) for broadcasting organizations, of fixations of their broadcasts, whether those broadcasts are transmitted by wire or over the air, including by cable or satellite."[128]

Until the proposal for the Directive and its outcome, the Community right had offered a reproduction right focused on computer programs, right holders of related or neighboring rights – performers, phonogram producers, film producers and broadcasting organizations – and databases; that is why the new proposal meant the definite establishment of this right in the Community principles of copyright, and at the same time an exhaustive intent to control all and singular possible ways to reproduce a work.

---

[128] Cf EUROPEAN PARLIAMENT and COUNCIL Directive on the Harmonization of Certain Aspects of Copyright and Related Rights in the Information Society (2001).

"The project of definition covers the direct or indirect, temporary or permanent reproduction by any means and in any form. The first element of the proposal concerns the terms 'direct' and 'indirect' reproduction. [...] This term implies the reproduction of a work or any other related material directly protected in the same or in any other medium. The term 'indirect' covers reproductions made by means of an intermediate stage, such as, for example, when an existing phonogram is recorded. This provision also aims to make it clear that the right is not affected by the distance existing between the place where an original work is located and the point where a copy of the same is made. The second element (temporary/permanent) aims to clarify the fact that in the network environment there can be many types of reproduction and all of them are acts of reproduction in the sense of this provision [...]".[129]

Logically, and based on the principles and doctrine of international protection, the future Directive imposes a number of exceptions and limits to this right, which is especially interesting when comparing the texts of 1997 and 1999 (italics), with the final Directive (underlined):

"Art. 5.

1. Temporary acts of reproduction referred to in Article 2, *such as transient and incidental acts of reproduction*, which are an integral and *essential* part of a technological process, *including those which facilitate effective functioning of transmission systems*, whose sole purpose is to enable use to be made of a work or other subject-matter, and which have no independent economic significance, shall be exempted from the right set out in Article 2.

1. Temporary acts of reproduction referred to in Article 2, which are transient or incidental and an integral and essential part of a technological process and whose sole purpose is to enable:

    a) a transmission in a network between third parties by an intermediary,

    b) a lawful use of a work or other subject-matter to be made, and which have no independent economic significance, shall be exempted from the reproduction right provided for in Article 2.

---

[129] Cf. EUROPEAN PARLIAMENT and COUNCIL Directive on the Harmonization of Certain Aspects of Copyright and Related Rights in the Information Society, COM (97) 27.

2. Member States may provide for exceptions or limitations to the reproduction right provided for in Article 2 in the following cases:

(a) in respect of reproductions on paper or any similar medium, *with the exception of musical works,* effected by the use of any kind of photographic technique or by some other process having similar effects, *provided that the right holders receive fair compensation;*

(b) in respect of reproductions on audio, visual or audio-visual *analog* recording media made by a natural person for private *and strictly personal* use and for non-commercial ends, on condition that the right holders receive fair compensation;

(b)bis, in respect of reproductions on audio, visual or audio-visual digital recording media made by a natural person for private and strictly personal use and for non-commercial ends, without prejudice to operational, reliable and effective technical means capable of protecting the interests of the right holders; for all digital private copying, however, fair compensation for all right holders must be provided;

(b) <u>in respect of reproductions on any medium made by a natural person for private use and for ends that are neither directly nor indirectly commercial, on condition that the right holders receive fair compensation which takes account of the application or non-application of technological measures referred to in Article 6 to the work or subject-matter concerned.</u>

(c) in respect of specific acts of reproduction made *for archiving or conservation purposes by establishments which are not* for direct or indirect economic or commercial advantage, *such as, in particular libraries and archives and other teaching, educational or cultural establishments;* <u>(this last part is not included in the final text of 2001).</u>

(d) *in respect of ephemeral fixations made by broadcasting organizations by means of their own facilities and for their own broadcasts;* <u>the preservation of these recordings in official archives may, on the grounds of their exceptional documentary character, be permitted.</u>

3. Member States may provide for limitations to the rights referred to in Articles 2 and 3 in the following cases:

(a) use for the sole purpose of illustration for teaching or scientific research, as long as the source is indicated and to the extent justified by the non-commercial purpose to be achieved, <u>unless this turns out to be impossi-</u>

ble, *on condition that the right holders receive fair compensation*; (this last line is not included in the text of 2001).

(b) *uses for the benefit of* visually-*impaired* and hearing-*impaired persons*, which are directly related to the disability and of a non-commercial nature and to the extent required by the specific disability;

(c) use of excerpts in connection with the reporting of current events, as long as the source and, *if possible, the author's name*, is indicated, and to the extent justified by the informatory purpose *and the objective of illustrating the event concerned*;

(c) reproduction by the press, communication to the public or making available of published articles on current economic, political or religious topics or of broadcast works or other subject-matter of the same character, in cases where such use is not expressly reserved, and as long as the source, including the author's name, is indicated, or use of works or other subject-matter in connection with the reporting of current events, to the extent justified by the informatory purpose and as long as the source, including the author's name, is indicated, unless this turns out to be impossible.

(d) quotations for purposes such as criticism or review, provided that they relate to a work or other subject-matter which has already been lawfully made available to the public, that the source *and, if possible, the author's name is indicated*, and that their use is in accordance with fair practice, and to the extent required by the specific purpose;

(e) use for the purposes of public security or *to ensure* the proper performance *or reporting* of an administrative, *parliamentary* or judicial procedure.

3 bis. Where Member States may provide for exceptions to the reproduction right by virtue of paragraphs 2 or 3, they shall likewise provide for exceptions to the distribution right under Article 4, in so far as they are justified by the purpose of the permitted reproduction."

4. The exceptions and limitations provided for in paragraphs 1, 2 and 3 shall only be applied in certain special cases and shall not be interpreted in such a way as to allow their application to be used in a manner which unreasonably

prejudices the right holders' legitimate interests or conflicts with the normal exploitation of their works or other subject-matter."[130]

In this regard, and after the adoption of a first agreement of the Council on the final text, on June 8, 2000, it was pointed out that the exhaustive enumeration of exceptions and limitations to the reproduction right and the right of communication to the public, would be optional. However, it was put straight that Member States could not incorporate new exceptions or limitations apart from the ones provided by the future Directive.

A clause would also be included permitting Member States certain exceptions on analog works which, on the other hand, could not be imposed on digital works and means.

Thus, the amendments of 1999 introduced the following exceptions to restricted acts:

a) Temporary copying, as may happen with computer programs, are excepted, as long as they are transient, incidental and essential for the technological process and to enable the use to be made of a protected work.

b) Reproductions on paper or any similar medium, provided that the right holders receive fair compensation. Such compensation, not included in the proposal of 1997, will mean a greater freedom in the acts of reprography, until then always sanctioned by national laws and international treaties.

Simultaneously, and thanks to the text of 1999, musical works in published form are not included in this provision.

c) The reproduction made by a natural person for private and strictly personal use and for non-commercial ends, on condition that the right holders receive fair compensation is another exception.

---

[130] Cf. COUNCIL Proposal for a Directive on the Harmonization of Certain Aspects of Copyright and Related Rights in the Information Society, COM (99) 23-25, European Parliament and Council Directive on the Harmonization of Certain Aspects of Copyright and Related Rights in the Information Society (2001) and COMMISSION, Commission welcomes Council agreement on a Directive on copyright in the Information Society, http://europa.eu.int/comm/internal_market/en/intprop/intprop/601.htm (Brussels 2000).

"Digital technology enables consumers, in principle, to make fast and multiple private copies of master quality. It is, however, still largely unknown whether digital private copying will be a widespread activity of consumers or not. It is expected that digital technology may allow the effective control of private copying and the replacement of levy schemes by individual licensing solutions that are under development (in the context of "electronic copyright management"), at least in the on-line environment. This may lead some Member States to abolish private copy exceptions for digital copying, as has already been done by one Member State [...]".[131]

Thus, digital copying will share the same legal conditions with analog copying, but with the disadvantage of technical systems limiting the digital private copying.

d) Acts of reproduction made for archiving or conservation purposes that are not for economic or commercial advantage, for the conservation of the cultural heritage of the Community.

e) Ephemeral fixations made by broadcasting organizations for their own broadcasts.

But, in spite of everything, the final text also added the following exceptions:

i) Political speeches and lectures, for reporting purposes and as long as the source is indicated.

ii) When a work is used during a religious or official celebration.

iii) When architecture or sculpture works are made to be located in open spaces.

iv) When the use of a work is made to advertise it.

v) When the use is made for caricature, parody or pastiche purposes.

vi) When it is used for the demonstration or repair of equipment.

vii) When a work of art is copied as a drawing for its eventual reconstruction.

---

[131] Cf. European Parliament and Council Proposal for a Directive on the Harmonization of Certain Aspects of Copyright and Related Rights in the Information Society, COM (97) 628 final, December 10, 1997, 34.

viii) When it is about other uses, not so important, according to national laws, regarding analog uses not affecting trade.[132]

2.3.5. Introduction of the Right of Making Available to the Public

Apart from the consolidation of the distribution right and the extension of the reproduction right, the proposal for a Directive foresees the adoption of an identical measure to the one established in the Protocol to the Berne Convention for the protection of digital dissemination. The introduction of the right of making available to the public, as a specific right of communication to the public.

It was the *Green Paper* of 1995, which first stated some interest in the protection of copyright in the digital dissemination or transmission. To find a possible solution, the *Book* proposed an examination of the main legal concepts applicable, among which there were: the right of communication to the public, the broadcasting right, the dissemination right and the rental right – which was aimed to be applied to on-demand transmissions, based on the idea of the transient nature of the work enjoyed.

However, in the *Follow-up to the Green Paper* the adoption of these approaches was discarded and instead the option of a general right of communication to the public was supported, which was considered a global but effective approach. In fact, with the Community consolidation of the right of communication to the public, and the creation of a specific right for interactive digital communication – the right to make available to the public – the adaptation of other concepts of copyright was postponed, while earlier they had been considered to protect various kinds of digital transmission.

> The *Green Paper* of 1995, referred to the possible application to the digital and multimedia environment of the public transmission and broadcasting categories, as well as to the creation of a new digital dissemination or transmission right.
>
> a) The WIPO Glossary defines communication to the public as the act of "Making a work, performance, phonogram or broadcast perceptible in any appropriate manner to persons in general, that is, not restricted to specific individuals belonging to a private group. This notion is broader than publication and also covers, among others, forms of use such as

---

132 Cf. European Parliament and Council Directive on the Harmonization of Certain Aspects of Copyright and Related Rights in the Information Society (2001).

public performance, broadcasting, communication to the public by wire, or direct communication to the public of the reception of a broadcast."

However, Community Law had never managed to give a harmonized definition of this concept, applicable in all Member States, in which the exceptions to this right were varied.

b) The extent of the digital dissemination or transmission right was justified from two different points of view: as a right covering any one point to one point and one point to many transmissions; and also as a term exclusively confined to the latter – which would exclude digital broadcasting.

c) Concerning the application of the broadcasting right and its extension to digital means, it was determined that this right, by definition, could be adapted to the new technological environment, although it could not cover all the new means of communication, leaving point-to-point transmissions out of its protection, that is, on-demand transmissions.[133]

Considering the problems posed by these types of transmission, the Commission focused on the classification of interactive on-demand transmissions which, due to their features, was problematic: on the one hand, their classification as broadcasting was not possible due to their unpredictable nature and because it was an individual communication; on the other hand, it was neither possible to classify them as a private communication, since one of the parties involved is always a broadcasting organization.

Interested parties were in favor of adapting an already existing right to new technologies, provided that its profile would be neutral enough to easily accept the controversial issue of interactive communication. Therefore, eventually the Paper opted for the right of communication to the public: because its content is so wide that it can cover different concepts such as performance, public performance or distribution by cable, to quote but a few examples. But, does this right not require an act of communication for an indeterminate public? Is this not the real nature of public communication?[134] How do then on-demand transmissions fit in?

---

[133] Cf. COUNCIL Green Paper on Copyright and Related Rights in the Information Society, COM (95) 382 final, 49-65 and COUNCIL Follow-up to the Green Paper on Copyright and Related Rights in the Information Society, COM (96) 508 final, November 20, 1996, 20-22.

[134] Cf. LIPSZYC, *op. cit.*, 183.

In the Community proposal, the introduction of the right of making available to the public is made as a specification of the right of communication to the public, such as it had been carried out in the Protocol to the Berne Convention of 1996. Actually, it could not have been done otherwise, since it was the Delegation of the Community that defended in the WIPO the use of this term for interactive communication over a network.

The proposal for the Directive of 1997, uses for the first time this term to emphasize, "[...] as was underlined during the WIPO Diplomatic Conference",[135] that it is essential to give to the public the opportunity to access a work; that is, "to offer a work in a place of public access, preceding the stage of its real on-line transmission."[136] Therefore, the Community legislative harmonization, was achieved together with the coherence and coincidence with the international treaty system:

"Art. 3.

1. Member States shall provide authors with the exclusive right to authorize or prohibit any communication to the public of originals and copies of their works, by wire or wireless means, including the making available to the public of their works in such a way that members of the public may access them from a place and at a time individually chosen by them.

2. Member States shall provide for the exclusive right to authorize or prohibit the making available to the public, by wire or wireless means, in such a way that members of the public may access them from a place and at a time individually chosen by them:

a) for performers, of fixations of their performances,

b) for phonogram producers, of their phonograms,

c) for the producers of the first fixations of films, in respect of the original and copies of their films, and

d) for broadcasting organizations, of fixations of their broadcasts, whether those broadcasts are transmitted by wire or over the air, including by cable or satellite.

---

[135] Cf. EUROPEAN PARLIAMENT and COUNCIL Proposal for a Directive on the Harmonization of Certain Aspects of Copyright and Related Rights in the Information Society, COM (97), 29.

[136] *Id.*

3. The rights referred to in paragraphs 1 and 2 shall not be exhausted by any act of communication to the public of a work and other subject-matter as set out in paragraph 2, including their being made available to the public.

4. The mere provision of physical facilities for enabling or making a communication does not in itself amount to an act of communication to the public within the meaning of this Article."[137]

What emerges from the text of the final proposal of 1999 is:

a) The creation at Community level of a general and broad right of communication to the public, capable of protecting any act of communication to the public, regardless the medium used. This way the legal protection of the future invention of new communication media is ensured.

b) The creation at Community level of a specific right of making available to the public, closely connected to the right of communication to the public, covering the possibility that members of the public may access a work from a place and at a time individually chosen by them and by any means – coaxial cable, optical fiber, radio waves, satellite or digital technology.

However, considering the terms of the proposal, it is necessary to explain the sense given to this new right. In the first place, the making available to the public refers more to the act of offering a work than to its transmission. Therefore, is there a real protection for this kind of transmission? Secondly, is the right of making available to the public so extensive as to cover on-demand, pay-per-view or public communication through Internet?

According to a literal interpretation of the proposal – and as indicated in Chapter III – the right of making available to the public seems to be aimed to protect the mere offer of access to a given work and not to protect its communication to the user. This way a creation saved or stored in computer hardware would be protected, which does not imply the protection of its later dissemination or transmission. Thus, this right would lack the features of the communication to the public, closely resembling an act of on-line distribution. So much so that to offer to the public a work does not imply its communication, but rather the possibility that this

---

[137] Cf. EUROPEAN PARLIAMENT and COUNCIL Proposal for a Directive on the Harmonization of Certain Aspects of Copyright and Related Rights in the Information Society, COM (1999), 22.

may happen, as the act of distribution does not involve an assured sale, but the possibility that this may take place.

In fact, according to the proposal definition of the act of distribution, it is possible to include this way of offering a work to the public:

"Art. 4.

1. Member States shall provide authors, in respect of the original of their works or of copies thereof, with the exclusive right to any form of distribution to the public by sale or otherwise."[138]

That is why, the right of making available to the public should be given a broader interpretation not only to include the act of offering a specific creation, but also its later communication.

On the other hand, the Commission insisted on excluding from this right such expressions as "pay-TV or pay-per-view, since the requirement of the 'individual choice' does not cover the so-called almost-on-demand-video, in which the offer of a non-interactive program is broadcast several times, simultaneously, beginning within short intervals on different channels."[139]

Finally, the adopted Directive stated the following:

"Art. 3.

1. Member States shall provide authors with the exclusive right to authorize or prohibit any communication to the public of originals and copies of their works, by wire or wireless means, including the making available to the public of their works in such a way that members of the public may access them from a place and at a time individually chosen by them.

2. Member States shall provide for the exclusive right to authorize or prohibit the making available to the public, by wire or wireless means, in such a way that members of the public may access them from a place and at a time individually chosen by them:

   a) for performers, of fixations of their performances;

   b) for phonogram producers, of their phonograms;

---

[138] Cf. EUROPEAN PARLIAMENT and COUNCIL Proposal for a Directive on the Harmonization of Certain Aspects of Copyright and Related Rights in the Information Society, COM (97), 50-51.

[139] *Id.*, 28-29.

c) for the producers of the first fixations of films, in respect of the original and copies of their films;

d) for broadcasting organizations, of fixations of their broadcasts, whether those broadcasts are transmitted by wire or over the air, including by cable or satellite."

3. The rights referred to in paragraphs 1 and 2 shall not be exhausted by an act of communication to the public of a work and other subject-matter as set out in paragraph 2, including their being made available to the public."[140]

However, the right of communication to the public is limited by certain exceptions, which may also be applied to the making available to the public, whose content is virtually similar to that of the principles established in the Berne Convention and supported by the doctrine, although the EU offers a broadened view of some of these exceptions and limits. In short, these are the same limitations imposed to the rights of reproduction and distribution, logically, whenever they are applicable.

Nevertheless, according to the proposal, these exceptions must always be interpreted in favor of the author or right holder, so that their application may be limited according to the case. In any case, their exceptional use shall not be detrimental to the normal exploitation of the work:

"4. The exceptions and limitations provided for in paragraphs 1, 2 and 3 shall only be applied in certain special cases and shall not be interpreted in such a way as to allow their application to be used in a manner which unreasonably prejudices the right holders' legitimate interests or conflicts with the normal exploitation of their works or other subject-matter."[141]

2.3.6. The Legal Promotion of the Protection of Electronic Copyright Management

Apart from the consolidation and creation of new rights in the Community legal framework of copyright, the Directive presents a realistic and practical approach of their protection by supporting the effectiveness of technical protection systems. Obviously, while digital technology prompted the need to "adjust" copyright to

---

[140] EUROPEAN PARLIAMENT and COUNCIL Directive on the Harmonization of Certain Aspects of Copyright and Related Rights in the Information Society (2001).

[141] *Id.*, 23-25.

new works and new ways of transmission, it is also true that it facilitates a better protection of creations.

In 1996 the Protocol to the Berne Convention recognized the value of these technical devices, encouraging signatory countries to condemn *de jure* their violation. A year before, the *Green Paper* had pointed out its relevance to attain two objectives: a better management in the acquisition of rights and a more effective control over identification and copy of works.

The first one was not considered by the Directive. Its study is limited to the considerations made in the *Green Paper* and, later, in its *Follow-up*; the second objective, on the other hand, is indeed one of the basic points of the new text.

In 1995 the *Green Paper* raised the possibility to identify digital works through the creation of a code, similar to the one used in the publishing – the ISBN – or in the record industry – the ISRC. This way, works would carry an electronic device which would allow invoicing of fees due to right holders when a specific work was incorporated into a new creation. The document referred specifically to two systems studied at that time within the Community project: Copyright in Transmitted Electronic Documents (CITED).

But, as it set out in the *Green Paper* of 1995, the issue of copyright management has always been characterized by the multiform nature of these rights and by their practice as follows: the direct granting of licenses by the first right holder – although he is not always their manager –the contractual assignment, before making a work; and the collective management, mainly used when right holders are granted compulsory licenses, or when they only have a right to remuneration.

Multimedia works management is more difficult in the Information Society, since their creators wish to use pre-existing works. For this, they should obtain the authorization of the right holder – if their term of protection has not expired – as well as to pay the costs derived from an expensive multiple negotiation. However, the Commission is against the use of this issue as an obstacle to developing a multimedia industry. Moreover, it recognizes that digitization may help to obtain a better work management, facilitating its identification and control by means of technical devices which would compel traditional rights managers to handle new duties.

Centralized schemes such as one-stop shops are proposed, which would allow users and creators to obtain more easily the information required for the legitimate use of works, allowing the private negotiation between the right holder and the multimedia creator.[142]

---

[142] Cf. COUNCIL Green Paper. Copyright and Related Rights in the Information Society, COM

Finally, the systems mentioned are:

a) *Cyphertech*, a digital tattooing system used to incorporate a digital distinguishing mark into each work which any receiver or recorder device can receive and decode. This will allow the determination of the period of time for which the work or other protected matter has been used, the features used and copyrights involved in such acts.

b) The Serial Copyright Management System (SCMS), which prevents a second digital copy from being made privately from the first copy. Its use would reduce the risks faced by copyright holders resulting from the acts of private users.

But the *Green Paper* barely offered a view on the possibilities presented by the technology of the moment. In the *Follow-up* of 1996 the wishes of the members of interested circles were translated into possible actions. For them, it was not just a question of requesting the manufacture of such devices, but rather that the Community laws regulate their different uses. It was requested, specifically, the adoption of legal measures aimed at punishing any type of violation of these systems. In short, the protection of the integrity of the devices would become a legal objective due to the existence and application of certain techniques that allowed "avoiding, evading, removing, deactivating or circumventing copyright protection systems."[143]

The proposal of 1997 would expressly state that technical identification systems are the most effective way to protect copyrights. This approach does not only seek the harmonization between the laws of the Member States, but also the adjustment between Community Law and treaties of the Protocol to the Berne Convention, whose content prohibited the circumvention of these systems and the destruction of the electronic data regarding a work and its author.

> "(30) Whereas technological development will allow right holders to make use of technological measures designed to prevent and inhibit the infringement of any copyright, rights related to copyright or *sui generis* rights provided by law; whereas the danger, however, exists that illegal activities might be carried out in order to enable or facilitate the circumvention of the technical

---

(95) 382 final, 69-79 and COUNCIL Follow-up to the Green Paper on Copyright and Related Rights in the Information Society, COM (96) 508 final, November 20, 1996, 24-27.

[143] *Id.*, 16.

protection provided by these measures; whereas, in order to avoid fragmented legal approaches that could potentially hinder the functioning of the Internal Market, there is a need to provide for harmonized legal protection against any activity enabling or facilitating the circumvention *without authority, whether granted by the right holders or conferred by law*, of such measures."[144]

"Art. 6.

1. Member States shall provide adequate legal protection against any activities, including the manufacture or distribution of devices or the performance of services, which have only limited commercially significant purpose or use other than circumvention, and which the person concerned carries out in the knowledge, or with reasonable grounds to know, that they will enable or facilitate without authority the circumvention of any effective technological measures designed to protect any copyright or any rights related to copyright as provided by law or the sui generis right provided for in Chapter III of European Parliament and Council Directive 96/9/EC (6).

2. The expression "technological measures," as used in this Article, means any technology, device or component that, in the normal course of its operation, is designed to prevent or inhibit the infringement of any copyright or any right related to copyright as provided by law or the *sui generis* right provided for in Chapter III of European Parliament and Council Directive 96/9/EC. Technological measures shall be deemed "effective" where the access to or use of a protected work or other subject-matter is controlled through application of an access code or any other type of protection process which achieves the protection objective in an operational and reliable manner with the authority of the right holders. Such measures may include decryption, descrambling or other transformation of the work or other subject-matter."[145]

The EU urges Member States to pass laws against the manufacture and distribution of systems used to infringe technical protection devices. At the same time, a defining standard of the effectiveness of such devices is established, based on the application by the user of a process or code to access the work wanted.

---

[144] *Id.*, 18.

[145] Cf. EUROPEAN PARLIAMENT and COUNCIL Proposal for a Directive on the Harmonization of Certain Aspects of Copyright and Related Rights in the Information Society, COM (97), 52.

Nevertheless, the proposal of 1999 gives a different wording to this article in order to facilitate its better understanding:

"Art. 6.

1. Member States shall provide adequate legal protection *against the circumvention without authority of any effective technological measures designed to protect any copyright or any rights related to copyright as provided by law or the* sui generis *right provided for in Chapter III of European Parliament and Council Directive 96/9/EC, which the person concerned carries out in the knowledge, or with reasonable grounds to know that he or she pursues that objective.*

2. Member States shall provide adequate legal protection against any activities, including the manufacture or distribution of devices, products or components or the provision of services, carried out without authority, which:

   a) are promoted, advertised or marketed for the purpose of circumvention of, or

   b) have only a limited commercially significant purpose or use other than to circumvent, or

   c) are primarily designed, produced, adapted or performed for the purpose of enabling or facilitating the circumvention of,

any effective technological measures designed to protect any copyright or any right related to copyright as provided by law or the *sui generis* right provided for in Chapter III of European Parliament and Council Directive 96/9/EC.

3. The expression "technological measures", as used in this Article, means any technology, device or component that, in the normal course of its operation, is designed to prevent or inhibit the infringement of any copyright or any right related to copyright as provided by law or the sui generis right provided for in Chapter III of Directive 96/9/EC.

Technological measures shall be deemed 'effective' where the access to or use of a protected work or other subject-matter is controlled through application of an access code or any other type of protection process which achieves the protection objective in an operational and reliable manner with the authority of the right holders. These measures may include decryption, descrambling or other transformation of the work or other subject-matter."[146]

---

[146] *Id.,* 24-25.

The revision allows to carefully detail the different activities involved in the manufacturing and distribution process of the infringing technical devices. This allows getting over the moderation of WIPO treaties, whose content is virtually similar regarding the alteration and/or removal of the electronic information present in digital creations.

"Art. 7. Proposal for a Directive of 1999.

1. Member States shall provide for adequate legal protection against any person performing without authority any of the following acts:

   (a) the removal or alteration of any electronic rights-management information;

   (b) the distribution, importation for distribution, broadcasting, communication or making available to the public, of copies of works or other subject-matter protected under this Directive or under Chapter III of Directive 96/9/EC from which electronic rights-management information has been removed or altered without authority, if such person knows, or has reasonable grounds to know, that by so doing he is inducing, enabling or facilitating an infringement of any copyright or any rights related to copyright as provided by law, or of the *sui generis* right provided for in Chapter III of Directive 96/9/EC.

2. The expression 'rights-management information,' as used in this Article, means any information provided by right holders which identifies the work or other subject-matter referred to in this Directive or covered by the *sui generis* right provided for in Chapter III of Directive 96/9/EC, the author or any other right holder, or information about the terms and conditions of use of the work or other subject-matter, and any numbers or codes that represent such information.

   The first subparagraph shall apply when any of these items of information are associated with a copy of, or appear in connection with the communication to the public of, a work or other subject-matter referred to in this Directive or covered by the *sui generis* right provided for in Chapter III of Directive 96/9/EC."[147]

---

[147] *Id.*, 53.

In this regard, and only since two years ago, within the "Info 2000" program, ten Community projects are being developed related to copyright management and protection systems:

a) *Indecs*, designed to obtain interoperability between different identification methods, such as CIS, ISRC, ISBN or ISSN.

b) *Efris*, focused on the public presentation of books to make them easily accessible.

c) *TV Files*, intended to create a file containing all European audiovisual works.

d) *Prisam*, intended to become a One-stop Shop for the multimedia works market.

e) *Ors*, with a similar purpose, although focused on the use of pre-existing works by creators of multimedia software.

f) *Bona Fide*, similar to the *Prisam* project.

g) b© (before copyright), office in charge of coordinating the activities of multimedia producers at the beginning of each project.

h) *Compas*, devoted to provide information on the use of multimedia works in the teaching and educational area.

i) RCRTIDW, focused on the management of radio, television and movie public archives, in minority languages areas.

j) *Verdi*, a project focused on the connection of rights management systems from several Member States.[148]

As for the final text of May 2001, there are only a few differences regarding the wording given to the proposal of 1999, in which it adds, however, a paragraph 4, within Article 6, emphasizing again the exceptions and limitations to copyright:

"Art. 6.

4. […] in the absence of voluntary measures taken by right holders, including agreements between right holders and other parties concerned, Member States shall take appropriate measures to ensure that right holders make available to the beneficiary of an exception or limitation provided for in national law in accordance with Article 5(2)(a), (2)(c), (2)(d), (2)(e), (3)(a), (3)(b) or (3)(e)

---

[148] Cf. SCHIPPAN, "Purchase and Licensing of Digital Rights: The Verdi Project and the Clearing of Multimedia Rights in Europe", *European Intellectual Property Review*, no. 1, Sweet & Maxwell (London 2000) 24-29.

the means of benefiting from that exception or limitation, to the extent necessary to benefit from that exception or limitation […]".[149]

2.3.7. Other Contents of Interest

Finally, the proposal for the Directive focused on three other important issues:

a) The delegation given to the Member States to establish the appropriate sanction
and remedy system in respect of the rights set out in the proposal. The sanctions
provided for shall be effective and dissuasive:

"Art. 8.

1. Member States shall provide appropriate sanctions and remedies in respect
of infringements of the rights and obligations set out in this Directive and
shall take all the measures necessary to ensure that those sanctions and remedies are applied. The sanctions thus provided for shall be effective, proportionate and dissuasive.

2. Each Member State shall take the measures necessary to ensure that right
holders whose interests are affected by an infringing activity carried out on its
territory can bring an action for damages and/or apply for an injunction and,
where appropriate, for the seizure of infringing material as well as of devices,
products or components referred to in Article 6(2)."[150]

b) The creation of a Contact Committee, informative in nature, whose mission will
be to monitor all the issues related to copyright, as well as to help Member States
to apply the provisions of the Directive:

"Art. 12.

*A contact committee is hereby established. It shall be composed of repre-
sentatives of the competent authorities of the Member States. It shall be chaired
by a representative of the Commission and shall meet either on the initiative
of the chairman or at the request of the delegation of a Member State.*"[151]

---

[149] EUROPEAN PARLIAMENT and COUNCIL Directive on the Harmonization of Certain Aspects of Copyright and Related Rights in the Information Society (2001).

[150] *Id.*

[151] *Id.*

The duties of the committee shall be as follows: to examine the impact of this Directive on the functioning of the internal market, and to highlight any difficulties to organize consultations on all questions deriving from the application of this Directive; to facilitate the exchange of information on relevant developments in legislation and case-law, as well as relevant economic, social, cultural and technological developments to act as a forum for the assessment of the digital market in works and other items.

c) Finally, the setting of a deadline for Member States to bring into force the laws, regulations and administrative provisions necessary to comply with this Directive which is January 22, 2002. However, it must be taken into account that this provision shall not affect contracts and acts of exploitation made before the entry into force of the Directive, although it may affect contracts that will still be in effect as of the fifth year following its entry into force.

Bibliography[1]

Reference Books

AA VV, *Colloque mondial sur l'arbitrage des litiges de propriètè intellectuelle*, OMPI (Geneve 1994)

AA VV, *L'audivisuel et le GATT. Actes des 7èmes journées d'actualité du Droit de l'Audiovisuel*, Presse Universitaires de France (Paris 1995)

ABBOT, COTTIER y GURRY, *The international intellectual property system: commentary and materials*, 2ª parte, Kluwer Law International (Then Hague 1999)

ABRISQUETA, *La construcción de Europa. Antecedentes, actualidad y futuro de la Unión Europea*, Colex (Madrid 1995)

AGENCE DE L'INFORMATIQUE ed., *Le droit criminel face aux technologies nouvelles de la communication. Actes du VIII Congrés de l'Association Française de Droit Pénal* (Paris 1986)

ALABAU, *La Unión Europea y su política de telecomunicaciones. En el camino hacia la sociedad de la información*, Fundación Airtel Móvil (Madrid 1998)

ALPISTE, BRIGOS y MONGUET, *Aplicaciones multimedia: presente y futuro*, Ediciones Técnicas Rede (Barcelona 1993)

AMBROSINI, *Derecho de autor*, tesina, *pro manuscripto*, Facultad de Comunicación, Universidad de Navarra (Pamplona 1983)

ANDERMAN, *EC competition law and intellectual property rights. The regulation of innovation*, Clarendon Press (Oxford 1998)

AÑÓN, *Derechos Humanos. Textos y casos prácticos*, Tirant lo Blanch (Valencia 1996)

---

[1] All the books and text contained in this bibliography are quoted in the original language in which they were employed for the development of this work.

ARMAÑANZAS, DÍAZ NOCI y MESO, *El periodismo electrónico. Información y servicios multimedia en la era del ciberespacio*, Ariel Comunicación (Barcelona 1996)

ARROYO, *200 años de informática*, Espasa-Calpe (Madrid 1991)

ASSERAF-OLIVIER y BARBRY, *Le droit multimédia*, Presses Universitaires de France (Paris 1996)

AVRIN, *Scribes, script and books. The book arts from antiquity to the renaissance*, American Library Association (Chicago 1991)

AZURMENDI, *El derecho a la propia imagen. Su identidad y aproximación al derecho a la informacion*, 2ª edición, Fundación Manuel Buendía y Universidad Iberoamericana (Mexico 1998)

BAERT, THEUNISSEN y VERGULT, *Digital audio and compact disc technology*, 2ª ed., Reed International Books (United Kingdom 1992)

BAINBRIDGE, *Intellectual property law. Cases and materials*, Pitman Publishing (Glasgow 1995)

BAINBRIDGE, *Software copyright law*, Butterworths (London 1997)

BEIER, SCHRICKER y FIKENTSCHER, *German industrial property, copyright and antitrust laws*, VCH (Munich 1996)

BENNETT, *English books & readers. 1475 to 1557. Being a study in the history of book trade from Caxton to the incorporation of the Stationers' Company*, 2ª ed., Cambridge University Press (Cambridge 1970)

BENSOUSSAN, *Le multimedia et le droit. Off line, on line, Internet*, Hermes (Paris 1996)

BERENBOOM, *Le droit d'Auteur*, Maison Larcier (Brussels 1984)

BERGÉ, *La protection internationale et communautaire du droit d'auteur. Essai d'une anlyse conflictuelle*, LGDJ (Paris 1996)

BETTIG, *Copyrighting culture*, Westview Press (United States 1996)

BISHOP, *Conceptos de informática*, Anaya Multimedia (Madrid 1989)

BOGSCH, *The law of copyright under the Universal Convention*, RR. Bowker (New York 1964)

BONET, *El derecho a la información en el Convenio Europeo de Derechos Humanos*, PPU (Barcelona 1994)

BORDERÍA, LAGUNA y MARTÍNEZ, *Historia de la comunicación social. Voces, registros y conciencias*, Síntesis (Madrid 1996)

BOSTWORTH, *Intellectual property rights*, Pergamon Press (London 1986)

BROOKHART, LEACH y TOBOR eds., *Current international legal aspects of licensing and intellectual property*, American Bar Association (United States 1980)

BRINSON y RADCLIFFE, *Multimedia Law Handbook*, Ladera Press (United States 1994)

BROWN, *Poets, patrons and printers. Crisis of authority in late medieval France*, Cornell University Press (United States 1995)

BUGBEE, *Genesis of American Patent and Copyright Law*, Public Affairs Press (Washington 1967)

CALABI, *Studi sulla società romana. Il lavoro artistico*, Istituto Editoriale Cisalpino (Milano-Varese 1958)

CAMPBELL y COTTER eds., *International intellectual property law. European jurisdictions*, John Wiley & Sons (United Kingdom 1995)

CARR y WILLIAMS eds., *Computers and law*, Intellect Books (Oxford 1994)

CARREAU, *Mérite et droit d'auteur*, Librairie General de Droit et Jurisprudence (France 1981)

CAUGHIE ed., *Theories of Authorship*, (United Kingdom 1981)

COALITION FOR NETWORKED INFORMATION ed., *Technological strategies for protecting intellectual property in the networked multimedia environment* (Annapolis 1994)

COLOMBET, *Propriété littéraire et artistique et droits voisins*, Dalloz (Paris 1994)

COLOMBET, *Grandes principios del derecho de autor y los derechos conexos en el mundo. Estudio de derecho comparado*, 3ª edición, UNESCO/CINDOC (Madrid 1997)

COLOMER, *El pensamiento alemán de Kant a Heidegger. Tomo I: la filosofía trascendental: Kant*, Herder (Barcelona 1986)

CONSEJO DE EUROPA, *La lucha contra la piratería sonora y audiovisual. Vademécum*, EGEDA y Consejo de Europa (Spain 1997)

CORNISH, *Piracy and counterfeiting of industrial property and copyright*, The Common Law Institute of Intellectual Property (London 1983)

CORREA, *Acuerdo TRIPs. Régimen internacional de la propiedad intelectual*, Ediciones Ciudad Argentina (Buenos Aires 1996)

COTTON y OLIVER, *The cyberspace lexicon. An illustrated dictionary of terms from multimedia to virtual reality*, 2ª ed., Phaidon Press Limited (Spain 1995)

COULTON, *Medieval village, manor and monastery*, 1ª ed., Harper Tochbooks (New York 1960)

COUNCIL OF EUROPE ed., *Data protection and the media*, Council of Europe Press (Estrasbourg 1991)

CRISTIE y GARE eds., *Statutes on intellectual property*, Blackstone Press Limited (United Kingdom 1997)

CZARNOTA y HART, *Legal protection of computer programs in Europe. A guide to the EC Directive*, Butterworths (London 1991)

CHENET, *Éléments pour la conception d'un systeme multimedia*, ADBS (Paris 1992)

DAVARA, *De las autopistas de la información a la sociedad virtual*, Aranzadi (Pamplona 1996)

DAVID HUME INSTITUTE ed., *Privacy and Property*, Edinburgh University Press (United Kingdom 1994)

DE MIGUEL y PIATTINI, *Fundamentos y modelos de bases de datos*, Ra-Ma (Madrid 1997)

DE SOLA, *Talking back: citizen feedback and cable technology*, The Massachussetts Institute of Technology (United Kingdom 1973)

DEMNARD-TELLIER ed., *Le multimedia et le droit. Internet, off line, on line*, Hermes (Paris 1996)

DEN BOER, *Private morality in Greece and Rome. Some historical aspects*, E. J. Brill (Leiden 1979)

DENIS, POULLET y THUNIS, *Banques de données: quelle protection juridique?*, Story – Scientia (Belgique 1988)

DEPARTMENT OF TRADE AND INDUSTRY ed., *Intellectual property and innovation*, Her Majesty's Stationer Office (London 1986)

DESBOIS, FRANÇON y KEREVER, *Les conventions internationales du droit d'auteur et des droits voisins*, Dalloz (Paris 1976)

DETTIENNE dir., *Les savoirs de l' écriture. En Grèce Ancienne*, Presses Universitaires de Lille (France 1988)

DÍAZ DE SANTOS ed., *Diccionario Oxford de Informática. Inglés-español/español-inglés*, Díaz de Santos (Madrid 1985)

DIETZ, *Le droit d'auteur dans la Communauté Européenne*, Comisión de las Comunidades (Bruxelles 1976)

DIETZ, *Copyright law in the European Community. A comparative investigation of national copyright legislation, with special reference to the provision of the Treaty establishing the European Economic Community*, Sijthoff & Noordhoff (1978)

DIETZ, *Le droit d' auteur dans la Communauté européenne. Analyse comparative des législations nationales relatives au droit d' auteur face aux dispositions du traité instituant la Communauté économique européenne*, Commission des Communautes Européennes (Luxembourg 1978))

DÍEZ BORQUE coord., *Métodos de estudio de la obra literaria*, Taurus (Madrid 1985)

DÍEZ DE VELASCO, *Las organizaciones internacionales*, 10ª edición, Tecnos (Madrid 1997)

DOMMERING Y HUGENHOLTZ, *Protecting woks of fact*, Kluwer (Netherlands 1991)

DOWNING, *EC Information Technology Law*, John Wiley & Sons (United Kingdom 1995)

DRAHOS, *A philosophy of Intellectual Property*, Dartmouth (Australia 1996)

EDELMAN, *Droits d'auteur, droits voisins: droit d'auteur et Marché Commune*, Dalloz (Paris 1993)

EISENSTEIN, *Le rivoluzioni del libro. L'invenzione della stampa e la nascita dell' età moderna*, 1ª ed., Il Mulino (Bologna 1995)

EISENSTEIN, *La revolución de la imprenta en la Edad Moderna europea*, Akal Ediciones (Madrid 1994)

ERCOLANI, *La creativitá in Europa e la sfida digitale*, Giuffré Editore (Milano 1996)

EUROPEAN COMISSION ed., *Practical guide to copyright for multimedia producers*, EUR 16128 EN (Luxembourg-Brussels 1996)

EUROPEAN LEGAL OBSERVATORY y AUDIOVISUAL EUREKA eds., *Audiovisual landscape and copyright legislation. Central and Eastern Europe*, Maklu (Netherlands1994)

FAUS, *La era audiovisual*, EUNSA (Pamplona 1995)

FEDERACIÓN INTERNACIONAL DE PERIODISTAS ed., *Derecho de autor. Un manual para periodistas* (Bruselas 1989)

FELDMAN, *Multimedia*, Blueprint (United Kingdom1994)

FEVRE y MARTIN, *La aparición del libro*, UTEHA (Mexico 1962)

FIDLER, *Mediamorphosis. Understanding new media*, Pine Forge Press (United States 1997)

FIRTH ed., *Perspectives on intellectual property. The prehistory and development of intellectual property systems*, Sweet & Maxwell (London 1997)

FIRTH, LANE y SMYTH ed., *Readings in Intellectual Property*, Sweet & Maxwell (London 1998)

FISHER, *Hybris. A study in the values of honour and shame in ancient Greece*, Aris & Phillips (United Kingdom1992)

FISHMAN, *The copyright law handbook. How to protect and use written works*, Nolo Press – Berkeley (United States 1997)

FLORY dir., *La Communauté Européenne et le GATT. Evaluation des accords du cycle d'Uruguay*, Apogée (Rennes 1994)

FUIANO, *Libri, scrittorii e biblioteche nell'alto medievo*, Librería Scientifica Editrice (Napoli 1973)

FUNDESCO ed., *La sociedad de la información. La tecnología y la información en la década de los ochenta*, vol. 1, Tecnos (Madrid 1983)

FUNDESCO ed., *Multimedia 1996. Tendencias*, serie Informes Anuales de Fundesco (Madrid 1997)

GANZ, *The role of the book in medieval culture*, vol. II, Brepols-Turnhout (Belgium 1986)

GARCÍA GARCÉS, *Compendio de metodología científica general*, Coculsa (Madrid 1945)

GARCÍA GARRIDO, *Derecho Privado Romano. Edición abreviada*, Dykinson (Madrid 1993)

GARMIER, *L' UIT et les télécommunications par satellites*, Bruylant (Bruxelles 1975)

GATT ed., *Los resultados de la Ronda Uruguay de negociaciones comerciales multilaterales*, Centre William Rappond (Geneve1994)

GILLENSON, *Introducción a las bases de datos*, McGraw-Hill (Mexico 1988)

GINGUAY, *Diccionario de informática y tecnologías afines. Inglés-español*, 2ª ed., Masson (Barcelona 1985)

GINSBURG, BOTEIN y DIRECTOR, *Regulation of the electronic mass media. Law and policy for radio, television, cable and the new technologies*, West Publishing Co. (Minnesota 1991)

GIURATI, *El plagio*, Imprenta de Gabriel L. Horno (Madrid 1922)

GLENISSON dir., *Le lívre au moyen age*, Brepols-Turnhout (France 1988)

GORMAN y GINSBURG, *Copyright for the nineties. Cases and materials*, 4ª ed., The Michie Company (Virginia 1993)

GRAFF, *Storia dell' alfabetizzazione occidentale*, Il mulino (Italia 1987)

GROVES, MARTINO, MISKIN y RICHARDS, *Intellectual Property and the Internal Market of the European Community*, Graham & Trotman (United Kingdom 1993)

GUILERA, *Los fundamentos de la informática*, EUNIBAR (Barcelona 1983)

GUINGUAY, *Diccionario de informática y tecnologías afines. Inglés-español*, 2ª ed., Masson (Barcelona 1985)

GUTUSSO y PAPPALARDO, *La disciplina comunitaria delle licence di know-how*, Francoangeli (Milanno 1991)

GUY y LEIGH, *The EEC and Intellectual Property*, Sweet & Maxwell (United Kingdom 1981)

HALBERT, *Intellectual property in the information age: the politics of expanding ownership rights*, Quorum Books (United States 1999)

HARRISON, *The law of Athens. The family and the property*, Clarendon Press (Oxford 1968)

HART y FAZZANI, *Intellectual Property Law*, Macmillan (United Kingdom1997)

HOCHRATH y HOCHRATH, *Diccionario Internet. Inglés-español*, Océano (Barcelona 1998)

HOEREN, *An assesment of long term solutions in the field of copyright and electronic delivery services and multimedia products*, European Commission (Luxembourg 1995)

HOLYOAK y TORREMANS, *Intellectual property law*, Butterworths (London 1995)

HUGENHOLTZ ed., *The future of copyright in a digital enviroment*, Kluwer (Netherlands 1996)

HUGENHOLTZ, *Copyright problems of electronic document delivery*, European Commission (Luxembourg 1995)

INSTITUT DE RECHERCHE EN PROPRIÉTÉ INTELLECTUELLE HENRI-DESBOIS ed., *L'avenir de la propriété intellectuelle*, Librairies Techniques (Paris 1993)

JANKOWSKI y HANSSEN eds., *The contours of multimedia. Recent technological, theoretical and empirical developments*, Luton Press (United Kingdom 1996)

JIMÉNEZ BLANCO, *El derecho aplicable a la protección internacional de las patentes*, Comares (Granada 1998)

JOHANNES, *Industrial Property and Copyright in European Community Law*, A. W. Sijthoff International Publishing Company B. V. (Netherlands 1976)

JONGEN y MEIJBOOM eds., *Copyright and software protection in the EC*, Kluwer Law & Taxation Publishers (Netherlands 1993)

KAMPERMAN, *Unfair competition law. The protection of intellectual and industrial creativity*, Clarendon Press-Oxford (Estados 1997)

KATZEN ed., *Multi-Media communications*, Fraces Pinter (London 1982)

KEEN, *Business multimedia explained. A manager's guide to key terms and concepts*, Harvard Business School Press (United States 1997)

KEITH y KRAUSE, *The radio station*, 3ª ed., Focal Press (Boston 1993)

KELLEHER y MURRAY, *IT law in the European Union*, Sweet & Maxwell (London 1999)

KENT y LANCOUR, *Copyright. Current view points on history, laws and legislation*, R. R. Bowker Company (New York-London 1972)

KOCH, *Journalism in the 21 st century. Online information, electronic databases and the news*, Adamantined Press Limited (United Kingdom 1991)

KOOPS, *The crypto controversy. A key conflict in the Information Society*, Kluwer Law International (Netherlands 1999)

LADDIE, PRESSCOTT y VITORIA, *The modern law of copyright,* vol. II, Butterworths (London 1995)

LARRÉGOLA, *De la televisión analógica a la televisión digital*, CIMS (Barcelona 1998)

LATCHEM, WILLIAMSON y HENDERSON, *Interactive multimedia. Practice and promise*, Kogan Page (London 1993)

LECLERCQ, *The love of learning and the desire for God. A study of monastic culture*, 1ª ed., New American Library (New York 1962)

LEHMAN y BROWN, *Intellectual property and the National Information Infraestructure. The report of the Working Group on Intellectual Property Rights*, Information Infraestructure Task Force (United States 1995)

LINANT de BELLEFONDS ed., *Le multimedia face au droit*, Editions des Parques (Paris 1995)

LIPSZYC, *Derecho de autor y derechos conexos*, UNESCO y CERLALC (Buenos Aires 1993)

LIVELY, *Modern communications law*, Praeger (United States 1991)

LÓPEZ-BARAJAS, *Fundamentos de metodología científica*, UNED (Madrid 1988)

LUCAS, GARCÍA y RUÍZ, *Sociología de la comunicación*, Trotta (Madrid 1999)

LUQUE y GÓMEZ NIETO, *Diseño y uso de bases de datos relacionales*, Ra-Ma (Madrid 1997)

LUQUE y GÓMEZ NIETO, *Ingeniería del software. Fundamentos para el desarrollo de programas informáticos*, Servicio de Publicaciones de la Universidad de Córdoba (Córdoba 1999)

MacDONALD, MANIATIS y SUTHERSANEN, *Design and copyright protection of products. World law and practice*, vols. I y II, Sweet & Maxwell (London 1998)

MacQUEEN, *Copyright, competition and industrial design*, Edinburgh University Press (Edinburgh 1995)

MARANDOLA, *Diritto d'autore*, Associazione Italiana Biblioteche (Roma 1996)

MARCEL, *Etudes sur la propriété industrielle, littéraire, artistique*, Sirey (Paris 1960)

MARETT, *Information Law and practice*, Gower Publishing Company Limited (Aldershot 1991)

MARTIN, *Le livre français sous l'Ancien Règime*, PROMODIS (France 1987)

MARTÍNEZ BONATI, *La estructura de la obra literaria*, Seix Barral (Barcelona 1972)

McCRACKEN y GILBART, *Buying and clearing rights. Print, broadcast and multimedia*, Blueprint (London 1995)

McGONAGLE ed., *Law and the media. The views of journalists and lawyers*, Sweet & Maxwell (Dublin 1997)

MERKINS, *Copyright designs and patents: the new law*, Longman (United Kingdom 1989)

METAXAS-MARAGHIDIS ed., *Intellectual property law of Europe*, John Wiley & Sons (United Kingdom 1995)

MILLER, *Legal aspects of technology utilization*, Lexington Books (London 1974)

MONDELO, *L'auteur multimedia*, Pratiques (Paris 1991)

MONTAÑÁ, *La OMC y el reforzamiento del sistema GATT*, McGraw-Hill (Madrid 1997)

MORENO, *Introducción a la comunicación social actual*, Playor (Madrid 1983)

MORENO MORENO, *La música en la radio: transformación de un contenido en un concepto de programación*, tesis doctoral, *pro manuscripto*, Facultad de Comunicación, Universidad de Navarra (Pamplona 1998)

NASRI, *Crisis in copyright*, Marcel Dekker Inc. (USA 1976)

NEGROPONTE, *El mundo digital*, 1ª reimpresión, Ediciones B (Barcelona 1996)

NOLL, *Highway of dreams. A critical view along the information superhighway*, Lawrence Erlabaum Associates (New Yersey 1997)

NORDEMAN, VINCK, HERTIN Y MEYER, *International Copyright*, VCH (Winheim 1990)

ORGANISATION MONDIALE DE LA PROPRIÉTÉ INTELLECTUELLE ed., *Colloque mondial sur l'arbitrage des litiges de propriété intellectuelle* (Geneve 1994)

ORIHUELA y SANTOS, *Diseño de comunicación digital. Concepción y desarrollo de proyectos interactivos*, Digitalia (Mutilva Baja 1999)

OWEN, *Selling rights*, 3ª ed., Routledge (London-New York 1997)

PADELLARO, *Il diritto d'autore. La disciplina guiridca degli strumenti di comunicazione sociale*, Società Editrice Libraria (Milanno 1972)

PALAU, *Historia del cine*, Seix Barral (Barcelona 1946)

PARASCHOS, *Media law and regulation in the European Union. National, transnational and U.S. perspectives*, Iowa State Universtiy Press (United States 1998)

PATTERSON, *Copyright in historical perspective*, Vaderbilt University Press (Nashville 1968)

1993)

PHILLIPS ed., *Butterworths intellectual property law handbook*, Butterworths (Edinburgh 1994)

PHILLIPS y FIRTH, *Introduction to intellectual property law*, Butterworths (London 1995)

PLOMAN y HAMILTON, *Copyright. Intellectual Property in the information age*, Routledge & Kegan Paul (United Kingdom 1980)

PORTER, *Beyond the Berne Convention. Copyright broadcasting and the european single market*, John Libbey & Company (London 1991)

PRIME, *The law of copyright*, Format Publishing (London 1992)

PRIME, *European intellectual property law*, Ashgate-Dartmouth (United Kingdom 1999)

PUTNAM ed., *The question of copyright. A summary of the copyright laws at present in force in the chief countries of the world*, The Knickerbocker Press (New York-London 1891)

RAITT ed., *Online information*, Learned Information (Oxford 1991)

RASHDALL, *The universities of Europe in the Middle Ages*, vol. I, 2ª ed., Oxford University Press (London 1936)

RATZKE, *Manual de los nuevos medios. El impacto de las tecnologías en la comunicación del futuro*, GG Mass Media (Barcelona 1986)

RAYNARD, *Droit d'auteur et conflits de lois. Essai sur la nature juridique du droit d'auteur*, Litec (Paris 1990)

RECODER, ABADAL y CODINA, *Información electrónica y nuevas tecnologías*, ESRP-PPU (Barcelona 1991)

RICKETSON, *The Berne Convention for the protection of literary and artistic works: 1886-1986*, Kluwer (London 1987)

ROCA, *La Ronda Uruguay sobre negociaciones comerciales multilaterales*, Mundi-Prensa (Madrid 1994)

ROSE, *Authors and Owners*, Harvard University Press (United Kingdom 1993)

SAUNDERS, *Authorship and copyright*, Routhledge (London 1992)

SEIGNETTE, *Challenges to the creator doctrine*, Kluwer (Netherlands 1994)

SEMETEYS, *Le multimedia*, Dunodtech (Paris 1992)

SEMPERE, *La galaxia McLuhan*, Fernando Torres-Editor (Valencia 1975) 21-24

SIMARD, *Naturaleza y alcance del método científico*, Gráficas Condor (Madrid 1961)

SMITH, G. ed., *Internet Law and Regulation*, Bird & Bird (London 1996)

SOBRINO, *Nuevas tecnologías aplicadas a la educación universitaria. Valoración de un sistema hipermedia*, tesis doctoral, *pro manuscripto*, Facultad de Filosofía y Letras, Universidad de Navarra (Pamplona 1995)

STEWART, *International copyright and neighbouring rights*, Butterworths (London 1989)

STEWART, T. ed., *The GATT Uruguay Round. A negotiating history (1986 – 1992)*, vol. I y II, Kluwer (Netherlands 1993)

STOCKMAIR, *The protection of technical innovations and designs in Germany*, VCH (Germany 1994)

STONE, *Copyright law in the United Kingdom and the European Community*, The Atholone Press (London 1990)

STRÖMHOLM, *Le droit moral de l'auteur en droit allemand, français et scandinave*, P. A. Norstedt & Söners Förlag (Suede 1967)

STROWEL, *Droit d'auteur et copyright*, Librairie Générale de Droit et Jurisprudence (Belgique 1993)

TANNENBAUM, *Theoretical foundations of multimedia*, W. H. Freeman and Company (New York 1998) 3.

THE COMMON LAW INSTITUTE OF INTELLECTUAL PROPERTY ed., *Feist/Magill and the draft base directive* (London 1992)

TRABANT, *Semiología de la obra literaria. Glosemática y teoría de la literatura*, Gredos (Madrid 1975)

TREJO, *La nueva alfombra mágica. Usos y mitos de Internet, la red de redes*, Fundesco (Madrid 1996)

TRITTON, *Intellectual property in Europe*, Sweet & Maxwell (London 1996)

TRUDEL, BENYEKHLEF y HEIN, *Droit du cyberspace*, Les Éditions Thémis (Quebec 1997)

TRUYOL y SERRA, *Los derechos humanos*, Tecnos (Madrid 1984)

U.G.A. ed., *Digest of Case-Law relating to the European Conventions on Human Rights (1955-1962)* (Belgique 1970)

VAUGHAN, TREJO y VIVANCO, *Todo el poder de multimedia*, 2ª ed., McGraw-Hill (Mexico 1995)

VERCKEN, *Practical guide to copyright for multimedia producers*, Oficina de Publicaciones Oficiales de las Comunidades Europeas (Italia 1996)

VERDOOT, *Declaración Universal de los Derechos del Hombre. Nacimiento y significación*, Biblioteca Mensajero (Bilbao 1969)

WILLIS, *The age of multimedia and turbonews*, Praeger (London 1994)

WINTERNITZ, *Electronic publishing agreements*, Oxford University Press (United Kingdom 2000)

WOOD, *Periodismo electrónico*, Letras (Mexico 1969)

WOODMANSEE y JASZI eds., *The construction of authorship. Textual appropriation in law and literature*, Duke University Press (London 1994)

WORLD INTERNATIONAL PROPERTY ORGANIZATION ed., *Introduction to intellectual property. Theory and practice*, Kluwer Law International (United Kingdom 1997)

WORLD INTELLECTUAL PROPERTY ORGANIZATION ed., *WIPO glossary of terms of the law of copyright and neighbouring rights*, WIPO (Geneve 1980)

ZELEZNY, *Communications law. Liberties, restraints and the modern media*, Wadsworth Publishing Company (California 1993)

ZUBIRI ed., *Terminología de la informática*, Zubiri (Bilbao 1970)

Articles

AA VV, "El derecho y las nuevas tecnologías", *Revista de Derecho Industrial*, Depalma (Buenos Aires 1991)

AA VV, "La propiedad intelectual en los medios de comunicación", monográfico de *Comunicación y Estudios Universitarios*, no. 7/1997, CEU-San Pablo de Valencia (Valencia 1997) 9-95

AMERICAN SOCIETY OF JOURNALISTS AND AUTHORS (ASJA) ed., News Releases, http://www.realflorida.net/asja/cwarticle.php3?this_id=178 (United States 1999)

AMERICAN BAR ASSOCIATION ed., *Intellectual Property Law Newsletter*, vols. 1-16, años 1993-1998 (United States)

AMERICAN BAR ASSOCIATION ed., *PTC Newsletter*, vols. años 1981-1993 (United States)

BAUTISTA, "Interferencia de la tecnología digital sobre la protección del derecho de autor y de los derechos afines en las autopistas de la información europea: problemática y propuestas", *Boletín de Derecho de Autor*, vol. XXXIII, no. 3, UNESCO (Paris 1999) 4-22

BELSON, "Brand protection in the age of the Internet", *European Intellectual Property Review*, no. 10, Sweet & Maxwell (London 1999) 481-484

BENDER, "Copyright Law and the newer technologies", *Wilson Library Bulletin*, no. junio, The H. W. Wilson Company (United States 1993) 44-47

BOOTON, "Novelty of Inventions under the Patents Act 1977 and the European Patent Convention", http://spade3.ncl.ac.uk/1996/issue2.booton2.html (United Kingdom 1999)

CEDRÓN, "La gestión de los derechos de autor en el nuevo entorno de productos y redes multimedia", *Fundesco: Boletín de la Fundación para el Desarrollo de la Función Social de las Comunicaciones*, no. abril (Madrid 1996) 16-17

CERINA, "The originality requirement in the protection of databases in Europe and United States", *IIC: International Review of Industrial Property and Copyright Law*, vol. 24, VCH (Weinheim 1993) 589-601

CHARTERED INSTITUTE OF PATENT AGENTS ed., Patents, http://www.cipa.org.uk/cipa/patents.htm (United Kingdom 1999)

DAVARA, "Las autopistas de la información y los profesionales del derecho", *Actualidad Informática Aranzadi*, no. 21, Aranzadi (Pamplona 1996) 1-6

DAVIES, "The convergence of copyright and authors' right, reality or chimera?", *IIC: International Review of Industrial Property and Copyright Law*, vol. 26, VCH (Weinheim 1995) 965-989

DE LA HORADADA, http://www.internet.ad/mp3/intro.html (Spain 1999)

DERCLAYE, "Software copyright protection: can Europe learn from American case law?", *European Intellectual Property Review*, no. 1, Sweet & Maxwell (London 2000) 7-17

DÍAZ NOCI, "Periodismo y derechos de autor. Evolución histórica de la protección jurídica sobre la obra informativa", *ZER. Revista de Estudios de Comunicación*, no. 7, diciembre, Universidad del País Vasco (Bilbao 1999) 193-219

DOHERTY y GRIFFITHS, "The harmonisation of Europea Union copyright law for the digital age", *European Intellectual Property Review*, no. 1, Sweet & Maxwell (London 2000) 17-23

DREIER, "Authorship and new technologies from the view point of civil law traditions", *IIC: International Review of Industrial Property and Copyright Law*, vol. 26, VCH (Weinheim 1995) 989-999

DREIER, "Copyright in the age of digital technology", *IIC: International Review of Industrial Property and Copyright Law*, vol. 24, VCH (Weinheim 1993) 481-490

DUTFIELD, "The public and private domains: intellectual property rights in traditional knowledge", *Science Communication. An Interdisciplinary Social Science Journal*, vol. 21, no. 3, Sage Publications (United States 2000) 274-296

EDELMAN, "Reflexiones sobre el derecho de autor y su evolución en la Comunidad Europea", *Boletín de Derecho de Autor*, no. 4, UNESCO (Paris 1993) 10-21

ELSEMORE, http://www.ccls.edu/iplaw/qmw_web_page.html (United Kingdom 1996)

EVANS, "Whose web site is it anyway", *Internet World*, september 1997, Macklermedia (Westport 1997) 46-50

EUROPEAN FEDERATION OF JOURNALISTS, Journalism and author's rights, http://www.ifj.org/jetpilot/efjbook.htm (Bruxelles 1999)

FLACK, "Copyright and the digital revolution: the view of the phonographic industry", *European Institute for the Media Bulletin*, no. 1, vol. 13, Europäische Medieninstitut (Düsseldorf 1996) 6-8

GELLER, "Conflictos de leyes en el ciberespacio: el derecho de autor internacional", *Boletín de Derecho de Autor*, no. 1, UNESCO (Paris 1997) 3-16

GOLDSMITH, "Les nouveaux traités de l'OMPI et l'action législative européenne sur le droit d'auteur et les droits voisins", *Legipresse*, no. 139-II, Victoires (Paris 1997) 26-30

GONTHIER, "El mundo digital y la propiedad intelectual. Oportunidades y desafíos. Un tema de contenido social", *I & T Magazine*, no. invierno 1994-95, Comisión Europea (Bruxelles 1995) 21-23

GORDON, "The very idea!: why copyright law is an inappropriate way to protect computer programs?", *European Intellectual Property Law*, no. 1, Sweet & Maxwell (London 1998) 10-13

GRÉGOIRE, "L'action communautaire dans le secteur culturel", *Revue du Marché Commun*, no. 217, Editions Techniques et Economiques (Paris 1998) 2-11

HART, "The proposed Directive for copyright in the Information Society: nice rights, shame about the exceptions", *European Intellectual Property Review*, no. 5, Sweet & Maxwell (London 1998) 169-171.

HARVARD LAW REVIEW ed., "The criminalization of copyright infringement in the digital era", *Harvard Law Review*, vol. 112, no. 7, The Harvard Law Review Association (Masschusetts 1999) 1705-1722

HARVARD LAW REVIEW ed., "Nothing but Internet", *Harvard Law Review*, vol. 110, no. 5, marzo, The Harvard Law Review Association (Massachusetts 1997) 1143-1166

KEREVER, "Propiedad intelectual. Determinación de la ley aplicable a las transmisiones digitalizadas", *Boletín de Derecho de Autor*, no. 2, UNESCO (Paris 1996) 11-24

KOBOLDT, "The EU-Directive on the legal protection of databases and the incentives to update: an economic analysis", *International Review of Law & Economics*, vol. 17, no. 1, Elsevier Science (New York 1997) 127-138

KÖHLER y BURMEISTER, "Copyright liability on the Internet today in Europe (Germany, France, Italy and the E.U.)", *European Intellectual Property Review*, no. 10, Sweet & Maxwell (London 1999) 485-499

KUNZRU, "Pirates invade the web", *Wired,* december 1997, Wired Venture (San Francisco 1997) 192-202

KROKER, "The computer Directive and the balance of rights", *European Intellectual Property Review*, no. 5, Sweet & Maxwell (London 1997) 247-250

LOWENHEIM, "Multimedia and the European Copyright Law", *IIC: International Review of Industrial Property and Copyright Law*, vol. 27, VCH (Weinheim 1996) 41-52

LUCAS, "La propiedad intelectual y la infraestructura global de la información", *Boletín de Derecho de Autor*, no. 1, UNESCO (Paris 1998) 3-20

MILLÉ, "Aspectos jurídicos de la producción, la distribución y la explotación de obras multimedia", *Boletín de Derecho de Autor*, no. 2, UNESCO (Paris 1995) 6-16

MILLER, "Copyright protection for computer programs, databases and computer-generated works: is anything new since CONTU?", *Harvard Law Review*, vol.

106, no. 5, The Harvard Law Review Association (Massachusetts 1993) 982-1073

NORCONTEL, Economic implications of new communication technologies on the audio-visual markets, (Bruxelles 1997)

OKERSON, Who owns digital works?, http://www.sciam.com/0796issue/0796okerson.html (United States 1999)

OMAN, "El imperativo de responsabilidad compartida en Internet", *Boletín de Derecho de Autor*, no. 2, UNESCO (Paris 1998)

PÁEZ, "Derecho comunitario y nuevas tecnologías: Libro Verde y Directivas de Bases de Datos", *Informática y Derecho. Revista Iberoamericana de Derecho Informático*, no. 19/22, UNED (España 1998) 91-111

PUY TANG, "Intellectual property rights and Internet", *Inter Media*, no. 4, vol. 23, Staples Printers (London 1995) 22-25

REUBEN, "What is new in intellectual property", *Aba Journal*, no. enero, American Bar Association (United States 1993) 72-77

RINDL, "The magic of Magill: TV program guides as limit of copyright law?", *IIC: International Review of Industrial Property and Copyright Law*, vol. 24, VCH (Weinheim 1993) 60-82

RISHER, "El derecho de autor y las nuevas tecnologías: un desafío para los editores de libros", *Boletín de Derecho de Autor*, no. 3, UNESCO (Paris 1993) 4-13

RODRIGO, "Derechos de autor y editor en la edición electrónica", *Boletín de Derecho de Autor*, no. 3, UNESCO (Paris 1996) 6-16

RODRIGUES, "Impacto de la tecnología digital en el ejercicio y la gestión colectiva de los derechos conexos, en el marco de la Convención de Roma", *Boletín de Derecho de Autor*, no.4, UNESCO (Paris 1997) 16-24

RONY, "Piratage, musique et copie numerique: un mariage à risques", *Legipresse*, no. 159, Editions Victoires (Paris 1999) 31-32

SAMUELSON, "The copyright grab", *Wired*, enero 1996, Wired Ventures (San Francisco 1996) 134-138 y 188-191

SCHIPPAN, "Purchase and licensing of digital rights: the VERDI project and the clearing of multimedia rights in Europe", *European Intellectual Property Review*, no. 1, Sweet & Maxwell (London 2000) 24-29

SCHIUMA, "TRIPS and exclusion of software 'as such' from patentability", *IIC: International Review of Industrial Property and Copyright Law*, vol. 31, no. 1, VCH (Weinheim 2000) 36-51

SMITH, S., The changing approach of the European Court to intellectual property, http://www.southampton-institute.ac.uk/law/home.html (Southampton 1996)

SOMA, "Software licenses in the EU and the US", *IIC: International Review of Industrial Property and Copyright Law*, vol. 27, VCH (Weinheim 1996) 813-818

STERLING, "Creator's right and the bridge between author's right and copyright", *IIC: International Review of Industrial Property and Copyright Law*, vol. 29, VCH (Weinheim 1998) 302-308.

THE SECURE DIGITAL MUSIC INITIATIVE WEBSITE, http://www.sdmi.org (United States 2000)

WEBER, "Copyright and the digital revolution: the view of the broadcaster", *European Institut for the Media Bulletin*, no. 4, vol. 12, Europäische Medieninstitut (Düsseldorf 1995) 1-4

US PATENT & TRADEMARK OFFICE, What are patents, trademarks, servicemarks and copyrights?, http://www.uspto.gov/web/offices/pac/doc/general/whatis.htm (United States 1999)

Legal Texts

ALONSO GARCÍA ed., *Tratado de Amsterdam y versiones consolidadas de los Tratados de la Unión Europea y de la Comunidad Europea*, Civitas (Madrid 1998)

BUTTERWORTHS ed., UK Patents Act, http://www.butterworths.co.uk/academic/lloyd/Statutes/patents.htm (United Kingdom 2000)

CABINET BEAU DELOMENIE ed., Code de la Propriètè Intellectuelle. Livre VI. Protection des inventions et des connaissances techniques, http://www.cabinetbeaudelomenie.com/fr/code/CPIL/2197.html (France 1999)

COMISIÓN DE LAS COMUNIDADES EUROPEAS, "Relance de l'action culturelle dans la Communauté européenne", *Boletín de las Comunidades Europeas*, suplemento 4/87 (Luxembourg 1988)

COMISIÓN DE LAS COMUNIDADES EUROPEAS, Propuesta de Directiva del Consejo sobre protección jurídica de programas informáticos, COM (88) 816 final, de 5 de enero de 1989, *Diario Oficial de las Comunidades Europeas*, de 12 de abril de 1989, no. C 91, Oficina de Publicaciones Oficiales de las Comunidades Europeas (Luxemburgo 1989)

COMISIÓN DE LAS COMUNIDADES EUROPEAS, *Libro Verde .sobre los derechos de autor y el reto de la tecnología. Temas relativos a los derechos de autor que exigen una actuación inmediata*, COM (88) 172 final (Bruselas 1989)

COMISIÓN DE LAS COMUNIDADES EUROPEAS, *El libro y la lectura: dos retos culturales para Europa*, COM (89) 258 final (Bruselas 1989)

COMISIÓN DE LAS COMUNIDADES EUROPEAS, Comunicación de la Comisión al Consejo y al Parlamento sobre la política audiovisual, COM (90) 78 final, de 28 de febrero de 1990, en COMISIÓN DE LAS COMUNIDADES EUROPEAS, *La política de la Comunidad Europea para la industria audiovisual. Recopilación de textos legislativos y políticos*, Oficina de Publicaciones Oficiales de las Comunidades Europeas (Bruselas-Luxemburgo 1990)

COMISIÓN DE LAS COMUNIDADES EUROPEAS, *Acciones derivadas del Libro Verde. Programa de trabajo de la Comisión en el ámbito de los derechos de autor y derechos afines*, COM (90) 584 final, de 17 de enero de 1991 (Bruselas 1991)

COMISIÓN DE LAS COMUNIDADES EUROPEAS, Propuesta modificada de Directiva del Consejo sobre protección jurídica de programas informáticos, COM (90) 509 final, *Diario Oficial de las Comunidades Europeas*, de 20 de diciembre de 1990, Oficina de Publicaciones Oficiales de las Comunidades Europeas (Luxemburgo 1990)

COMISIÓN DE LAS COMUNIDADES EUROPEAS, *El derecho de autor y los derechos afines en la Comunidad europea*, Documentos Europeos 9/1991 (Luxemburgo 1991)

COMISIÓN DE LAS COMUNIDADES EUROPEAS, *El derecho de autor y los derechos afines en la Comunidad Europea. La aparición de un espacio europeo de creatividad*, Serie Documentos Europeos 9/1991, Oficina de Publicaciones Oficiales de las Comunidades Europeas (Luxemburgo 1991)

COMISIÓN DE LAS COMUNIDADES EUROPEAS, Propuesta de Directiva del Consejo relativa a la protección jurídica de las bases de datos, COM (92) 24 final, de 15 de abril de 1992, *Diario Oficial de las Comunidades Europeas*, no. C 156, de 23 de junio de 1992, Oficina de Publicaciones Oficiales de las Comunidades Europeas (Luxemburgo 1992)

COMISIÓN DE LAS COMUNIDADES EUROPEAS, Propuesta de Directiva del Consejo relativa a la protección jurídica de las bases de datos, COM (93) 464 final, de 4 de octubre de 1993, *Diario Oficial de las Comunidades Europeas*, no. C 308, de 15 de noviembre de 1993, Oficina de Publicaciones Oficiales de las Comunidades Europeas (Luxemburgo 1993)

COMISIÓN DE LAS COMUNIDADES EUROPEAS, *Libro Blanco sobre crecimiento, competitividad y empleo. Retos y pistas para entrar en el siglo XXI*, COM 700 (93) (Luxemburgo 1993)

COMISIÓN DE LAS COMUNIDADES EUROPEAS, *Europa en marcha hacia la Sociedad de la Información*, COM (94) 347 final (Bruselas 1994)

COMISIÓN DE LAS COMUNIDADES EUROPEAS, Propuesta de decisión del Consejo relativa a la aprobación del Convenio Europeo sobre aspectos de los derechos de autor y derechos afines en el ámbito de la radiodifusión transfronteriza vía Satélite, COM (95) 154 final, de 3 de mayo de 1995 (Bruselas 1995)

COMISIÓN DE LAS COMUNIDADES EUROPEAS, *Libro Verde. sobre los derechos de autor y los derechos afines en la Sociedad de la Información*, COM (95) 382 final (Bruselas 1995)

COMISIÓN DE LAS COMUNIDADES EUROPEAS, *Propuesta de decisión del Consejo relativa a la aprobación del Convenio Europeo sobre aspectos de los derechos de autor y derechos afines en el ámbito de la radiodifusión transfronteriza vía satélite*, COM (95) 154 final (Bruselas 1995)

COMISIÓN DE LAS COMUNIDADES EUROPEAS, *Seguimiento del Libro Verde sobre derechos de autor y derechos afines en la Sociedad de la Información*, COM (96) 568 final (Bruselas 1996)

COMISIÓN, Seguimiento del Libro Verde sobre derechos de autor y derechos afines en la Sociedad de la Información, COM (96) 508 final, de 20 de noviembre de 1996, (Bruselas 1996)

COMISIÓN DE LAS COMUNIDADES EUROPEAS, *Libro Verde sobre la convergencia de los sectores de telecomunicaciones, medios de comunicación y tecnologías de la información, y sobre sus consecuencias para la reglamentación*, COM (97), de 3 de diciembre de 1997 (Bruselas 1997)

COMISIÓN DE LAS COMUNIDADES EUROPEAS, Propuesta de Directiva del Parlamento Europeo y del Consejo relativa a la armonización de determinados aspectos de los derechos de autor y derechos afines en la Sociedad de la Información, COM (97) 628 final, de 10 de diciembre de 1997, http://europa.eu.int/comm/dg15/en/intprop/intprop/1100.htm (Bruselas 1998)

COMISIÓN DE LAS COMUNIDADES EUROPEAS, *Política Audiovisual: próximas etapas*, COM (98) 446 final, de 14 de julio de 1998, Oficina de Publicaciones Oficiales de las Comunidades Europeas (Luxemburgo 1998)

COMISIÓN DE LAS COMUNIDADES EUROPEAS, Informe del Grupo de Alto Nivel de Política Audiovisual, http://europa.eu.int/comm/dg10/avpolicy/key_doc/hlg3_es.html (Bruselas 1998)

COMISIÓN DE LAS COMUNIDADES EUROPEAS, Propuesta modificada de Directiva del Parlamento Europeo y del Consejo, relativa a la armonización de determinados aspectos de los derechos de autor y derechos afines en la Sociedad de la Información, COM (1999) 250 final, de 21 de mayo de 1999, http://europa.eu.int/comm/dg15/en/intprop/intprop/copy2.htm (Bruselas 1999)

COMISIÓN DE LAS COMUNIDADES EUROPEAS, Comunicación de la Comisión al Consejo, al Parlamento Europeo y al Comité Económico y Social. Fomento de la innovación mediante la patente. El seguimiento que debe darse al Libro Verde sobre La patente comunitaria y el sistema de patentes en Europa (sin referencias), (Bruselas 1999)

COMISIÓN DE LAS COMUNIDADES EUROPEAS, Propuesta modificada de Directiva del Parlamento Europeo y del Consejo relativa a la aproximación de los regímenes jurídicos de protección de las invenciones mediante el modelo de utiidad, COM (1999) 309 final, de 25 de junio de 1999, http://europa.eu.int/comm/dg15/en/intprop/indprop/utility.htm (Bruselas 1999)

COMISIÓN DE LAS COMUNIDADES EUROPEAS, Informe sobre el grado de aplicación de las normas comunitarias relativas a la propiedad industrial e intelectual, (Bruselas 1999)

COMITÉ ECONÓMICO y SOCIAL, Dictamen sobre la propuesta de directiva del Consejo sobre protección jurídica de programas informáticos (89/C 329/02), *Diario Oficial de las Comunidades Europeas*, de 30 de diciembre de 1989, Oficina de Publicaciones Oficiales de las Comunidades Europeas (Luxemburgo1989)

COMMISSION DES COMMUNAUTÉS EUROPÉENNES, "Le renforcement de l'action communautaire dans le secteur culturel", *Bulletin des Communautés Europeénnes*, suplemento 6/82, Office des Publications des Communautés Européennes (Luxembourg 1983)

COMMISSION DES COMMUNAUTÉS EUROPÉENNES, "Relance de l'action culturelle dans la Communauté Européenne", *Bulletin des Communautés Europeénnes*, suplemento 4/87, Office des Publications Officielles des Communautés Européennes (Luxembourg 1987)

COMMISSION OF THE EUROPEAN COMMUNITIES, White Paper on growth, competitiveness and employment: the challenges and ways fordward into the 21st century, COM (93) 700 final, http://europa.eu.int/en/record/white/c93700/ch5_1.html (Bruxelles 1999)

COMMISSION OF THE EUROPEAN COMMUNITIES, Green Paper on tackling the problem of counterfeiting and piracy in the single market, (Bruxelles 1999)

COMMISSION OF THE EUROPEAN COMMUNITIES, Amended proposal for a Council Directive on the legal protection of databases (93/C 308/01), COM (93) 464 final, (United Kingdom 1999)

COMMISSION OF THE EUROPEAN COMMUNITIES, Copyright: Commision decides to take Ireland to the Court of Justice for failing to implement the Directive on rental right, (Bruxelles 1999).

COMMISSION OF THE EUROPEAN COMMUNITIES, Copyright: infringement procedures against Ireland and Portugal, http://europa.eu.int/comm/dg15/en/intprop/intprop/13.htm (Bruxelles 1999).

COMMISSION OF THE EUROPEAN COMMUNITIES, Intellectual property: Commssions decides to refer Greece, Ireland, Luxembourg and Portugal to Court, (Bruxelles 1999).

CONGRESS OF THE UNITED STATES OF AMERICA, US Code. Title 35, http://thomas.loc.gov/cgi-bin/query/z?c104:S652.enr (United States 1999)

CONSEJO DE LAS COMUNIDADES EUROPEAS, Directiva sobre la protección jurídica de programas de ordenador, (91/250/CEE), de 14 de mayo de 1991, *Diario Oficial de las Comunidades Europeas*, de 17 de mayo de 1991, Oficina de Publicaciones Oficiales de las Comunidades Europeas (Luxemburgo) L 122/42-L 122/46

CONSEJO DE LAS COMUNIDADES EUROPEAS, Resolución del Consejo, de 14 de mayo de 1992, encaminada a fortalecer la protección de los derechos de autor y derechos afines, en Diario Oficial de las Comunidades Europeas, de 28 de mayo de 1992, http://europa.eu.int/eur-lex/es/lif/dat/1992/es_392Y0528_01.html (Bruselas 1999)

CONSEJO DE LAS COMUNIDADES EUROPEAS, Directiva sobre derechos de alquiler y préstamo y otros derechos afines a los derechos de autor en el ámbito de la propiedad intelectual, (92/100/CEE), de 19 de noviembre de 1992, *Diario Oficial de las Comunidades Europeas*, L 346, de 27 de noviembre de 1992, Oficina de Publicaciones Oficiales de las Comunidades Europeas (Luxemburgo 1992)

CONSEJO DE LAS COMUNIDADES EUROPEAS, Directiva sobre coordinación de determinadas disposiciones relativas a los derechos de autor y derechos afines a los derechos de autor en el ámbito de la radiodifusión vía satélite y de la distribución por cable, (93/83/CEE), de 27 de septiembre de 1993, *Diario*

Oficial de las Comunidades Europeas, L 248, de 6 de octubre de 1993, Oficina de Publicaciones Oficiales de las Comunidades Europeas (Luxemburgo 1993)

CONSEJO DE LAS COMUNIDADES EUROPEAS, Directiva relativa a la armonización del plazo de protección del derecho de autor y de determinados derechos afines, (93/98/CEE), de 29 de octubre de 1993, *Diario Oficial de las Comunidades Europeas*, L 209, de 24 de noviembre de 1993, Oficina de Publicaciones Oficiales de las Comunidades Europeas (Luxemburgo 1993)

CONSEJO DE LAS COMUNIDADES EUROPEAS, Decisión del Consejo por la que se adopta un programa plurianual comunitario para estimular el establecimiento de la sociedad de la información en Europa (Programa Sociedad de la Información), 98/253/CE, de 30 de marzo de 1998, *Diario Oficial de las Comunidades Europeas*, L 107, de 7 de abril de 1998, Oficina de Publicaciones de la Comunidades Europeas, Oficina de Publicaciones Oficiales de las Comunidades Europeas (Luxemburgo 1998)

CONSEJO DE LAS COMUNIDADES EUROPEAS, Recomendación 98/560/CE del Consejo, de 24 de septiembre de 1998, relativa al desarrollo de la competitividad de la industria europea de servicios audiovisuales y de información mediante la promoción de marcos nacionales destinados a lograr un nivel de protección comparable y efectivo de los menores y de la dignidad humana, http://www.europa.eu.int/eur-lex/lif/dat/1998/es_398X0560.html (Bruselas 1999)

CONSEJO DE LAS COMUNIDADES EUROPEAS, Propuesta de Decisión relativa a la aprobación, en nombre de la Comunidad Europea, del Tratado de la OMPI sobre Derecho de Autor y del Tratado de la OMPI sobre Interpretaciones o Ejecuciones y Fonogramas (98/C 165/08) COM (1998) 249 final-98/1141 (AVC), presentado el 27 de abril de 1998, http://europa.eu.int/eur-lex/es/com/dat/1998/es_598PC0249.html (Bruselas 1999)

CONSEJO DE LAS COMUNIDADES EUROPEAS, Conclusiones de los ministros de cultura, reunidos en el seno del Consejo, sobre las directrices para la actuación cultural comunitaria, del 12 de noviembre de 1992, Diario Oficial de las Comunidades Europeas, no. C 336, de 19 de diciembre de 1992, http://europa.eu.int/eur-lex/lif/dat/1992/es_492Y1219_01.html (Bruselas 1999)

CONSEJO DE LAS COMUNIDADES EUROPEAS, Conclusiones del Consejo, de 10 de noviembre de 1994, sobre la comunicación de la Comisión titulada "Acción de la Comunidad Europea a favor de la cultura", Diario Oficial de las Comunidades Europeas, no. C 348, de 9 de diciembre de 1994, http://europa.eu.int/eur-lex/es/lif/dat/1994/es_394Y1209_01.html (Bruselas 1999)

CONSEJO DE LAS COMUNIDADES EUROPEAS, Resolución sobre cultura y multimedios, de 4 de abril de 1995, Diario Oficial de las Comunidades Europeas, no. C 247, de 23 de septiembre de 1995, (Bruselas 1999)

CONSEJO DE LAS COMUNIDADES EUROPEAS, Resolución sobre los aspectos industriales para la Unión Europea en el desarrollo de la Sociedad de la Información, de 17 de noviembre de 1995, (Bruselas 1999)

CONSEJO DE LAS COMUNIDADES EUROPEAS, Resolución relativa a las nuevas prioridades políticas en materia de Sociedad de la Información, de 21 de noviembre de 1996, Diario Oficial de las Comunidades Europeas, no. C 376, de 12 de diciembre de 1996, http://europa.eu.int/eur-lex/lif/dat/1996/ es_396Y1212_01.html (Bruselas 1999)

CONSEJO DE LAS COMUNIDADES EUROPEAS, Resolución por la que se adopta un programa plurianual comunitario para estimular el establecimiento de la Sociedad de la Información en Europea, de 30 de marzo de 1998, Diario Oficial de las Comunidades Europeas, no. L 107, de 7 de abril de 1998, http:// europa.eu.int/eur-lex/es/lif/dat/1998/es_398D0253.html (Bruselas 1999)

CONSEJO DE LAS COMUNIDADES EUROPEAS, Decisión por la que se adopta un programa plurianual de la Comunidad para fomentar el desarrollo de la industria europea de los contenidos multimedia y la utilización de éstos en la naciente Sociedad de la Información (INFA 2000), 96/339/CE, de 20 de mayo de 1996, Diario Oficial de las Comunidades Europeas, no. L 129, de 30 de mayo de 1996, (Bruselas 1999)

CONSEJO DE LAS COMUNIDADES EUROPEAS, Resolución relativa a las nuevas prioridades políticas en materia de Sociedad de la Información, de 21 de noviembre de 1996, Diario Oficial de las Comunidades Europeas, no. C 376, de 12 de diciembre de 1996, http://europa.eu.int/eur-lex/es/lif/dat/1996/ es_396Y1212_01.html (Bruselas 1999)

COUR DE JUSTICE DES COMMUNAUTÉS EUROPÉENNES, *Recueil de la Jurisprudence de la Cour*, vols. años 1955-1998 (Luxembourg)

DEUTSCHE PATENTMAT ed., *Germany Patent Law*, (Munich 1993)

EUROPEAN PARLIAMENT and COUNCIL, Directive 2001/29/EC, of 22 may 2001, on the harmonisation of certain aspects of copyright and related right in the information society, *Official Journal* L 167 (Luxembourg 2001) 0010-0019.

HERVADA Y ZUMAQUERO eds., *Textos internacionales de Derechos Humanos. 1776-1976*, EUNSA (España 1978)

MARTINUS NIJHOFF ed., *Yearbook of the European Convention of Human Rights*, vols. 1973 y 1977 (La Haya)

MINISTROS DE CULTURA COMUNITARIOS, Conclusión de los Ministros de Cultura reunidos en el seno del Consejo sobre las directrices para la actuación cultural comunitaria, de 12 de noviembre de 1992, Diario Oficial de las Comunidades Europeas, no. C 336 de 19/12/1992, http://europa.eu.int/eur-lex/es/lif/dat/1992/es_492Y1219_01.html (Bruselas 1999)

NATIONAL PATENT ASSOCIATION, The US Constitution and the patent, http://www.nationalpatent.com/const.htm (United States 1999)

ORGANISATION MONDIALE DE LA PROPRIÉTÉ INTELLECTUELLE ed., *Actes de la Conférence de Stockholm de la propriété intelletuelle 1967* (Ginebra 1971)

ORGANISATION MONDIALE DE LA PROPRIÉTÉ INTELLECTUELLE ed., *Convention de Berne pour la protection des ouvres littéraires et artistiques. Acte de Paris du 24 juillet 1971 et tel que modifié le 2 octobre 1979* (Geneve 1989)

ORGANIZACIÓN MUNDIAL DE LA PROPIEDAD INTELECTUAL ed., *Tratado de sobre Derecho de Autor*, OMPI (Ginebra 1997)

ORGANIZACIÓN MUNDIAL DE LA PROPIEDAD INTELECTUAL ed., *Tratado de la sobre Interpretación o Ejecución y Fonogramas*, OMPI (Ginebra 1997)

ORGANIZACIÓN MUNDIAL DE LA PROPIEDAD INTELECTUAL ed., Acuerdo entre la Organización Mundial de la Propiedad Intelectual y la Organización Mundial de Comercio, (Ginebra 1999)

ORGANIZACIÓN MUNDIAL DE LA PROPIEDAD INTELECTUAL ed., Convenio de Paris para la Protección de la Propiedad Industrial, http://www.wipo.org/spa/iplex/wo-par01.htm (Ginebra 1999)

ORGANIZACIÓN MUNDIAL DE LA PROPIEDAD INTELECTUAL ed., Tratado de Cooperación en Materia de Patentes (PCT), http://www.wipo.org/spa/iplex/wo-pct01.htm (Ginebra 1999)

ORGANIZACIÓN MUNDIAL DE LA PROPIEDAD INTELECTUAL ed., Reglamento del Tratado de Cooperación en Materia de Patentes, http://www.wipo.org/spa/iplex/wo-pcr01.htm (Ginebra 1999)

ORGANIZACIÓN MUNDIAL DE LA PROPIEDAD INTELECTUAL ed., Información General, http://www.wipo.org/spa/iplex/infbroch/infbro98.htm#P22_2453 (Ginebra 1999)

ORGANIZACIÓN MUNDIAL DE LA PROPIEDAD INTELECTUAL ed., Convenio de Berna para la Protección de las Obras Literarias y Artísticas, htpp://www.wipo.org/spa/iplex/wo-ber01.htm (Ginebra 1999)

ORGANIZACIÓN MUNDIAL DE LA PROPIEDAD INTELECTUAL ed., Convenio que establece la Organización Mundial de la Propiedad Intelectual, http://www.wipo.org/spa/iplex/wo-wipo01.htm (Ginebra 1999)

ORGANIZACIÓN MUNDIAL DE LA PROPIEDAD INTELECTUAL ed., Informe Definitivo de la OMPI sobre el Proceso de Nombres de Dominio de Internet, http://wipo2.wipo.int/process/esp/final_report.html (Ginebra 1999)

ORGANIZACIÓN MUNDIAL DE LA PROPIEDAD INTELECTUAL ed., Convenio para la Protección de los Productores de Fonogramas contra la Reproducción No Autorizada de sus Fonogramas, (Ginebra 1999)

ORGANIZACIÓN MUNDIAL DE LA PROPIEDAD INTELECTUAL ed., Arreglo de Estrasburgo relativo a la Clasificación Internacional de Patentes, http://www.wipo.org/spa/iplex/wo-ipc01.htm (Ginebra 1999)

ORGANIZACIÓN MUNDIAL DE LA PROPIEDAD INTELECTUAL ed., Centro de Arbitraje, http://arbiter.wipo.int/arbitration/ny-convention/text.html (Ginebra 1999)

ORGANIZACIÓN MUNDIAL DE LA PROPIEDAD INTELECTUAL ed., Propuesta básica de Tratado sobre el Derecho de Patentes, http://www.ompi.org/spa/document/pt_dc/doc/pt_dc3.doc (Ginebra 2000)

ORGANIZACIÓN MUNDIAL DE LA PROPIEDAD INTELECTUAL ed., Propuesta básica de reglamento de aplicación del Tratado sobre el Derecho de Patentes, http://www.ompi.org/spa/document/pt_dc/doc/pt_dc4.doc (Ginebra 2000)

PARLAMENT EUROPÉENNE, Resolution sur la proposition de résolution présentée, au nom du group des libérux et apparantés sur la sauvagarde du patrimoniel culturel européen, DOC 62/74, *Journal Officiel des Communautés Européennes*, de 30 de mayo de 1974, Office des Publicationes Officielles des Communautés Européennes (Luxembourg 1974)

PARLAMENT et CONSEIL DES COMMUNAUTÉS EUROPÉENNES, Proposition de directive du Parlament Européen et du Conseil relative à certains aspects juridiques du commerce électronique dans le Marché intérieur, *Communications Commerciales. Le journal de la politique et de la pratique de la publicité et du marketing dans la Communauté Éuropéenne*, no. 13, Dirección General XV de la Comisión Europea (Bruxelles 1999)

PARLAMENTO EUROPEO, Resolución legislativa que contiene el dictamen del Parlamento Europeo sobre la propuesta de la Comisión al Consejo referente a una directiva relativa a la protección jurídica de programas informáticos, COM (88) 816 final, *Diario Oficial de las Comunidades Europeas*, de 17 de septiembre de 1990, no. C 231, Oficina de Publicaciones Oficiales de las Comunidades Europeas (Luxembourg 1990)

PARLAMENTO EUROPEO y CONSEJO DE LAS COMUNIDADES EUROPEAS, Directiva sobre la protección jurídica de las bases de datos, (96/9/CE), de 11 de marzo de 1996, *Diario Oficial de las Comunidades Europeas*, L 77, de 27 de marzo de 1996, Oficina de Publicaciones Oficiales de las Comunidades Europeas (Luxembrugo 1996)

PARLAMENTO y CONSEJO DE LAS COMUNIDADES EUROPEAS, Directiva relativa a la protección de las personas físicas en lo que respecta al tratamiento de datos personales y a la libre circulación de estos datos, (95/46/CE), de 24 de octubre de 1995, *Diario Oficial de las Comunidades Europeas*, L 281, de 23 de noviembre de 1995, Oficina de Publicaciones Oficiales de las Comunidades Europeas (Luxemburgo 1995)

PARLAMENTO EUROPEO y CONSEJO, Propuesta de directiva relativa al derecho de participación en beneficio del autor de una obra de arte original, de 25 de abril de 1996, (Bruselas 1999)

PARLAMENTO EUROPEO y CONSEJO, Directiva relativa al Tratamiento de los Datos Personales y a la Protección de la Intimidad en el Sector de las Telecomunicaciones, (97/66/CE), de 15 de diciembre de 1997, en *Diario Oficial de las Comunidades Europeas*, L 24, de 30 de enero de 1998, Oficina de Publicaciones Oficiales de las Comunidades Europeas (Luxemburgo 1998)

PARLAMENTO EUROPEO y CONSEJO, Propuesta de decisión por la que se establece un único instrumento de financiación y de programación a favor de la cooperación cultural (Programa "Cultura 2000"), http://europa.eu.int/eur-lex/es/com/dat/1998/es_598PC0244.html (Bruselas 1999)

PARLAMENTO EUROPEO y CONSEJO, Propuesta de Directiva relativa a la armonización de determinados aspectos de los derechos de autor y derechos afines en la Sociedad de la Información, COM (97) 628 final, http://europa.eu.int/eur-lex/es/com/dat/1997/es_597PC0628.html (Bruselas 1999)

REPRESENTANTES DE LOS ESTADOS MIEMBROS DE LAS COMUNIDADES EUROPEAS, Resolución de los representantes de los Estados miembros relativa a la lucha contra la piratería audiovisual (84/C 204/01), de 24 de julio de 1984, *Diario Oficial de las Comunidades Europeas*, de 3 de agosto de 1984, 16/vol. 01, Oficina de Publicaciones Oficiales de las Comunidades Europeas (Luxemburgo) 194-195

TRIBUNAL DE JUSTICIA DE LAS COMUNIDADES EUROPEAS, Jurisprudencia reciente, http://curia.eu.int/jurisp (Luxemburgo 1997-1999)

TRIBUNAL PERMANENTE DE JUSTICIA INTERNACIONAL ed., *Receuil des avis consultatifs*, vols. 1970-1998 Kraus Reprint (Netherlands)

UNIVERSITY OF CORNELL, Title 15 of the US Code. Lanham Act, http://www.law.cornell.edu/lanham/lanham.act/html (United States 2000)

WHITE HOUSE, A framework for global electronic commerce, http://www.ecommerce.gov/framework.htm (United States 1999)

WORLD INTELLECTUAL PROPERTY ORGANIZATION ed., Contracting parties of treaties administered by WIPO. Convention establishing the World Intellectual Property Organization, (Geneve 2000).

WORLD INTELLECTUAL PROPERTY ORGANIZATION ed., Agreement between the World Intellectual Property Organization and the World Trade Organization, (Geneve 1999)

WORLD INTELLECTUAL PROPERTY ORGANIZATION ed., *Basic proposal for the substantive provisions of the treaty on intellectual property in respect of databases to be considered by the diplomatic conference*, fotocopia facilitada por la WIPO (Geneve 1996)